Russia may be a 'riddle, wrapped in a mystery inside an enigma,' but this book does more to unravel its post-Communist experience than any other I can think of. One of its most original aspects is a large-N analysis of subnational variation in democracy and autocracy, drawing on an extensive databank. No study of democratization – east or west – has done this so thoroughly. Another finding of potentially wider significance is their demonstration that the size and loyalty of the local bureaucracy inherited from the *ancient regime* is a major contributor to a more autocratic outcome. Highly recommended to those condemned to making sense of post-Communist Russia, but also of interest to students of democratization elsewhere.

**Philippe C. Schmitter**, *Professor Emeritus,*
*European University Institute*

In their book, Obydenkova and Libman provide the most comprehensive and up to date account of Russia's sub-national politics. Using a variety of historical and contemporary datasets and rigorous statistical analysis, they offer a nuanced and well-grounded explanation of the causes and effects of the diversity of political regimes within the country. A must read for scholars of Russian and comparative politics.

**Vladimir Gel'man**, *European University at St. Petersburg,*
*and Aleksanteri Institute, University of Helsinki*

One of the landmarks in comparative democratisation studies in the last decade has been the development of studies of sub-national regime variation and dynamics. This book takes this approach to a new level of sophistication in a study of regional democratisation in Putin's Russia. It thereby offers several novel insights into one of the most conspicuous and threatening autocracies in the world today.

**Jan Teorell**, *Professor of Political Science, Lund University*

Libman and Obydenkova have written an impressive book that takes full advantage of Russia's regional diversity to test long-standing arguments about the sources of democracy and the economic impacts of political regimes. Rich in empirical detail and far ranging in its analysis, this work offers fresh insights into the relationship between economic performance and democracy. It deserves a wide audience in comparative political economy and Russian studies.

**Timothy M. Frye**, *Director, Harriman Institute,*
*and Marshall D. Shulman Professor of Post-Soviet Foreign*
*Policy, Columbia University*

T0352804

# Causes and Consequences of Democratization

In recent decades, the regions of Russia have taken different paths of regime transition. Despite the consolidation of an autocratic regime at the national level and the centralization steered by Vladimir Putin's government, the variation across sub-national regimes persists.

Using an innovative theoretical framework, this book explores both causes and consequences of democratization in the regions of Russia. It is the first study in the field to systematically integrate structural and agency approaches in order to account for economic, social, historical and international causes of democratization and to trace its consequences. By focusing on the challenging and under-studied topic of sub-national regimes, the book provides a unique perspective on regime transition, and the new theoretical framework contributes to a better understanding of democratization world-wide.

The book will be of key interest to scholars and students of democratization, sub-national regimes, East European politics, comparative politics, post-communism and international relations.

**Anastassia V. Obydenkova** is a senior researcher (Ramón y Cajal) at the Universitat Pompeu Fabra (Barcelona, Spain), and a research fellow at the Centre for International Studies of London School of Economics, UK.

**Alexander Libman** is associate, German Institute for International and Security Affairs SWP, Berlin, Germany.

# Democratization Studies
## (Formerly Democratization Studies, Frank Cass)

Democratization Studies combines theoretical and comparative studies with detailed analyses of issues central to democratic progress and its performance, all over the world.

The books in this series aim to encourage debate on the many aspects of democratization that are of interest to policy-makers, administrators and journalists, aid and development personnel, as well as to all those involved in education.

# Causes and Consequences of Democratization

## The regions of Russia

**Anastassia V. Obydenkova
and Alexander Libman**

Routledge
Taylor & Francis Group

LONDON AND NEW YORK

First published 2015
by Routledge
2 Park Square, Milton Park, Abingdon, Oxon OX14 4RN

and by Routledge
711 Third Avenue, New York, NY 10017

First issued in paperback 2017

*Routledge is an imprint of the Taylor & Francis Group,
an informa business*

*British Library Cataloguing in Publication Data*
A catalogue record for this book is available from the British Library

*Library of Congress Cataloging-in-Publication Data*
Obydenkova, Anastassia.
   Causes and consequences of democratization : the regions of Russia /
Anastassia V. Obydenkova and Alexander Libman.
      pages cm
   1. Democratization—Russia (Federation)   2. Russia (Federation)—
Politics and government—1991—Regional disparities.   3. Post-
communism—Russia (Federation)   I. Libman, Alexander.   II. Title.
   JN6699.A15O28 2015
   320.947—dc23
   2014049106

ISBN 13: 978-1-138-50497-4 (pbk)
ISBN 13: 978-1-138-81818-7 (hbk)

Typeset in Times New Roman
by Apex CoVantage, LLC

# Contents

# Acknowledgements

While working on various aspects of Russian regions and sub-national politics, we have received substantial feedback from a number of scholars who should to be mentioned. The authors are very grateful to Philippe C. Schmitter, Donatella Della Porta, Tomila Lankina, Vladimir Gel'man, Timothy Frye, Valerie Jane Bunce, Kathleen Collins, Wade Jacoby, Michael Keating, Stephen E. Hanson, Andrei Yakovlev, Lars P. Feld, Carsten Herrmann-Pillath and Nikolay Marinov for their generous feedback on the ideas discussed in this book. They also wish to express gratitude to Tanja Börzel and Steven Levitsky for their comments on various issues that are raised in the book. The various papers that became chapters of the book were presented at conferences in political science: American Political Science Association, European Consortium of Political Research, International Political Science Association, European Political Science Association, International Studies Association; and in the conferences on economics: European Economic Association, International Institute of Public Finance, European Public Choice Society, Public Choice Society, International Society for New Institutional Economics. Some of the ideas were also presented and discussed within the framework of various seminars at academic centers world-wide: University of Oxford, London School of Economics and Political Science, the Davis Centre for International Relations (Jerusalem), University of Edinburgh, the Center for Political and Constitutional Studies (Madrid), Jena School of Social Sciences, Goethe University Frankfurt, University of Helsinki, University of Mannheim, Stockholm School of Economics, New Economic School and Higher School of Economics. We are very grateful to their participants for insightful comments and suggestions. Part of the research presented in the book was conducted within the research grant of the Ministerio de Economía y Competividad of Spain (reference CSO2012–37126). Yet another part of the book was written during the research fellowship at the

London School of Economics and Political Science, at the Institute of Economic Analysis, and at the Centre for Russian and Eurasian Studies of the University of Uppsala (Sweden).

All opinions expressed in the book and possible mistakes are solely our own.

# 1 Introduction

Understanding the causes of democratization can probably be considered one of the major scholarly endeavors in political science in the last half century. Numerous studies have investigated the role of various factors in this process – from the early contributions of the modernization theory to the more recent studies of the role of culture, history and external actors in this process. At the same time, democratization, being the dependent variable in the causes of democratization literature, became the key explanatory variable in the studies of consequences of democratization. In economics, obviously, the effect of democratization on economic growth, but also on economic liberalization, has been carefully studied. Other fields have investigated implications of democratization in other areas. Our book provides yet another contribution to this literature – however, it systematically explores a number of angles that have received insufficient attention in the existing scholarly literature. Our goal is to study the consequences and causes of unequal paths to democratization in various regions of the Russian Federation in the first decade of the 2000s.

There are several theoretical issues important for this endeavor. First, while approaching democratization theoretically, the inevitable departure point traditionally was cross-national studies. However, recently scholars noticed that sub-national political regimes present quite an exciting laboratory for study world-wide. The research on sub-national regimes started from the analysis of the American South with enormous power concentration, exceeding that existing in the United States at the national level in the mid-20th century. Over time, numerous other countries have been discussed from the point of view of sub-national regime variation, including India (Lacina 2009), South Africa (Inman and Rubinfeld 2005), the Philippines (Sidel 2014); Mexico (Giraudy 2013), Argentina (Gervasoni 2010), Venezuela (Garcia-Guadilla and Perez 2002), Brazil (Samuels and Abrucio 2000) and even Italy (Gel'man 2010a). The precise meaning of the concept of a 'sub-national regime' varied from country to country, depending on the organization of sub-national governance. However, in any case the switch of empirical focus from national to sub-national level produced many new insights for the theory of regime transition. This book contributes to this new, growing field of studies. The empirical focus of the book is at the sub-national level of the regions of Russia that had led to the formation of a new concept in democratization studies – a multi-level approach to democratization (Obydenkova 2011; Obydenkova and Libman 2015a). The second premise is related to terminological clarity of the concepts used throughout the book (specifically, understanding of democracy, democratization and regime transition as central to this research along with a number of other concepts far less conventional, such as limiting factor, autocratic diffusion, etc.) These notions will be clarified in the theoretical discussion presented in this chapter.

As a number of studies proved, national democratization may be paralleled by sub-national autocratization. The direction of diversion of national and sub-national vectors of regime development can be also the opposite: the autocratization of the national level may be paralleled by democratization at the sub-national level due to various reasons, such as, for example, the resistance of regional political elites to the pressure of national ones. In the long run, national autocratization might eventually result in seizing total control over sub-national politics through, for example, centralization policy among many other reforms that might be launched by the central autocratic government. Similarly democratization at the national level may well result in democratization at the sub-national level in the long run (the case of the EU regional policy provides an excellent example). In some cases, sub-national regime deviation may spur over the national level and cause the change in the national regime development. Examples of the later are less numerous but highly important in modern political development of the states (e.g., the Ukraine case and the importance of the sub-national regions and their different regime development over the period from 2013–2014 for the development of the Maidan movement).

The more general questions we address in this book are the following: To what extent were existing theories on the causes and consequences of democratization confirmed by the experience of the regions of Russia over the 25 years of regime transition, over the research period from 1991–2014? What *novel insights* may the sub-national democratization in Russia add to these theories? How can strategy and agency perspectives on causes of democratization be united in one study? What new can this combined perspective uncover about the nature and the dynamic of transition? How may agency be applied to the studies of the consequences of democratization? Finally, how can the theoretical and empirical discoveries from the case of Russia be generalized to the post-Communist regime transition and world-wide? Does the theory of democratization hold in the context of the sub-national regions of modern Russia? Does the empirical analysis confirm or reject existing theories? What new can be added to theory of democratization, if anything at all? Are there any factors not considered previously that are to be taken into account to explain the success or failure of democratization? If yes, which ones? What causes of the previous successful transitions to democracy still account or may account in the success of the fourth wave? Focusing on the sub-national regions of the same country creates a laboratory-like setting for empirical analysis and allows for controlling many intervening variables that cannot be controlled in cross-national analysis. This empirical approach adopted in this volume allows for detailed testing of the theories.

## Concepts and definitions

Before we proceed to the subsequent analysis, it is necessary to clarify the key concepts and definitions we use in this book. By 'democratization' we mean the process of the regime change toward democracy. 'Democratization' is cautiously used interchangeably with 'regime transition'. However, there is some difference between the two. Regime transition conventionally covers the first few first years after the collapse of a previous non-democratic regime. With certain reservations, one may suggest that the transition is a period with a high likelihood of arrival of the regime at the 'target', i.e., the democracy, and followed by the consolidation of democracy.

However, the difference between democratization and regime transition became more pronounced with the fourth wave of regime transition – in other words, the post-Communist states. Central European states indeed passed over the regime transition in the 1990s and managed to consolidate democratic regimes. In a sharp contrast, none of the 12 post-Soviet states – former republics of the USSR – has have experienced proper democratization resulting in establishing democracy.[1] The specificity of the fourth wave is that even 25 years after the collapse of Communism (1990s–2015), democracy was not actually established, let alone consolidated. Indeed, since the early 1990s, regime transition took place in many post-Soviet states and in all of them (with exception of the Baltic republics) resulted in either consolidated authoritarian regimes (like in Belarus and Russia) or various shadows of hybrid regimes. Thus, the notions of regime transition and democratization are not to be applied as synonyms with the ease as in the case of Southern European transition. However, though there are some differences as described earlier, this study will use both notions interchangeably. In this book, democratization and regime transition will imply the transition from a less democratic to a more democratic regime.

By democracy we mean a broad phenomenon that goes beyond the presence (or absence) of political liberties and their recognition in the constitution. It also implies the actual implementation of those freedoms and rights not only on the part of the government but also the society. Thus, democracy is taken as a quite encompassing phenomenon (inclusive definition) that incorporates the presence of civil society, freedom of mass media, market economy or economic liberalization and many other political, social, cultural and behavioral aspects associated with democracy. In what follows, we will discuss the implications of this definition for measuring democracy in our study more specifically.

Similarly, by 'regime' we mean not only a set of rules and an institutional design of a polity (be that a state or a region). The regime also includes a set of cultural and social norms and the interaction between the institutions and society. Thus, both regime and the level of democracy would include political, social, cultural and legal aspects. The notion of a regime is also used in a broader sense to reflect the political climate, the civil society, the relations between the power and the people and many other interrelated aspects.

Along with democracy, the book also consistently uses the term 'autocracy', which also needs a bit of theoretical elaboration here. Given that the discourse on modern autocracy is emerging, it might be handy to elaborate our meaning of another term – 'autocratic diffusion' – used throughout the book. In what follows, we provide the definitions of 'external influence', 'autocracy' and 'external autocratic diffusion' as important for our book concepts.

The notion of 'external influences' is used interchangeably with 'international influences' throughout this book and can be defined as an impact increasing or decreasing the level of democracy coming outside of the borders of the state. This impact may be caused intentionally, by, for example, EU democracy-promotion initiatives, or non-intentionally, through the communication of elite across the borders and value transmission mechanisms. Further on, the impact can be either democracy promoting or autocracy promoting. We also distinguish between 'promotions' and 'diffusion'. Both refer to the impact of external factors; however, both underline different natures of this impact. The promotion is more associated with *intentionality* of the actors and of their initiatives. In contrast, diffusion can be both intentional and non-intentional.

That brings us to the need to define 'autocracy' and 'autocratic diffusion' as key concepts used throughout the chapter. By 'autocracy' is meant is a multi-faceted phenomenon that goes beyond the formal institutional setting. Some studies argued that modern autocracy is different from historical autocracy (such as Nazi Germany or Imperial Japan; see e.g., Obydenkova and Libman 2015a). Modern autocracy is defined as a non-democratic regime, a set of values, principles and mechanisms (or tools) and practices used normally by the executive branch (the president) to exercise or to achieve control over various political, social, economic and informational aspects of the life of the state and its population. One of the key differences between modern autocracies and historical ones is that democracy in the 21st century is widely acknowledged as the best possible regime. Therefore modern autocracies often imitate democracies in terms of founding documents and political parlance. The modern autocracies are more hidden regimes that can be discovered beyond the democratic veil (an example is Belarus, a truly autocratic state, with an extremely democratic Constitution and main laws, regular popular elections, equality of rights, etc.).

Yet another significant difference between historical and modern external anti-democratic impact is the intentionality of the international players. Historically, the USSR intentionally tried to spread its ideology to the neighboring states, expanding into Central European states, for example. Similarly, Franco's Spain, Fascist Germany and Mussolini's Italy used their respective ideological programs as an important strategic step in their domestic and foreign policies. Thus, the presence of clearly anti-democratic ideology was historically highly important. Further difference, as specified earlier, is the intentionality. Historically, the spread of autocratic and totalitarian regimes was *intentional* (e.g., Communist bloc and Fascism). In contrast, in modern autocracies, their international influences are far less ideological, if at all, and in most of the cases also non-intentional. Intentionality of actions remains in some of the cases, but they are not directly linked to establishing autocratic regimes abroad but rather to solving other strategic purposes.

This definition goes beyond the institutional approach based on founding documents and actual institutional design as the only criteria of the regime. The modern autocracy and the definition used in this book might include formal democratic legal founding documents but present a strong type of regime that is dominated by a leader and that aims at total control over many other aspects of the population and a state – control over mass media, control over the most important entrepreneurialism, control over various aspects of the society (control over the access of the information). Given these differences between historical and modern autocracy, and between external democratic and external autocratic influence, new theories are to be created and tested to account for this new phenomenon of the modern world. The question that is important in this context is whether the mechanisms, channels and tools of autocracy diffusion are exactly the same as in democracy diffusion. While the book is bound to be limited, it focuses on only one important channel of diffusion that previously had been proved to be highly important in external democratic influence – geography (geographic proximity and borders). Previous research successfully demonstrated the powerful role of geography in the spread of democracy from the West east-ward. We test this important mechanism of diffusion by applying it to exter-nal autocracy-reinforcing influences.

Finally, external autocratic diffusion is defined as an influence emerging outside of a polity (a state or a region) that leads to a decrease of democ-racy either intentionally or not. The book further argues that when it comes to modern external autocratic diffusion the division into intentional and non-intentional is more important than in the case of external democratic influences. The difference is that modern external autocratic actors may pursue goals that do not imply the change of the regime per se but are more pragmatic – that is, maintaining beneficial trade deals, security of the bor-ders and geopolitical space (access to the sea ports) (Obydenkova and Lib-man 2014). Out of multiple mechanisms of external influences, geography presents an important phenomenon for a few reasons. Theoretically, geog-raphy was proved to be one of the most successful factors in democracy promotion world-wide (Kopstein and Reilly 2000) and in the regions of Russia (Lankina and Getachew 2006; Obydenkova 2012). The geographic proximity of the states and their regions to Brussels along with other factors was proved to be one of the most significant contributing factors to success-ful democratization. Does geography serve as a mechanism in the process of autocracy diffusion? Does geographic proximity to the capitals of consoli-dated autocracies matter for consolidation of autocracy in the neighboring states and regions? How do the borders with non-democratic states matter? These questions were never previously raised and addressed as the main focus of study. Chapter 7 will attempt to fill this gap and will focus in detail on the role of geography in autocracy diffusion.

## Organization of the book

The book is organized as follows. The next chapter looks into the existing theory of causes of democratization that had been applied to explain the previous three waves of regime transition and more modern theories that emerged to account for peculiarities of the fourth wave of transition – the post-Communist ones. Then we proceed with the theoretical analysis of the con-sequences of transition. The following chapter looks at the Russian context – we briefly discuss the development of the sub-national political regimes in Russia over the last two decades, as well as the issues associated with mea-suring democracy. Chapters 4 to 7 investigate the specific causes of democ-ratization: we start with looking at conventional literature (paying particular attention to the modernization theory and to the studies of culture), proceed to the discussion of historical and external factors, as well as introduce the novel concept of a limiting factor. Chapters 8 to 12 give a comprehensive review of the consequences of democratization: in terms of economic development, happiness and well-being, public policy in the area of resource management, identity formation and national politics. Thus, we cover not only issues that have received a lot of attention in the extant literature (like economic growth) but also look at more recent additions to the academic scholarship. Chapter 13 concludes our investigation.

Some of the discussions of this book are based on our previous work, published in particular in Obydenkova and Libman (2012, 2013, 2015a); Libman and Obydenkova (2013, 2014a, 2014b, 2015) and Libman (2010, 2013a) However, the econometric analysis of the book is entirely new: while in the previous work we looked only at the period of the first half of the first decade of the 2000s, this book uses data for the entire period from 2001–2010. We will show that this change of time period has important implications: not only did we find a number of novel results, but also some previously established findings changed massively (in one case we find the very opposite to our previous research). Furthermore, the book systematically discusses the role of bureaucratic agency, which has been an omitted topic in our previous studies. Methodologically, we have re-designed all regressions to follow the common standard, use common data, if possible, and so forth. The effects of democracy on happiness and identity formation have not been investigated in any previous study. Another contribution of this book from the methodological point of view is the consistent use of semi-parametric analysis. Thus, the book is not merely a collection of individual articles and is of interest even for those who looked at our previously published papers.

The book's analytical part is augmented by a detailed appendix, reporting primary data on the specifics of Russian sub-national regions we have applied in our study. We hope that these processed data could be of use for other researchers studying Russian sub-national regimes.

## Note

1 By post-Soviet states we refer to only 12 former Soviet Republics, excluding the three Baltic states (Estonia, Latvia and Lithuania) from this group.

# 2 Theory of democratization
## Causes and consequences

Scholars debate the variety of explanations of the success or failure of democratization and its consequences. An extensive literature emerged covering various predictors for the success or failure of democratization. This debate also changes a lot over time, and new explanatory factors have been recently taken into account. The theories of democratization can be conditionally divided into structural and procedural (agency-actors) perspectives. The book takes these debates further from theoretical and empirical perspectives. Theoretically, it presents a few new, previously undiscovered theories of democratization. Second, it unites the structural and agency approach in one single systematic empirical analysis. Third, it offers a new operationalization of the agency. Fourth, it applies this integrative approach of structure and agency not only to the analysis of the causes of democratization but also to the analysis of its consequences. This chapter presents the structural causes and consequences of democratization and then introduces the theoretical understanding of agency and its specific importance for the post-Communist regime transition.

The various traditional explanations for the success or failure of democratization can be classified according to various groups – economic, social, historical and cultural predictors. More recently, scholars also distinguished between national and international causes of democratization; the later became especially important with the so-called fourth wave of democratization – the post-Communism. Within these groups, the literature further debates the importance of these competing explanatory variables. Moreover, the relationships between some of them are even debated in terms of their endogeneity. Even within the set of causes, the relationship between a set of variables and democratization was analyzed from the opposite grounds: for examples, economic wealth as a factor increasing the level of democracy (Lipset 1959) and as damaging or decreasing democracy (Dimitrov 2009); civil society as a prerequisite (cause) of democracy or rather its consequences; and so on. Moreover, the division into short-run versus long-run causes and consequences became also pronounced in theoretical literature.

The long-run causes are important and were addressed in the literature at the national level in general and in the case of the USSR in particular. The national-level approach allows for clear division into structural and procedural causes of democratization. Among the long-run structural causes at a national level are accumulated problems of economic development, economic crisis and world-wide economic and political context. In contrast, among procedural one, it is easy to distinguish the role of national leaders who radically influenced the dynamic of democratization – in this case, Mikhail Gorbachev followed by a more ambiguous role played by Boris Yeltsin and by autocracy-consolidator Vladimir Putin clearly demonstrate the importance of actor-related approach to democratization. All these topics and issues of national-level analysis had been well covered by previous literature that provided further insights into the theory of democratization. However, the intriguing question is to what extent the theory of democratization can be applied and tested on the different sub-national political regimes? None of the existing books had raised and addressed this question so far. In our analysis of both causes and consequences, we will be referring to the short-run perspective. Therefore, this book focuses on the theory of democratization in short-run perspective. With this in mind, we proceed to outline the existing explanations of democratization and explain how they are applicable to our laboratory – the regions of Russia.

## 2.1 The causes of democratization

This chapter has a double purpose. First, it aims only *briefly* to outline the *well-established* theories of democratization. Some of the structural and procedural theories had been successfully developed in literature theoretically and tested empirically. Thus, it is highly important to account for them and to control for a number of factors outlined in this literature. However, it is impossible to develop all of them in depth theoretically and empirically as any book is bound to be limited in its scope and size. Instead, this book poses the second theoretical and empirical purpose. The most important aim here is to identify and analyze in more detail some of the most *recent* theories and approaches to democratization. The reason behind this asymmetrical approach to various theories is a straightforward one – new and recent theories require further validation and development in contrast to well-established theories of democratization. As the literature on democratization keeps on growing, the more detailed approach will be applied to the most recent approaches.

Among the most traditional and well-known causal explanatory factors of democratization are economic factors; social, cultural and historical factors; and geography. Among the most recent theories, we distinguish two for the purpose of this book: first, international dimension of democratization and its somewhat overlooked dimension, external *autocratic* influences; and, second, the limiting factor theory (also known as dependence of economic growth).

## Economic factors

The nexus of economic factors and democracy has been analyzed from very different angles and direction of causality. A set of literature has addressed the nexus of economic growth as a cause of democracy (e.g., Lipset 1959, Boix 2003, Inglehart and Welzel 2005, Acemoglu and Robinson 2006b) and explored the causal link from economic growth to political transition (Przeworski et al. 2000, Boix and Stokes 2003, Epstein et al. 2006). The economic group of factors was among the most frequently cited predictors of democratization. This group includes various causes such as economic growth and economic development, level of market economy and more recent theories such as resource curse and limiting factor theory.

As for economic development, its relationship with democratization has been debated in the literature: Are economic development and market economy causes or rather consequences of democratization? Among one of the most traditional explanations is the theory of modernization that links economic development and successful democratization as well as consolidation of newly established democracies (Przeworski et al. 2000). This set of studies highlights the positive correlation between the level of economic development and the level of democracy (Przeworski et al. 2000). Economic development is often associated with wealth and is traditionally measured with the GDP.

Second, the economic prerequisite of democratization is sometimes considered to be market economy. According to this approach, market economy increases the culture of the respect for law and the rule of law, decreases corruption and so forth, thus contributing to successful democratization (Mousseau, 2000). However, similarly to previous debates, the market economy plays an ambiguous role in regime transition – some studies consider it simply another aspect of liberties (economic liberties, that is, paralleled by political liberties); it might also be viewed as proper cause to democratization – in a society without democracy – as well as its consequence. Another economic factor impacts the democratization process – the presence of natural resources. A number of studies dedicated to the role of natural resources in political regime transition demonstrated that if the wealth and economic development of the state are based on rich natural resources or heavily dependent on them, then it might favor undemocratic political development (Ross 2001; Balmaceda 2008).

This gave rise to a new way of thinking and theorizing about the relationship between the structure of economy and political regime, and yet another theory emerged recently – the dependence of economic growth or limiting factor theory. According to this theory, not only the presence of rich natural resources may impact political regime development, but any kind of not-diversified and highly localized economic factor. That is, a mechanism similar to the natural resource curse is at work in any other situation in which economic development and economic wealth is dependent on one single factor (for example, if the economy of a state is totally dependent on revenue from the *transit* of natural resources –as in the case of Belarus – the state is *without* natural resources, and thus the theory of natural resource curse cannot be applied to explain autocratic consolidation). This single factor is the presence of non-diversified trade of limited product, or total dependence of economic development on one single foreign producer or so forth. The limiting factor theory is a new step in the literature on democratization and has been tested in the post-Communist context, and it will be tested in application to the regions of Russia along with other theories.

### *The role of society*

Another set of the prerequisites to democracy can be defined as a social group and includes, for example, the existence of a middle class, education and social equality; urban population versus rural population; age of the population.

Education of the population is naturally considered one of the most important social factors that may contribute to democratization and the consolidation of a new democratic regime. An educated population is more likely to actively participate in the elections and to vote for more democracy-prone candidates and parties. An educated population is also considered to have more responsiveness to irregularities of electoral results (e.g., fraud) or to pay more attention to political programs and agendas (that leads us to yet another potential cause – civil society). Civil society may be properly considered as one of the most endogenous factor to democratization – it can be a cause and a consequence of democratization. We argue, however, that civil society is the dynamic process of the social development that also incorporates the development of such ingredients of democratization per se as education, freedom of mass media and expression and, in the 21st century, access to the Internet (that in its turn is also associated with modernization and urbanization). In contrast, the emergence of multi-faceted civil society (that is not only passive but also active) is the proper outcome and consequence of democratization. In contrast the passive form of civil society might be considered as the cause. The following chapters will address this issue of the role of civil society in terms of causes and consequences.

Another two social causes are social equality and the presence of a middle class. Both are related ambiguously to democracy (Acemoglu and Robinson 2006b; Boix 2003). On the one hand, in a more egalitarian society, the population, as argued, is less inclined to protest against a non-democratic regime. On the other hand, in an extremely economically hierarchical society, the political actors may lose a lot if it is decided to redistribute wealth and income. As a result, the political and economic elite in such a society will try to prevent democratization to protect their assets. Democratization may emerge in societies where political actors fear the possibility of revolution on the part of the population and where they are willing to offer more redistribution and wealth as long as the costs are not harmful for them.

Yet another social factor of democratization is associated with the average age of the population. Some studies provided evidence toward the argument that age of the population may play an important role in the consolidation and stability of the democratic regime. That is, the older the population of a state is, the more stable the democracy (Cincotta 2008). However, while it is quite an important discovery, this cannot be applied to our case study. The analysis of Cincotta is derived based on the studies of already established and consolidated democracies, not on the causes of transition or democratization. The difference between the two processes is thus to be highlighted here – the process of regime transition is different from the process of the consolidation of already established democracy. The variable of age actually may well be expected to have the opposite effect in transitional societies. The younger generation may be more perceptive of the plurality of views and opinions and extended liberties associated with the transition period as compared to the liberties of a previous non-democratic regime. Chapter 12 will address this issue.

## The role of culture

A number of culture-related factors can be tentatively united into one group, conditionally labeled as 'cultural causes'. A number of studies highlighted the importance of such preconditions to democracy as, for example, ethnicity and religion (e.g., Christianity and Islam), Western culture versus Eastern culture and so on. Thus, Almond and Verba (1963, 1980) stated that some societies are more inclined to democracy than others due to the specificity of their culture. They argued that the presence of certain values and principles makes democracy inevitable for some societies. Similarly,

Inglehart and Welzel (2005) also stated the importance of such social values as equality of opportunities and freedom of expression as associated with modernization and democracy. This approach was further developed in Inglehart, Klingemann and Welzel (2003) and in Welzel and Inglehart (2008). Welzel (2006; 2013) argued that emancipative values are crucial for democratization and the establishment of new democracies as well as for sustaining old democracies. Further on, he argued that values are also a contributing factor to the mass protests and social movements against non-democratic elite and their politics. Social movement is indeed one of the key factors of democratization and keeps its importance in already consolidated democratic regimes.

Naturally, as this brief overview demonstrates, there is some overlapping and possible correlation between many modern economic, social, political and cultural causes of democratization outlined here – the middle class and social equality; education and urbanization; civil culture and social culture or religion; and so forth. Thus, the division into social, economic and cultural groups is meant to be rather suggestive. It also might be problematic to include all of them into statistical analysis due to multicollinearity problem (when a few explanatory variables are highly correlated between themselves – as can be, for example, the case with urbanization and education, among others). The third chapter will address the operationalization and choice for control variables in detail.

The previous sections outlined causes of democratization that can be considered overlapping to some extent and even endogenous to democratization. In contrast, the following sections will consider the causes of democratization outlined in the following and analyzed in the subsequent chapters of the book that are more clearly divided among themselves – these are historical factors, external factors (international dimension of democratization) and geography.

### *History and legacies*

The literature emphasized the importance of the previous experience of a state in democratization and the role of the democratic past in the future development and success of democratization. While the previous historical experience with democracy had been analyzed, there is also broader historical context and factors that only start gaining attention – the role of anti-democratic factors in the state's history. One of the most obvious is a set of factors related to Communism. Given that all states faced very different entrenchment of Communism (in terms of institutionalization, control, value diffusion, penetration of ideology into the system of education at all levels – in schools and universities) this difference may be one of the contributing factors explaining the success or failure of democratization in a state. This book considers and tests this hypothesis in detail.

The role of history in democratization has been addressed in literature (Pridham 2000). The studies argue that history is one of the major contributing factors to democratization world-wide: it has been analyzed in the application to various parts of the world (e.g., in Latin America by Mainwaring and Perez-Linan 2008; in Asia by Varshney 1998; in Africa by Gennaioli and Rainer 2007; in India by Lankina and Getachew 2012). The historical legacies also have received a lot of attention in the studies of post-Communist regime transition in general (Frye 2012). Communist and pre-Communist legacies became the subject of intensive analysis in the research on regime transition of the fourth wave (Bunce 2005; Pop-Eleches 2007; Hanson 1995; Eickert 2003; Frye 2010).

Yet a separate set of literature argues that the sub-national regional regimes within single nation-states may also be the political products of their specific historical development. Among the historical factors were considered, for example, British legacies in India (Lankina and Getachew 2012); pre-Communist Imperial legacies in Russia (Lankina 2012); and legal traditions across the British American colonies (Berkowitz and Clay 2005).

In this book, we choose to analyze in detail one single historical legacy that we consider one of the most crucial ones for the formation of various political regimes in the regions of Russia – the role of Communist Party of the Soviet Union (CPSU) membership in the 1970s and 1980s. In the chapter on historical legacies, we raise and address an intriguing question as to how and why the Communist membership of the 1970s was transmitted and preserved in the 21st century, 20 years after the collapse of the Soviet Union.

## International dimension of democratization and geography

The focus on the impact of external influences on democratization has received special attention of scholars, with the fourth wave of transition, in studies of post-Communism. Compared to the theories of democratization outlined earlier, the international dimension is relatively recent literature, and scholars continue debate its importance. Two controversial events gave a push to the post-Communist transition – the disintegration of the USSR and the rapid development of the integration within the European Union. Thus, only in the 1980s and 1990s have scholars focused on the synergy of national and international factors and its role in regime transition (Schmitter 1996; Whitehead 1996). The EU became a particularly pronounced external factor in democratization of the Central and Eastern European states and led scholars to focus on the nature and mechanisms of *democracy*-reinforcing external factors to explain the external impact of the EU, World Bank, and the United States (Bunce 2003, Carothers 1999, 2004, Pridham 2005). The direct external impact of the EU's projects and the EU's financial aid was analyzed beyond the EU's borders and beyond the border of former EU candidates, and its actual role in successful democratization at a regional sub-national level in Russia was recognized (Obydenkova 2006a, 2006b, 2007, 2012). A few other studies have traced the EU's positive impact not only on democratization but also on the independence of mass media across the regions of Russia that were involved in the EU's various programs and received the EU's aid targeted to facilitate the level of democratization and to help to build civil society in the regions of Russia (Obydenkova 2008).

However, it is only recently that scholars made one more step in developing the theory of international dimension, and they pointed out the existence of external autocratic influences (in additional to external democratic ones). Thus, two main types were finally distinguished: the democracy-*reinforcing* and autocracy-*reinforcing* ones (can also be described as democracy *decreasing*). Some studies argued that the external impact can be either democratic or anti-democratic depending on the nature of external actors (Obydenkova and Libman 2012). If democracy may spread from the West eastward, it is reasonable to suggest that autocracy may also move from the East westward. Given that external autocratic influence is a new highly debated topic, and as any new concept needs further theoretical consolidation and empirical validation, we have chosen to address this topic properly in one of the chapters of this book.

The theory of external influences in general on regime transition was mainly built on the analysis and experience of *democracy*-promoting actors and their mechanisms, with geography as one of the main elements of it. In the literature on the international dimension of democracy, a few successful attempts had been made in classification of these democratic external influences. Thus, for example, Jacoby (2006) distinguished three types of external impact – inspiration, coalition and coercion. Levitsky and Way (2010) specified two types of external impacts – linkages and leverages. Leverage is similar to the coalition approach as both are interpreted as intentional strategies of democracy-promoting factors. The mechanisms of inspiration can be tentatively associated with mechanism of linkages as both can be non-intentional and unplanned, and both may imply the diffusion of (democratic) values, principles and imitation mechanisms. The inspiration, coalition and linkages (in contrast to leverages and coercion) are more likely to take place if there is a geographic proximity or a border with a democratic neighbor. This scholarship on external democratic impact gave rise to the research on external autocracy promotion (or diffusion). The distinction had been made between intentional (promotion) and non-intentional (diffusion) types of external anti-democratic influences.

Further on, scholars faced a challenge to address the *mechanisms* of external influences. In some cases, those mechanisms were obvious, as stated in guiding principles of the EU's enlargement, for example. However, in other cases, those mechanisms at work were much more subtle. One of the studies that addressed this challenge was the theory of geographic diffusion by Kopstein and Reilly (2000). According to this analysis, democratic values and principals may spread across borders, and geography and distances were analyzed as important factors of democratic diffusion. The theory of the international dimension of democratization was successfully applied and tested in the regions of Russia.

## *Limiting factor – the dependence of economic growth*[1]

The dependence of economic growth argument, based on the notion of a limiting factor, has been developed in Libman and Obydenkova (2014a). The limiting factor theory explains the cases of the failure of democracy where both natural resource curse and international dimension in their original form do not apply. It can be tentatively argued that the limiting factor theory lies at the nexus of the resources curse and the international dimension approach but was proved to be critically different from both.

The limiting factor is a specific economic resource that is crucial for the economic development and well-being of the society, and the presence of it is an equally crucial obstacle for successful democratization in a region or a state. More specifically, the limiting factor is a particular resource with a highly localized source that is in short supply and that leads to the dependence of economic growth of the total state or region on this one source; as a result, it presents a strong obstacle to successful democratization or even makes it impossible (adjusted from Libman and Obydenkova 2014a). Originally, the concept of limiting factor was employed in ecological economics to refer to a situation where productivity is conditioned and dependent on the least available factor. This concept can be used, however, for political science purposes to explain unsuccessful democratization in the post-Communist world.

Limiting factors can be tentatively distinguished into internal and external types. It is important to state that in most of the case, there is a certain interplay between internal and external aspects that creates a mechanism of the dependency of the economic development on one single source and that leads to the establishment and consolidation of autocracy (even if the initial departure point was transition to democracy). The external type of limiting factor is associated with resources located outside the polity that are essential for the polity's growth. We will, in fact, focus on a particular example of this external type of limiting factor in the remaining part of the book.

Typically, an external limiting factor occurs if economic relations between the polity and a single foreign partner are very intensive – for example, if there is strong path dependency in trade patterns or if international institutions frame the trade patterns in a particular way. The internal type of limiting factor is associated with resources that are located within the polity but that are equally crucial for economic growth. Natural resources obviously often qualify as meeting the definition of a limiting factor, but, as we will discuss in what follows, other examples of limiting factors are also possible. These limiting factors, anyway, should be of crucial importance for the polity's economic growth – hence the reference to the 'dependence of economic growth'.

There are three criteria the polity should satisfy to exhibit the dependence of economic growth–driven logic of regime transition. First, the economic development should be dependent on one particular source (Libman and Obydenkova 2014a). This logic should be present at both the macro level and the micro level (e.g., the access to this source is important for both growth of the region as a whole and performance of key companies). If the access to the source were restricted, growth would become impossible. Second, there should be high switching costs: in case the polity or its companies decide to search for a substitute to the source we discuss, accessing this substitute should be particularly costly (Libman and Obydenkova 2014a). Third, it should be possible for the incumbent to seize control of the source (i.e., the limiting factor). If we look at an internal limiting factor, control is determined by the power balance in the society; for an external limiting factor, it is driven either by the extent incumbent that controls foreign trade in general or by the willingness of the foreign partner to engage in any deals or transactions only if approved by the incumbent (Libman and Obydenkova 2014a). It means that in this case international trade is not organized based on free market principles, but rather follows the informal structure of political connections existing between elites of different polities. Very often dependence of economic growth is also associated with the fourth condition: having access to the limiting factor, the incumbent is capable of maintaining a relatively high level of well-being of the population (thus preventing protests and revolutions and buying loyalty of the population through providing benefits from the source the incumbent controls; see also Allina-Pisano 2010). In this case, the regime transition is affected as follows: the incumbent uses the control over the limiting factor to ensure economic power (i.e., loyalty of companies, which, in exchange for access to the limiting factor, will back the incumbent), which is then transferred into political power (which, as mentioned, can also be associated with the use of the limiting factor for redistribution purposes).

The limiting factor is universal chronologically and geographically, meaning it can be found present in history and the modern world and across different content. Thus, although it helps explain heterogeneous outcomes of post-Communist democratization, it is not exclusively linked to modern Eurasia. The limiting factor slightly resembles the mechanism present in the natural resource curse theory, where the economic development of a state is dependent on one single source – that is, the presence of natural resources (normally oil and/or gas resources) that provides abundant revenue for the economic survival of a state and for the relative well-being of its population. However, the limiting factor is more encompassing mechanisms that account for a number of types of economic development where the natural resources are not necessarily present or crucial. In contrast to the natural resource curse, the limiting factor can demonstrate itself in various forms that are nor related at all to the presence of oil and gas resources and allows researchers to explain a few counter-intuitive failures of democratization in Eastern Europe that other theories of democratization are unable to explain.

The external types of limiting factors are probably somewhat easier to find in the modern world. To provide a recent example outside the post-Soviet context, Libman and Obydenkova (2014a) consider the case of Fiji as another example of the presence of a limiting factor. Fiji passed over the transition period in the 1970s when it became independent. Historically, starting from colonial period, Fiji has been specialized in sugar exports. After Fiji became independent, it continued exporting sugar to Europe as part of the European Union Sugar Protocol, which was abolished only in 2009. The Sugar Protocol created a system of preferential access to the European market for the member-states of the protocol and favorable conditions for importing states like Fiji with prices for sugar much higher than at the international market. Again, the four features of limiting factor mechanism can be found in the case of Fiji: (1) it is organized within a market with high barriers to entry as protected by the protocol; (2) this became the main source of the economic development of Fiji and provided a certain well-being level of its population; (3) the switching costs were too high; (4) this only source was captured by the political leaders and resulted in seizing control over the economy and politics of a state (Libman and Obydenkova 2014a). The mechanism of the limiting factor had been so pronounced in the case of Fiji that even after the initial period of transition in the 1970s and the establishment of the democratic political system, the state was slowly but steadily converted into a autocracy that, according to research, had been promoted and sustained by political elites holding major stakes in sugar production and trade (Barbalich 2009).

Internal varieties of the limiting factor mechanisms can, for example, be found in history (e.g., the case of a polity with a centralized infrastructure – one that can be only managed and organized by the central government). Historically, one may find similar case in the Ancient East hydraulic civilizations when strong control over the irrigation systems was established by the central authority. The economic performance of these hydraulic civilizations was totally dependent on the irrigation and, thus, on the center. Central governments of these civilizations became highly despotic, although with prosperous and stable economies (see Wittfogel 1957). A modern mechanism, resembling some of these features, can be found in the cases of external pro-democratic aid-dependent countries when the aid is linked to the presence of the specific leader in power. These examples are present in the modern post-Communist world, as some studies have demonstrated (see Fish 2001). Other scholars have noticed certain similarities between these cases of foreign aid and resource-curse mechanisms (Morrison 2012). As all other aforementioned theories of democratization, the limiting factor mechanism will be tested in application to the regions of Russia, where it can be identified easily and where a set of intervening variables can be controlled, unlike in the case of nation-states.

## 2.2 Consequences of democratization

The literature on the consequences of democratization is far less developed than the literature on the causes of democratization in political science; these topics have been mostly considered in other fields, in particular in economics, where political regime is a standard explanatory variable in many models of economic growth (Durlauf et al. 2005). While studies focused mainly on democracy as a dependent variable, very few approached it as an independent variable. Recently the consequences of democratization attracted more and more attention, and the first attempts at the systematization of consequences of democratization took place. While approaching the consequences of democracy, it became more important than ever to disentangle the concept of democratization in a more nuanced way: Is civil society an aspect of democracy or its consequences? Is independent mass media the result of democratization or part of it? Is economic liberalization a process that is paralleled by democratization or rather prerequisite of it or even its consequences?

When it comes to democratization – the process of increase in the level of democracy, but not the democracy per se – the analysis of its consequences is more straightforward and can be grouped into a few fields of research. It is also important to highlight that when it came to the studies of the consequences, the literature often used 'democracy' and 'democratization' interchangeably. Among the first and detailed attempts at classification of the consequences of democracy was given by Giovanni Carbone (2009), who distinguished the consequences into seven groups and with the eighth group demonstrated that his classification was actually open-ended. Among the most studied consequences is probably the group of economic consequences: nexus of democracy and economic liberalization, economic growth and, related to it, well-being of the population. Among economic consequences, the following can be distinguished: promotion of openness of trade and financial openness, privatization, reduction in taxation, makes external financial aid more effective and so on. Even in this first group of consequences, it is important to highlight the intrinsic presence of the internal-external nexus: democratization is associated with a number of external factors (that are also considered among its causes). Democracy is also associated with a higher level of satisfaction of life in the population of a given state (this is explained though increase of welfare and well-being and increase of the importance of population through raises of social spending, raises of wages, better education, etc.)

Another group of consequences is far more disputable: that democracy is meant to promote national and international peace and prevent wars and conflicts. However, the establishment and consolidation of democracy is often accompanied by civil conflicts, wars, demonstrations and social unrest.

Yet another group of consequences is related to the better nation-building and strengthening of the state through making authority more legitimate in the eyes of the population, advancing the rights of the citizens, reducing corruption, introducing into society new values and political principals, providing new norms of political behavior (e.g., respect for the law and introducing the rule of law) and increasing the responsibility of the citizens (through, for example, participation in elections).

In the last group of this classification are separately considered various consequences such as increase of happiness of the population and its trust, respect for human rights and protection of the environment.

### Economic consequences: economic growth and economic liberalization

Although the format of this book does not allow testing all the groups of consequences that have been discussed in the literature, we have selected some of the important consequences of democratization that hopefully will contribute further to the studies on this topic. Inevitably, we consider the most studied nexus of democracy and a number of economic variables. While this nexus has received substantial attention in the literature, the studies still debate on its place (economic factors were considered among the causes of democratization and the consequences, and these debates have been ongoing up to the present). Thus, a set of studies has explored the issue of how democracy influences economic growth (e.g., Przeworski and Limongi 1993) and how political transition impacts economic growth (e.g., Fidrmuc 2003, Giavazzi and Tabellini 2005). Economics research, where this literature comes from, originally was very skeptical toward democracy. In economics, there exists an established tradition of looking at democracy as a harbor of populism, which would undermine economic growth. On the contrary, restriction of democratic control could allow the 'autonomous government' to implement the necessary (although occasionally socially painful) reforms and achieve higher growth levels. However, this original skepticism has also been challenged by numerous investigations that criticize non-democratic regimes as being particularly prone to rent-seeking (Acemoglu and Robinson 2012), harming economic growth. Instability of economic policy is another issue that has been debated in this context, again with some studies treating authoritarianism as less likely to implement consistent economic policies (due to the lack of checks and balances) and others being more critical toward democracy (due to the time inconsistency problem inevitably occurring for governments ruling for a limited period of time) (Kyland and Prescott 1977).

This theoretical debate has been paralleled by skyrocketing empirical research, which put substantial effort into overcoming the econometric difficulties studies of democracy and growth often encounter (especially the endogeneity). As of now, the literature is extremely heterogeneous (Doucouliagos and Ulubasoglu 2008). The consensus, which most economists would subscribe to, is that economic growth on average is the same in democracies and in non-democracies, but the variation of economic growth rates is higher in non-democratic regimes – the least and the most successful countries in terms of growth are autocracies (Weede 1996).[2] Modern literature also argues that growth effects may differ depending on the type of autocracy (Besley and Kudamatsu 2008; Gilson and Milhaupt 2011). Another point, which is often made in the contemporary studies, is that one needs to carefully investigate particular *channels* of effects of democracy on economic growth – for example, the impact of regimes on public goods provision and on human capital formation. Even if there is no evidence that democracy directly affects economic growth, there may be indirect effects through changing other growth fundamentals (quality of labor and capital, population growth, technological progress, etc.) (Tavares and Wacziarg 2001; Baum and Lake 2003). Finally (and this is the point we develop in depth in this book), more and more researchers focus on the potential non-linearity of effects of democracy on economic growth.

Somewhat less studied consequences of democratization are related to the management of public resources. Among many, we decided to focus on the quality of forest management and mineral resource management. We consider these two areas of management to evaluate their relationship to the democratization that took place across the regions. The implications of democratization for renewable natural resources and ecosystems (such as forests) are, to our knowledge, discussed only in very few studies. Elinor Ostrom's (1990, 1999, 2010, 2012) powerful research agenda suggests looking at the specifics of local governance systems, which could affect the management of natural resources. She in particular refers to the concept of 'local tyrannies' (Andersson and Ostrom 2007) – in other words, regimes with extremely restrictive access to resource rents. Furthermore, she looks at the problem of predatory resource use by unaccountable officials. This discussion, however, has to our knowledge almost never been integrated in the actual literature on democratization: for example, it is not self-evident that Ostrom's 'local tyrannies' and sub-national authoritarian enclaves, which have been studied in the democratization research, indeed share the same features. Our book tries to make the connection more explicit. With respect to mineral resources, again, the discussion mostly happened in economics research and to some extent can be reduced to the same contradiction we have discussed earlier – populism versus rent-seeking (Collier and Hoeffler 2009). Generally, there is a consensus among economists that high-quality economic institutions allow reducing the otherwise negative effect of resource rents on economic growth. However, whether democracies are particularly good at creating these high-quality institutions is unclear; furthermore, there are other channels as to how political regimes can affect the management of natural resources (e.g., redistribution schemes for resource revenue) (Eifert et al. 2002). Our book discusses this problem as well.

### *Formation of civil society as a consequence of democratization: political behavior through elections and social protests, new values and principles*

One of the consequences of democratization is the formation of a civil society (though there are some studies arguing that it is a prerequisite of democratization and others stating that it is an aspect of democracy). Based on the existing studies, one can safely state that civil society is indeed one of the main consequences of democratization; however, it can be endogenous with the process of democratization as one of the contributing factors. Civil society implies understanding and incorporating into the everyday life certain democratic values, principals, civil responsibility and political behavior. In practice, it is implemented through such activities of the civil society as active participation in elections (understanding civil responsibility) and demonstration of consent as well as discontent through, for example, civil protests. In contrast, non-democratic regimes (totalitarian or authoritarian) demonstrate very low if any at all mass activities in the form of protests and demonstrations. Throughout the history of the USSR, there were no open demonstrations against the state power. However, while suppressed by the state, the population used to find different forms of fighting (not protesting) against the state. Here it is important to highlight the difference between fight and protest. A protest implies the public demonstration of disagreement on the part of the population about certain actions by the state (e.g., enactment of specific laws or their implementation). In contrast, a fight may be both open but also frequently hidden and may find the way of more implicit demonstration through, for example, art (e.g., artistic sarcasm and metaphors in literature or music or poetry). Specifically, in Soviet totalitarian society, where open fight against the state power was out of the question and the population was scared to protest in open and explicit ways, the fight took place in artistic forms and mainly in literature and in even more hidden, indirect ways in various though admittedly few published mass media (the TV and the radio were under strict control of the government, while control over the press was slightly more relaxed). From this historical perspective and for the specific region under study, only some very few aspects of civil society can be tentatively considered to be a prerequisite for democratization. The formation of civil society started with the disintegration of the USSR and followed up the emergence of the newly independent state. From the beginning of the 1990s, the population became more independent in the demonstration of their protests and discontent or disagreements with the state policy across former Soviet republics in general and in Russia in particular.

Apart from civil protests and demonstrations, there is yet another characteristic of mature civil society – the responsibility to participate in national politics through legitimate elections and the choice made over the elections. During the totalitarian regime, elections were insignificant, and the population was not enthusiastic to vote. Despite the massive falsification in elections starting from the beginning of the 2000s, the attitude toward elections had changed significantly as compared to the Soviet period. Participation in elections became one of the important ways of manifestation of public opinion, and it can be considered properly as one of the aspects of the formation of proper civil society (that had been previously absent).

Yet another aspect of civil society can be distinguished and related to political behavior of the population and separately to the formation of democratic values and principles. As for the former, it can be seen, as explained earlier, in mass protests and changed attitude toward elections. As to the later, the changes taking place in values and principals are more difficult to trace but not impossible. For example, principals of behavior that can be captured, such as respect for honesty and transparency and respect for the rule of law, did take place. Indeed, democracy and associated with it civil society are highly associated with respect for the law and transparency in politics and public affairs and the everyday life of the citizens, as well as honesty. Partly, this category is overlapping with corruption. There can be two ways of analyzing the relationship between then. Democracy may directly reduce corruption due to various reasons. Democracy may increase civil society and through this decrease corruption. The changes taking place after the beginning of democratization may occur in parallel with each other. However, it is not the main purpose of the book to disentangle this nexus, rather to find a better approach to operationalization. Thus, one of the good aspects to measure the level of the development of civil society as a result of democratization could be not the corruption per se, but rather the attitude toward the corruption, for example. Based on this, we can safely distinguish between two different consequences of democratization – the actual corruption (bribe offering and bribe taking) and civil society, defined as values and principles of the behavior (participation in elections, electoral choice, attitude to violation of the rule of law – through, for example, attitude to corruption) – and the actual manifestation of civil society (demonstrations and mass protests). This approach allows analyzing corruption and civil society as two different consequences of democratization, although admittedly interrelated between themselves as all other consequences.

## 2.3 Agency

The preceding discussion concentrated primarily on the role of structural causes of democratization. One of the most debatable issues in political science has been the relation between the role of structure and of agency in this context, as well as generally in politics (O'Donnell and Schmitter 1986; Keller 1996; Mahoney and Snyder 1999). While structure has previously been frequently studied in econometric large-$n$ papers, agency has typically been an exercise of small-N case studies. It is reasonable due to the very nature of the agency factors, strongly associated with choices and backgrounds of individuals and not generic characteristics of regions (like structure). Our book, however, attempts to provide a large-$n$ investigation of agency, thus complementing the existing case study literature.

Very few studies look at agency in Russia, and most concentrate on the background of regional governors (Libman et al. 2012; Schultz and Libman 2015; Sharafutdinova and Kisunko 2014; Vasilyeva and Nye 2013; Buckley, Frye, et al. 2014). Heads of the regions are certainly of crucial importance for their development, and this approach is entirely justified. However, we do not use it for two reasons. First, in Russia governors do not act alone; therefore, investigating agency of other actors in regional politics is of crucial importance, although it has almost never been done in the past.[3] Second, we look at a relatively long period from 2001–2010. During this time, most Russian regions experienced a change in governor, and many had several governors appointed and removed. The correlation between characteristics of old and new governors is typically very low; thus, we would find it difficult to use any governor characteristics to explain the index of democracy for the period from 2001–2010 (using an average would lead to results hard to interpret).

Therefore we took a different approach, which has, to the best of our knowledge, almost never been used in the preceding literature to account for agency: we concentrate on the variation in the composition of regional bureaucracy as part of agency. We use this variable throughout the book in two contexts. In the first part of the book (chapters 4–7) we look at the regional bureaucracy as a *predictor* of democratization. More specifically, we investigate how regional bureaucracy *as such* affects the process of democratization and how it influences the *conditional* effect other variables have on democratization. It is possible that some of the determinants of democratization have a different effect depending on the features of regional bureaucracy. In the second part of the book (chapters 8–12), we look at how the composition of regional bureaucracy changes the *effects* democratization has on various outcomes. Somewhat simplified, the logic of this analysis has to be understood as follows. A particular structure of bureaucracy is leading to higher (or lower) level of democracy *on average* across all Russian regions. However, since the effect of bureaucracy is statistical (as is always the case in social sciences), and not deterministic, there are always certain regions that have a too high or too low level of democracy given the structure of their bureaucracy. We argue that for these regions the consequences of democracy for various variables (e.g., economic growth) will be different than for other regions. Somewhat simplified, in the first part of the book we look at how human actions (agency) within certain structures affect the outcomes of democratization. In the second part, we look at how human actions within certain political regimes affect the implications of these regimes.[4]

Bureaucracy in Russia, with some exceptions (mostly in the military sector), is organized across the borders of the regions. Within each region, two types of bureaucrats are present: the regional bureaucrats (which serve the regional government with its own agencies) and the bureaucrats of the local branches of the federal offices (which in Russia are, as mentioned, organized within the regional borders). For federal offices, there is also a higher level – the so-called 'federal districts', seven (later eight) groups of regions, which were created by Putin in the early days of his presidency as a tool of political control over regional governors; the size of the staff of the districts is negligible, and after elections of governors were abolished, the importance of the districts disappeared. We look at both federal and regional bureaucrats in each region because they frequently interact with each other (and sometimes functions switch from the federal to the regional level – we will look at a particular example of this process while talking about forest resources – or vice versa). The fact that bureaucracies are organized into regional units allows us to argue that the characteristics of regional bureaucracy we are going to use in what follows can indeed be applied for research. Furthermore, there is substantial evidence that there is a spatial variation in the behavior of bureaucrats and that this variation is regional (e.g. Yakovlev and Zhuravskaya 2013) – again, supporting the approach we use.

   In what follows, we will attempt to develop a set of hypotheses regarding the possible role of the bureaucratic agency, which will guide our investigation. These hypotheses are based on two assumptions. First, we argue that the political leadership of the regions – the regional governors – *are generally interested in maximizing their power.* The idea that politicians should be looked at as 'power-maximizing beings' is extremely old and well established in social sciences; it is used as the basic assumption in many rational choice approaches (starting with the famous median voter theorem, which became the founding element of the Public Choice approach to politics). The assumption implies, however, that we ignore cases when governors promote democracy due to their ideological commitment to this form of governance. As any assumption, this argument is simplified – some Russian governors (like the Perm governor Nikita Belykh) have been known to have strong democratic convictions. However, the number of these governors is very small, and whether their ideological commitments actually affected their policy choices is debatable; hence, we believe our assumption to be generally valid for most cases. Second, in a democracy (or any other established regime) power maximization happens *within the given rules.* In a situation of regime transition, power maximization is happening *through the choice of the rules.* The natural outcome of successful power maximization by a governor is the establishment of a regional authoritarian regime. If the governor fails to achieve her goal and finds herself constrained by various other groups (e.g., elites, civil society, business, etc.), the region becomes more democratic. Of course, simple competition of various groups is not a sufficient condition for democratization (it may degrade into anarchy), but it is a necessary one. Therefore, any aspect of bureaucratic behavior, which can be used by the governor to consolidate her power, implies that the authoritarian trajectory of regime transition becomes more likely. Interestingly, many of these actions would have different consequences in a stable regime, where they could, under certain conditions, strengthen the democracy, but in the process of regime transition, they promote authoritarianism.

Bureaucracy (mostly composed of street-level public officials) generally received less attention in the literature on democratization in Russian regions than the actions of political elites. However, bureaucrats are important for three reasons. First, they have to execute most of the decisions of the political leadership in order to consolidate a regional authoritarian regime or to democratize a region. These are bureaucrats who, for example, are involved in electoral falsifications (which is as a major factor influencing the Russian politics, see also Gel'man 2013) or monitor and pressure private business in the regions ensuring support of the governors. If the bureaucrats are more reluctant to follow the demands of the governors, their ability to successfully consolidate their regimes is lower (while it is rarely the case that bureaucrats directly contradict the governors, they may decide to de facto sabotage the decisions of the regional leaders). To some extent, bureaucrats reluctant to follow the will of the governor create an additional, although informal, type of checks and balances *within* the executive, limiting the power of the governor, who is de facto unable to implement measures necessary to consolidate his regime. If the bureaucrats are fully compliant, authoritarian consolidation becomes very easy. This is again a nice example of the aforementioned contradictions: in an established democracy, non-compliant bureaucracy is a problem for the functioning of the democratic system, which finds it more difficult to implement political decisions democratically elected leaders make. But in a regime transition setting, governors make not just policy decisions, but also decisions concerning further regime transformation – and here non-compliance of bureaucrats can play a positive role.

Second, bureaucrats have a major impact on the information access of political leaders and therefore on their decisions. Russian sub-national regions are relatively large, and therefore the ability of governors to effectively collect information is crucial. The logic of our argument is essentially the same. Better informed governors find it easier to establish authoritarian control over a region. For example, information can be used to pressure private business; to establish a 'blackmail state' where officials are forced into submission due to the governor having sufficient information on their transgressions; or to monitor information flows between the region and the center (thus ensuring what the already discussed paper by Gibson 2005 calls the 'boundary control' – i.e., preventing the intervention of the federal government into regional conflicts). Again, in a democracy or in a non-democracy, lack of information merely reduces the efficiency of the political machine, but in a regime transition setting, it also affects the ability of the governor to consolidate the regime.

Third, it is the behavior of bureaucrats (e.g., while interacting with the recipients of public services) that influences public perception of the regional government – since in Russia enforcement of laws is very weak, the actions of bureaucrats are often more important in the public's eyes than any high-ranked decisions. Here the effects are more complex, since they relate not merely to the policy options a governor has, but to the general perception of the regional political system by the public. We expect these effects to manifest themselves at a later stage – in other words, when the regional regime starts forming. The behavior of bureaucrats might be related to an increase in corruption, which has a direct influence on public opinion, undermining public trust in institutions and their legitimacy. It also might settle or entrench norms of corrupted behavior in the society that will be accepted or supported on the part of the population. As a result, the existing regime will be undermined. If it is a democratic regime, democratic consolidation becomes more difficult; if it is an authoritarian regime, it will also find it more difficult to gain public trust and support.

## 2.4   Sub-national aspects

The theoretical discussion of this chapter would be incomplete if we did not explicitly mention another important issue, which we have tried to take into account in the remaining part of the book. The research on sub-national democratization has originally been based on the research on democratization at the national level. However, the literature has frequently pointed out that sub-national democratization is a phenomenon which has a number of specific features, not necessarily paralleling those of national-level democratization. Somewhat simplified, these features are associated with two aspects: instruments of control and actors involved.

In terms of instruments of control, sub-national regimes are much more often using indirect tools (like economic pressure, populist redistribution programs, etc.) than direct threats to the opposition and force. Certainly, force is used as well, but in most cases the options sub-national leaders have in this respect are, as we will discuss in what follows, limited; hence, indirect instruments have to be applied – in particular, economic control over businesses and fiscal flows (Sidel 2014). It matters not only for the nature of the regimes, but also for the consequences these regimes have for economic development – chapter 8 will provide a detailed discussion of this issue.

In terms of actors, sub-national politics is always intertwined with politics at the national level. Gibson (2005) suggests that if the national politics is democratic, the most important task any sub-national regime has to resolve is to limit the impact of federal politicians on what is happening in the region. If the national politics is autocratic, this task is equally important because the willingness of the central government to intervene in regional politics may be larger – authoritarian regimes often establish control over any alternative power centers in excess to what is actually needed to survive or to generate rents, since this excessive control is used as a signal to the supporters of the regime (Simpser 2013). Furthermore, interaction with federal politics (e.g., gains from federal transfers, which are discussed by Gervasoni 2010) can create additional tools of authoritarian consolidation at the sub-national level. Finally, sub-national politicians in their actions may also be driven by the concerns created by national-level politics – for example, they may have ambitions to become federal politicians at some point. In Russia there are some specific implications of this interdependence of the regions and the center, which we discuss in chapter 3.

The specific nature of sub-national regimes, of course, does not imply that the theories of national democratization are automatically to be treated as not applicable to them or that sub-national politics cannot be used as a testing ground for these theories – on the contrary, Snyder (2001) in an influential paper makes a strong case in favor of using sub-national samples. It merely means that if we investigate the sub-national politics, we need to subject the national-level theories and explanations to another plausibility check, associated with the sub-national political specificity. We will systematically do it in the remaining part of the book.

Summing up, the rich literature on democratization, its causes and its consequences provides us with a fruitful ground for empirical analysis of the Russian regions, which we will implement in the remaining part of the book. At the same time, there are also numerous gaps in the literature, which our book could help fill in.

## Notes

1 This section is adjusted from Libman and Obydenkova (2014a)
2 The very recent work by Acemoglu et al. (2014) again challenges this claim.
3 There are some papers, which look at vice-governors (Reuter and Buckley 2014) and mayors (Buckley, Garifullina, et al. 2014), but typically in relatively specific contexts.
4 This approach, certainly, faces a number of econometric challenges, multicollinearity being the most important one. The econometric analysis we will implement in the remaining part of the book attempts to take this problem into account.

# 3 Regions of Russia
## Sub-national regime heterogeneity

## 3.1 Sub-national regimes

This chapter presents the sub-national regime transitions that have occurred in Russia from 1991 until 2011. The aim of this chapter is to demonstrate the various paths that regions have taken over the last twenty years as well as the various outcomes of these paths. The outcome levels of sub-national democracy range from consolidated autocratic sub-national regimes to various hybrid regimes. This chapter presents the conceptualization and operationalization of the main phenomenon under study – the sub-national democracy. The main purpose here is to explain how sub-national democracy can be operationalized for research purposes – in general and in the Russian context. Specifically, we stress that the phenomenon of regional democracy cannot be solely reduced to its institutional aspects. While the institutions matter, other aspects of democracy such as the development of civil society, the independence of the mass media and the political behavior of the local bureaucrats are important ingredients of political regimes; the role of informal institutions in the process of sub-national democratization seems to be even larger than for national democratization. In what follows, the chapter will demonstrate heterogeneity of outcomes of democratic development in Russian regions. The research presented in this chapter is from multiple time periods and demonstrates the persistence of differences between sub-national regimes despite centralization trends.

While the differences in democratic development across the regions of Russia are the crucial issues to address, it is also important to outline so-called contextual differences of the regions. The regions of Russia traditionally have been highly heterogeneous in such factors as geography, climate, density of the population, historical path, economic development and the presence of different ethnic minorities as well as the presence of various religious confessions that seemed to have survived even over the atheism of the Soviet period.[1] In the beginning of the regime transition and the emergence of a new state – the Russian Federation – in the early 1990s, the sub-national regions of Russia became even more different from each other in terms of political development, which eventually resulted in various political regimes. While some variation in the governance mechanisms at the sub-national level existed already in the Soviet era (more on this in chapter 5), the collapse of the USSR and the subsequent regime transition in various regions followed multiple trajectories, resulting in very different outcomes.

The 1990s were characterized by a rapid and chaotic decentralization policy under the government of Boris Yeltsin. Many sub-national regions have asked for additional autonomy, and most were granted this autonomy in the form of bilateral contracts made between national and regional executives. In some cases, this autonomy was also grabbed unilaterally – Russian regions introduced legislation and norms explicitly contradicting the federal acts (Polishchuk 2001; Stoner-Weiss 2006). Furthermore, federal bureaucrats in the regions were often inclined to form coalitions with the regional elites. All in all, the regional governors received real autonomy and considerable independence from the national government for the first time in the 20th century. The result provided sub-national governments with ample opportunities to unilaterally change the political system of the regions. Depending on the specificity of the regions – the initial endowment, economic and social factors and so forth – the outcomes of the democratization process also varied dramatically.

On the one hand, while, during the 1990s, the national rating of Russia in such reputable think tanks as Freedom House was growing in terms of level of democracy at the national level, the sub-national political development in some of the regions went in the opposite direction. Back to the beginning of the 1990s, the sub-national leaders were mainly officials of the USSR who remained in power in the beginning of the transition in the 1990s, and only later did certain turnover take place. These governors had no experience of self-government and no experience or even understanding of democracy and its basic principles, such as the rule of law, electoral turnover, balance of powers and so on. They, however, had learned to use democratic parlance at ease without proper experience of implementation of basic democracy principles and values. The priority of many of the first regional executives in the 1990s was to keep recently gained control over politics in their respective regions and to seize the access to rents (which eventually resulted in a merger of political and business elite in many cases, as also will be demonstrated in some of the chapters of this book).[2] In other words, without being accountable to the national government (as it used to be during the Soviet period) and with lots of autonomy and power, they turned into kings of the region, often seizing control over politics and main economic enterprises. The result was the establishment of sub-national autocracies.

Among the most famous examples is the mayor of the City of Moscow, Yuriy Luzhkov, and his family, who took total control over the construction licensing in the Moscow City.[3] At the same time, Luzhkov was famous among the population for his democratic image. Among other examples where a higher level of autonomy from the central government was paralleled by an increasing level of autocracy at the sub-national level are two ethnic republics – Tatarstan and Bashkortostan. Both republics established and consolidated autocratic regimes, again controlling political development, electoral outcomes and the economy of the region. According to some studies, the rise of regional powerful autocrats became one of the reasons for the centralization launched by Putin's government from the early 2000s onward.[4]

In other regions, however, the outcomes of regime transition were different. In some cases strong regional civil society came into existence and constrained regional governors. In some regions legislatures remained powerful and independent players. In some regions old Soviet elites were driven away by the newcomers; these new incumbents partly created their own authoritarian regimes, but partly followed democratic principles. In some regions large corporations played the dominant role determining how the regional politics was organized (Gel'man 1999; Stoner-Weiss 1997; Hale 2003; Sharafutdinova 2006). Furthermore, conflicts between governors and elected mayors of the largest cities in the regions also contributed to the heterogeneity of the regime transition outcomes, which was clearly observable by the end of the 1990s, when most regions reached some sort of 'institutional equilibrium', reflecting itself in both the formal organization of regional government (varying from presidential to parliamentary republics) and, more importantly, informal rules and practices (Libman 2012).

Putin's territorial policy was described as radical centralization justified on the part of the national government in terms of the need for 'legal harmonization' and the need to fight against Chechen terrorism. The policy was paralleled by Chechen wars and resulted in rapid territorial centralization. Most power-sharing contracts were abolished in 2002. The national rating of Russia, according to Freedom House, fell radically from 2004 onward. In the rating of 2013, the Russian Federation has a score of 7 – the lowest one assigned by Freedom House – and is included into the group of non-democratic regimes (or authoritarian regimes). However, as previously explained, centralization and autocratization at the national level may be paralleled by democratization at the sub-national level. Some studies even argued that the centralization of Putin´s government was one of the factors of regional democratization: regional governors became weaker players at a national level and, as the result, had less control over regional politics as well. One of the unexpected consequences of this trend was the increase in political pluralism and the multiplicity of political players at the regional level (as less controlled by the regional governors) and the overall increase in the level of sub-national democracy (Petrov and Titkov 2013).

Thus, the dynamic change of the level of democracy at the national level of Russia was paralleled by the equally dynamic change of sub-national levels of democracy that often went into directions opposite from the national one. It makes investigation of sub-national political regimes an important and non-trivial task.

## 3.2  Operationalization of sub-national regimes

The empirical literature on measuring sub-national regimes in federations is still in its early stages. Unlike cross-national analysis, where established proxies like Polity IV or Freedom House ratings are available, at the sub-national level most of the proxies are debatable. The reason is, first, that measuring sub-national regimes is more difficult due to the predominantly informal nature of their variation – regional governments more frequently change informal practices and patterns of implementation of legal acts than laws themselves, and these informal rules are hard to observe. Second, the heterogeneity of federations also makes sub-national regimes in these federations heterogeneous; therefore, an approach applicable for some countries may fail to work in others. Frequent qualitative small-N case studies avoid these limitations by carefully investigating the logic of formation of individual sub-national regimes (Stoner-Weiss 1997; Gel'man 1999; Alexander and Gravingholt 2002; Herrera 2005; Evans 2014); for the design of this book, which is primarily based on large-N analysis, a formal proxy of sub-national regimes in Russia is, nevertheless, necessary.

Probably, the most popular approach to studying sub-national regimes involves looking at electoral outcomes. While in some regions a single party or politician could dominate the political landscape and thus de facto create an authoritarian regime, in others the system would be more competitive (Hiskey 2005). A certain limitation of this approach is that it is hard to distinguish electoral outcomes from public preferences. A recent literature looks at the extent of electoral fraud (Myagkov et al. 2009), which has also been studied for different Russian regions (Bader and van Ham 2014). Still, democracy is not limited to this concept, so further extensions of the measurement tool are needed. While studying Russia, we benefit from the availability of a systematic index of democracy at the sub-national level, which was published by the Carnegie Center in Moscow, a Russian branch of the reputable Carnegie Endowment. The index, meanwhile, became the standard tool for measuring democratization, which is used in numerous insightful studies (Akhmetov and Zhuravskaya 2004; Trochev 2004; Lankina and Getachew 2006; Freinkman and Plekhanov 2009; Remington 2011, among others).

Conceptually, the idea of the Carnegie index follows the definition of the 'liberal democracy', which, according to Bollen (1993), can be described as a combination of two elements: democratic rule and political liberties. Democratic rule implies the existence of government accountability; political liberties mean that the public is free to participate in political organizations and that the freedom of speech is ensured, among other aspects. Accountability, in turn, is determined by the system of checks and balances (Persson et al. 1997) and rule of law in the political sphere (Giraudy 2013). The Freedom House index has mostly followed the conception of the liberal democracy, and so did the index developed by the Carnegie Center. The index is based on systematic evaluations of the regional political system conducted by reputable experts, which assigned each region a score on a five-point scale for each of the 10 dimensions of democratization, which are listed in the following:

1) Openness of political life: transparency of regional politics and of its involvement into national politics;
2) Electoral democracy: Transparent and fraud-free elections at all level conducted in specific region (at national, regional and local/municipal); competitiveness of elections; the role of 'administrative factor' (meaning the direct involvement the executive and judicial power; limitations and obstructions in electoral right of the population in a passive or active way; irregularities in electoral process;
3) Political structure at the regional level: the real balance of executive, legislative, and judicial powers; independence of judicial power and police; obstructions of the rights of the citizens;
4) Political pluralism: the existence of stable political parties and political coalitions in legislative branch, coalitions during the pre-electoral process and after the elections; political competition and polycentrism;
5) Independence of mass media: absence of the pressure of regional government and their attempts to control mass media in the region; the role of mass media in political life; the existence of mass media that are independent on regional administration; their audience;
6) Civil society: non-governmental organizations, referendums, different forms of social activity not sanctioned by the government such as strikes, meetings, demonstrations, protests, etc.;
7) Elite: quality, turnover of political leaders through elections; heterogeneity of elite; efficiency of the mechanisms of their coordination of their interests and their consensus;

8) Local self-government: the activity and the role of electoral local government;
9) Corruption: merger of political and economic elites, corruption-related scandals, efficiency of the fight with corruption;
10) Economic liberalization: privatization (regional laws and their implementation; scandals related to property rights).

Of these 10 aspects, the first 7 clearly relate to the definition of the liberal democracy and would hardly cause any concern from this perspective. The local self-government dimension looks at the existence and strength of municipalities; while this measure is typically not included in the analysis of democracy at the national level, at the sub-national level it is relevant since the political liberties and the accountability of the government in general strongly depend on the development of municipalities. In Russia, many regions had almost non-existent municipal levels of governance (municipalities were under complete control of the federal center), but in other regions municipalities were sufficiently strong and independent. The last 2 dimensions are the most troublesome, but the Carnegie index explicitly attempts *not* to measure liberalization and corruption as such, but rather to investigate their role in political life – whether corruption is used as a tool of political control (from simply bribing the voters to more complex forms, e.g., rent-seeking coalitions of the elites or 'blackmail state', see Darden 2001) and whether property rights in the region are sufficiently safe to make sure that the expropriation of assets is not used as a tool of political fights (as we will show in chapter 7, in Russia economic control is indeed a crucial precondition for political control for most regions). Furthermore, the existing evidence (Obydenkova and Libman 2012; Libman and Obydenkova 2015) shows that excluding the last 2 dimensions almost never changes any results of the estimations. The final version of the index, which we use in our analysis, was obtained as a simple sum of the 10 listed dimensions.

The Carnegie Center has published numerous editions of the index, and most papers, which have applied this variable in the previous research, used the 2000–2004 edition of the index. The period of 2000–2004 is indeed an attractive period for investigating sub-national democracy. On the one hand, regional politics was less chaotic and uncertain than in the 1990s, when regional regimes were merely forming themselves. On the other hand, sub-national governments were not yet under very strong political pressure from Moscow. The Putin government has already limited the *formal* variation of regional constitutions and the policy prerogatives of the regions; however, the informal practices, decisive for regional politics, remained unaffected. More importantly, since 1996 regional governors in all constituent units of Russia were publicly elected (before 1996, some regions practiced elections, while in others governors were appointed). The election system could have been influenced by the federal government (and, indeed, there are cases when Moscow intervened, de facto forcing individual governors to resign or making their reelection more difficult), but it still guaranteed a certain level of sub-national autonomy. Moreover, in the first half of the first decade of the 2000s, sub-national elections were partly substantially more competitive than the well-controlled national ones. By the end of 2004, Putin unexpectedly abolished the elections of governors, who became de facto appointed by Moscow. While originally appointments were relatively cautious, and strong powerful leaders of the past stayed in their office, over time the central government managed to replace most sub-national leaders, creating a new generation of regional governors (Libman et al. 2012).

In our book, we pursue a different approach from the previous literature: for the first time in the extant studies of the Russian federalism, we use the Carnegie index for the entire decade, 2001–2010 (published in Petrov and Titkov 2013). This allows us to check whether sub-national variation of political regimes persisted even after the appointment system was created and the federal government became a much more powerful player in regional affairs. Indeed, the appointment practices were never uniform; in some regions, federal administration had almost unrestricted power, in other regions it had to negotiate with regional elites, de facto taking their position into account (Libman et al. 2014). But, more importantly, in the liberal democracy definition, democracy refers not only to how the regional government is formed (through free and fair elections – while there were differences in this respect in terms of regional parliaments, for the regional governors no differences were observed), but also how the regional government exercises its power. In more democratic regions, it may be forced to compromise with various regional political forces and with civil society; in less democratic regions, it would be much less constrained. Anecdotal evidence suggests that these differences indeed persisted in Russia – thus, Vladislav Surkov, a powerful advisor to Putin who was often described as one of the creators of Putin's political system and of the very concept of the 'sovereign democracy', as late as 2009 described Russia as a 'multi-speed' democracy, referring to differences in regional governance (Biryukova and Novikova 2009). However, no systematic large-N evidence exists in this respect – our book is the first attempt to provide one, also comparing the findings for the early 2000s and for the first decade of the 2000s in general.

This approach and the indicator we use, however, make it necessary to indicate two important caveats. First, the analysis of sub-national democracy we implement should be based on different arguments and mechanisms than the studies of national democracy. While some aspects of the 'national-level' literature, of course, can be borrowed, the specifics of the sub-national level have to be recognized explicitly. This is a well-known issue in the literature on sub-national political regimes, which frequently points out the need to take the interaction with the federal government into account (Gibson 2005). For us, however, the issue is even more important since, as mentioned, we look at sub-national democracy in regions with appointed governors. We will show (for example, in chapter 8) how this factor changes some of the more standard conclusions of the literature. Second, the concept of liberal democracy (and in particular the focus on how the power is exercised) is debatable in the political science. Our approach, on the one hand, does not cover the more general definitions of democracy. More importantly, on the other hand, it is broader than the more restrictive concept of 'procedural', or 'minimalist', democracy, which is advocated by a large part of the literature (see discussion of various concepts of democracy in Munck and Verkuilen 2002; Coppedge et al. 2011). The idea of the 'minimalist' democracy is to concentrate explicitly on how the regional government is formed, separating it from the way regional authority is exercised. Giraudy (2013), in another large project attempting to measure sub-national democracy in several Latin American countries, explicitly introduces two indices – one for the access to power and one for the exercise of power. We cannot do it because in Russia governors since 2005 were appointed. However, with all its caveats, the liberal democracy concept is highly influential in the political science and is relevant for many aspects of the discussion – thus, we find our approach to be relevant as well but think it is crucial to clearly separate what we can achieve and try to achieve from what is not relevant for the Russian case.

### 3.3 Variation of sub-national regimes: quantitative evidence

Let us briefly look at the variation of sub-national regimes across Russian regions before we proceed to more systematic analysis of the causes and consequences of democratization. From now on, we will look at a universe of 79 Russian regions. It includes almost all Russian regions, with a few exceptions: first, we, following the approach dominant in the literature, exclude Chechnya (for which no systematic data is available for most indicators and which has a very special status in the Russian political system); second, we exclude all autonomous okrugs – lower-level political units, which were parts of other constituent units of the federation and for which, therefore, many indicators were not available as well.[5] According to the Carnegie dataset, the democracy indicators vary from 18 (the lowest possible level, according to the way the index was constructed, could be 10) and 43 (50 is the highest potentially achievable score). The average score is about 30. We have to stress that this variation does *not* mean that the region with the highest score can be treated as a successful democracy of the European style, and the least democratic region is comparable with North Korea or Turkmenistan. The index is relative, not absolute. From this point of view, most Russian regions could be classified as different varieties of 'hybrid regimes'; this will be important for our discussion in a number of chapters. However, even within this limit, we find enormous variation in what regimes could look like and how they could function, which justifies our investigation.

Figure 3.1 reports the kernel density estimator of the distribution of the levels of democracy in Russia. It is almost perfectly symmetric, which is to be expected given the use of the relative measure of democracy in our data. The highest score is achieved in the Sverdlovskaia oblast (with the capital of Ekaterinburg), followed by Perm, Samara, St. Petersburg City and Irkutsk. All these regions have been known for competitive and independent politics, with multiple actors involved in the decision making. The lowest score is achieved by three ethnic regions – Chukotka and two Caucasian republics, Ingushetia and Kabardino-Balkaria. This is another important feature of the Russian data, which we will more formally discuss in chapter 4 – ethnic regions are frequently less democratic than the rest of the sample.

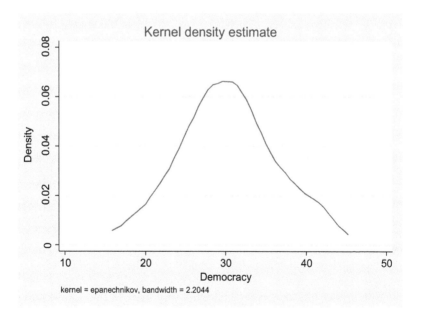

*Figure 3.1* Kernel density estimator, democracy scores

Source: Computed by authors based on Moscow Carnegie Center data.

Summing up, the variation of sub-national regimes in Russia can be considered an established phenomenon. From the next chapter on, we will systematically investigate the causes and the consequences of this variation.

## Notes

1 On survival of various religious confessions during the Soviet period, see Obydenkova (2015).
2 This observation is in line with similar trends in transitional societies in general, as was demonstrated by Hellman (1998).
3 Throughout the book, when we refer to the 'City of Moscow', we mean a constituent unit of the Russian Federation. If we refer to 'Moscow', it is typically used figuratively to describe the Russian federal government.
4 For detailed analysis of local politics in Russia and the centralization reforms of Putin, see Ross (2009) and Ross and Campbell (2009).
5 Besides, many autonomous okrugs were abolished in the 2000s. We do include Chukotka autonomous okrug in our dataset – it is the only okrug which is not part of another region; this specific construction is a legacy of the 'parade of sovereignties' Russia experienced in the early 1990s.

# Part I
# Causes of democratization

# 4 Determinants of democracy
## Structure and agency

As a starting point of our analysis, we apply the standard set of variables, which are typically used in research on causes of democratization outlined in the previous chapters, and investigate their effect on the level of subnational democracy in individual Russian regions. We start with structural variables, reflecting long-term patterns specific for particular regions. Our analysis concentrates, in particular, on four possible causes of democratization: those derived from the *modernization literature*; those from the *literature on resource curse*; those from studies of *economic openness*; and *cultural explanations of democratization*. The second part of the chapter focuses on the procedural-agency approach to democratization. It makes the first attempt in all literature on democratization to find the quantitative operationalization of the agency – something that has never been done previously. Thus it introduces the agency into the analysis, looking at the variable, which will play the central role in our investigation for the remaining part of the book – the composition of regional bureaucracy.

## 4.1 Structural perspective

Modernization literature, pioneered by Lipset (1959), belongs to the most powerful explanations of democratization in the extant political science, as discussed in chapter 2. In order to account for this approach, we distinguish three main explanations within the theory of modernization – the level of economy, the role of urbanism and education. The economy-related explanation is operationalized through monthly income per capita; the level of urbanization through the share of urban population versus rural; and level of education of the regional population is captured by the share of people in the region holding a university or other tertiary education degree.[1] All of these variables are derived from the official statistics of the Rosstat, the Russian official statistical agency. The theory of modernization suggests that these three variables – economy, urbanism and education – are the most important explanation for the success of democratization. We expect them to be positively and significantly correlated with the level of democratization in the regions. Since the index of democracy we use is computed for the period from 2001–2010, we also average the income and the urbanization levels over this period; annual income data is re-computed to ensure that they are measured in the same price units using the GDP deflator for Russia (reported by the World Bank). The education level is extracted from the data of the 2010 census; annual variation of this variable is not reported by the Russian statistical authorities.

The resource curse literature, which we have also briefly mentioned in chapter 2, particularly focusing on mineral resources (oil and gas), forcefully argues that abundance of natural resources is likely to decrease the level of democratization by affecting the behavior of both the political elites and the general population (Ross 2001). This factor is obviously of great importance for Russia, which is a resource-rich country; however, resources are unequally distributed throughout its territory – while for some regions resource extraction is important (like, for example, the Tiumen region in Western Siberia, where Russian oil fields are located), others have no reasonable natural resources. We proxy the impact of natural resources by the share of mineral resource extraction in the regional GDP. Unfortunately, this variable has been published only since 2005, so we use the average for the period from 2005–2010. This is, however, to some extent, an advantage for our analysis, since the second half of the first decade of the 2000s was associated with major changes in how resource rents were allocated in Russia. Resource curse theory suggests that the variable should have a negative sign.

Finally, this chapter also focuses on testing the role of culture in the success of democratization. There are a few ways we account for the cultural explanation. First, we proxy the cultural specifics of the Russian regions by the share of ethnic Russians (which, again, is extracted from the census 2010). Ethnic identity in modern Russia is self-reported (and not based on birth records, like in the Soviet era), yet it is unlikely that people massively misreported their perceived identities while responding to the census questions. The share of ethnic Russians is relevant for democratization for two reasons. First, regions which are different in terms of the ethnic composition from the rest of the Russian Federation are likely to have a different political culture, which in turn affects the level of democratization (Giuliano 2006). In this case we cannot make clear predictions regarding the sign of the variable. Second, a high share of non-Russian population is typically present in ethnic republics, which have been very successful in consolidating sub-national authoritarian regimes in the 1990s (and partially managed to keep their isolated political systems in the 2000s or integrated them into Putin's new hierarchical political system – 'power vertical' (Matsuzato

2004; Mikhailov 2010; Sharafutdinova 2013; Golosov 2014). In this case, we predict a positive sign for this variable – regions with larger share of ethnic Russians should be more democratic.

Second, in an additional specification we also add a further variable, which is linked to a large recent body of literature in political science (e.g., Fish 2002) and economics (e.g., Rowley and Smith 2009) and may be of relevance for Russia. Being not only a multi-ethnic, but also a multi-religious, country, Russia contains a number of regions with a high share of Islamic population. The literature frequently argues that Islamic countries may be less likely to develop democratic political systems; does it, however, also apply to Islamic regions within a single state? The literature has often attempted to integrate Islamic heritage into the analysis of variation of democracy in Russian regions, and typically (including our own earlier work, see Obydenkova 2012; Obydenkova and Libman 2012; Libman and Obydenkova 2015) did it controlling for a dummy, equal to regions, which traditionally have a Muslim majority (some of the Volga republics and some of the republics of the Northern Caucasus). This is also the approach we use in our analysis. In this specification we also drop the share of ethnic Russians from the set of controls to avoid multicollinearity.

Economic openness in our analysis is proxied by the share of foreign trade (exports plus imports) in the GDP of Russian regions. The literature on the role of economic openness as a factor predicting democratization is substantial (Milner and Mukherjee 2010); however, it mostly comes to ambiguous conclusions. While trade with foreign countries could increase the level of democracy, if it strengthens the value transmission from the democratic trade partners, it is likely to reduce the level of democracy, if it increases inequality. One possible explanation of puzzling heterogeneity of findings in different studies could be that they refer to different trade patterns established with different partners; we will provide a more detailed investigation of this problem in chapters 6 and 7. At this stage, however, we merely add the standard proxy of economic openness, as is done, for example, in our previous work cited earlier, but remain agnostic about possible direction and strength of effects.

## 4.2 Results of the structural perspective

Table 4.1 reports the results of the estimations. We add variables one by one to prevent multicollinearity problems. The findings are, however, robust to different permutations of the set of control variables. Three variables stand out as highly significant. First, urbanization has a significant and positive effect. If the share of urban population in the region goes up by 10 percent points, the democracy score increases by 2–3 points. The robust effect of

*Table 4.1* Baseline regressions; dependent variable: Carnegie index of democracy, 2001–2010, OLS

|  | (1) | (2) | (3) | (4) | (5) |
|---|---|---|---|---|---|
| Income per capita | −0.001 (0.000) | −0.000 (0.001) | −0.000 (0.001) | −0.000 (0.001) | −0.000 (0.000) |
| Urbanization | 0.269*** (0.075) | 0.275*** (0.078) | 0.272*** (0.078) | 0.184** (0.083) | 0.238*** (0.080) |
| Economic openness | 0.028 (0.020) | 0.031 (0.021) | 0.032 (0.021) | 0.024 (0.019) | 0.031 (0.020) |
| Education |  | −12.376 (15.372) | −18.256 (17.479) | −3.927 (18.143) | −11.300 (18.749) |
| Natural resources |  |  | −0.039 (0.048) | −0.006 −0.052 | −0.029 (0.047) |
| Share of ethnic Russians |  |  |  | 6.525** (3.017) |  |
| Dummy Islamic regions |  |  |  |  | −3.423* (1.975) |
| Constant | 12.685*** (4.172) | 14.741*** (4.839) | 15.738*** (5.330) | 13.505*** (4.922) | 17.002*** (5.239) |
| Observations | 79 | 79 | 79 | 79 | 79 |
| R-squared | 0.304 | 0.311 | 0.318 | 0.359 | 0.339 |

Note: robust standard errors in parentheses. *** significance at 1% level, ** 5%, * 10%. OLS stands for ordinary least squares estimates.

Source: Computed by authors using the data of Rosstat, Russian Census 2010 and Moscow Carnegie Center.

urbanization is consistent not only with the theoretical literature on modernization, but also with area-specific investigations of Russia: Zubarevich (2011) indicates that large urban centers in Russia differ greatly from the rest of the country in terms of culture and the extent of connections to the West. And it was large cities that became centers of the most recent wave of political protests against the Putin regime in 2011 and 2012 (Volkov 2012). Second, share of ethnic Russians is, as expected, significant and positive. Ethnic composition of the population has an impact on the political evolution of the Russian regions, which remains consistent throughout the 1990s. Dummy Islamic regions is significant and negative, again, as expected from the literature. Other variables, however, are insignificant. The lack of effect of education could be related to the specifics of the Russian educational system, which is strongly influenced by the Communist legacies; we will discuss it in chapter 5. Natural resources evidently play no effect because of strict central control over how the rents are allocated, which precluded sub-national autocracies in the second half of the first decade of the 2000s to use them as a resource strengthening their power. The effect of economic openness, as expected, is ambiguous – the variable is insignificant.

From now on, we will use specification (4) as the baseline regression, which will be subjected to modifications throughout the first part of the book. We do not use specification (5) for this purpose because the significance of the share of ethnic Russians as an explanatory variable is higher. In the next step in this chapter, we add a number of additional factors, which either are less relevant in the mainstream literature on structural causes of democratization or are more specific for the Russian case. To account for this, we control for the share of young (below 18 years) and of elderly (above 55 years for women and 60 years for men)[2] in the total population of the region. Elderly population may have experienced stronger indoctrination from the Soviet era or generally may be unaccustomed to democratic procedures due to life experience; thus, Soviet nostalgia (White 2010) in elderly regions may prevent effective democratization. Young population may be more open to new Western ideas and values but, at the same time, having grown up under Putin's rule, may be more accustomed to Putin's non-democratic system (this feature of the Russian young population became evident in 2014, when there was massive support of the youth for Putin's actions in Ukraine as well).

Yet another important factor is the role of geographic distances (where we distinguish the national geography – the distance to Moscow – and international dimension – the distance to foreign democratic and autocratic capitals). To account for national geography, we control for the distance between the capital city of the region and the city of Moscow. Distance from the capital has been shown to be a forceful predictor of any institutional variation (Libman 2010) and in particular of democracy (Obydenkova and Libman 2012; Libman and Obydenkova 2015) in the 1990s and in the first half of the first decade of the 2000s. On the one hand, regions more distant from Moscow may be more difficult for the center to control.[3] On the other hand, they may exhibit preferences regarding democratization, which differ substantially from those predominant in the regions close to Moscow. In some cases, these differences have caused distant regions (e.g., Primorsky krai in the Far East or Kaliningrad enclave in Europe) to experience mass protests against the policy implemented by Moscow (Libman 2011). Third, we control for the average temperature of January in Russia. This variable captures the climatic differences between Russian regions. The tradition linking climate to political specifics is very old and well established in social sciences (see the survey in Hardin 2009); in the Russian context it is possible, for example, that regions with less favorable climatic conditions are *ceteris paribus* more dependent on the central government and thus unable to develop a strong regional political scene or that the population of these regions is less interested in promoting democracy or any local institutions and rather focuses on the possibility of migration into a more favorable climatic environment, treating their current region of residency as temporary.[4] The results reported in Table 4.2 are unambiguous: none of the additional variables reported are significant. For age structure of the population, it may indicate that differences between elderly and young in Russia in terms of their lasting political values are not as strong as one could expect, at least in terms of their ability to affect the pattern of democratization. The same applies to the effect of climate. More puzzling and innovative is our finding

*Table 4.2* Additional determinants of democratization: dependent variable Carnegie index of democracy, 2001–2010, OLS

|  | *(1)* | *(2)* | *(3)* | *(4)* |
|---|---|---|---|---|
| Income per capita | 0.000 | 0.000 | 0.000 | 0.000 |
|  | (0.001) | (0.001) | (0.001) | (0.001) |
| Urbanization | 0.198** | 0.193** | 0.184** | 0.181** |
|  | (0.086) | (0.081) | (0.082) | (0.084) |
| Economic openness | 0.022 | 0.023 | 0.025 | 0.023 |
|  | (0.019) | (0.019) | (0.020) | (0.019) |
| Education | −1.329 | −1.134 | −1.919 | −5.182 |
|  | (18.791) | (18.467) | (18.849) | (18.243) |
| Natural resources | −0.008 | −0.013 | −0.008 | −0.003 |
|  | (0.053) | (0.054) | (0.053) | (0.052) |
| Share of ethnic Russians | 8.122* | 7.986** | 6.494** | 6.497** |
|  | (4.661) | (3.961) | (3.020) | (3.046) |
| Share of young population | 0.166 |  |  |  |
|  | (0.311) |  |  |  |
| Share of elderly population |  | −0.136 |  |  |
|  |  | (0.207) |  |  |
| Average January temperature |  |  | −0.031 |  |
|  |  |  | (0.074) |  |
| Distance from Moscow |  |  |  | 0.000 |
|  |  |  |  | (0.000) |
| Constant | 8.075 | 14.576*** | 12.920** | 14.060*** |
|  | (11.410) | (5.345) | (5.055) | (4.980) |
| Observations | 79 | 79 | 79 | 79 |
| R-squared | 0.361 | 0.362 | 0.36 | 0.36 |

Note: see Table 4.1.

Source: Computed by authors using the data of Rosstat, Russian Census 2010, various Internet sources (for distances) and Moscow Carnegie Center.

with respect to distance from Moscow since, as mentioned, previous research (including our own work) indicated a strong and significant effect of this variable. A likely explanation for the novel results we obtain in this book is that the effect of the internal (national, or domestic) geographical factors changed while Russia became more centralized.[5] It means that the central government is able to exercise a much closer control even over remote regions, which in the past managed to escape the attention of Moscow. Furthermore, since the second half of the 2000s, Russia has successfully instituted a system of rotation of heads of federal agencies (including security services and prosecutors) in individual regions. As a result, on the one hand, their connections to the regional elites were broken, and on the other hand, Moscow managed to establish more effective control over distant territories.

## 4.3   Agency perspective

As already discussed in the previous chapters of this book, our goal is to combine a structural perspective on democratization with an agency perspective in a single systematic investigation, and for this purpose we look at regional bureaucrats. In order to describe the regional bureaucracy, we use the data published by the Rosstat. They include both *regional officials* and *officials of the federal agencies working in the region* (Russian law includes both of them into the state civil service). Military personnel, policemen and security officers are not included, but civilian personnel of law enforcement agencies are included. The data do not cover employees of state-owned companies, as well as other personnel employed by the state (teachers, university professors, medical personnel, employees of state-owned railroad and local traffic companies etc.), which are officially not part of the civil service – the variables we are going to use measure bureaucrats in the narrow sense of this word only. Most of the bureaucrats in the data are, of course, street-level public officials. In the first step, we look at four sets of variables: size, age, tenure and education of the bureaucracy in the regions. Again, none of these characteristics have been previously systematically included in regressions of determinants of democratization in Russian regions (the research on the impact of civil service on democratization in cross-national comparisons is also extremely limited). We will discuss the hypothetical effects of these variables on democratization, as well as the way they are measured, in what follows.

### Size of regional bureaucracy

To start with, we compute the share of the public officials in the regional population. The variable reflects how large the bureaucratic machine is. The expansion of bureaucracy can be seen as evidence of bureaucratic power; Public Choice scholarship (Mises 1944; Niskanen 1973; Migue and Belanger 1974) suggests that bureaucracies are interested in growth in terms of size and the budget they control. This, in turn, is likely to have three implications for democratization:

First, large bureaucracy is likely to even further limit the development of the civil society, which is anyway an endangered species in many regions of Russia. Furthermore, it can be much more successful in backing the political leadership in its attempts to consolidate a regional autocratic regime (again, recall that we exclude the option of the regional leadership consciously willing to consolidate the democratic regime – if the regional governor is interested only in power maximization, the easiest way to achieve the goal in a regime transition environment is to consolidate the authoritarian system).

Second, large bureaucracy improves the ability of political leaders to collect information and to identify the causes of dissent. Certainly, one should not over-estimate the ability of a bureaucratic hierarchy to collect information – bureaucrats often report only favorable news to the political leadership (Prendergast 1993) and are appointed rather based on political loyalty than on competence (Egorov and Sonin 2011). But it is still more likely that a large and developed bureaucracy will be better at collecting information than a small and understaffed public service.

Third, large bureaucracy could affect public attitudes regarding the government – but the direction of this effect is unclear. On the one hand, larger bureaucracies may be better able to provide public services and thus make people more content with the existing regime (giving rise to paternalistic autocracies; see Eifert et al. 2003). The causal chain is in this case the following: regional governor requires public support to consolidate his power (which, as mentioned, will lead to the establishment of an authoritarian regime). If bureaucracy is better at providing public goods, public support is higher. Excellent examples of this logic are the City of Moscow and Tatarstan – in both bureaucracy functioned relatively well in the 1990s, and the regional leaders gained enormous popularity, creating authoritarian regimes and becoming influential players at the federal arena. This causal effect, however, can change over time: if a democratic system manages to emerge and establish itself in a region, the efficient bureaucracy becomes a factor supporting this system as well (as it happens in most well-established democratic states of the West). On the other hand, large bureaucracy, if it behaves predatorily, substantially increases pressure on the regional population. This could probably increase public disapproval of the government and encourage political activism.[6] For Russia, different papers find different effects of the size of bureaucracy on rent-seeking (Dininio and Orttung 2005; Brown et al. 2009; Libman 2012).

The first two effects have a clearly negative effect on democratization; the third effect is ambiguous: an 'honest' bureaucracy may improve the popularity of the regional regime, while a 'rent-seeking' bureaucracy is likely to increase public disapproval of the regime, but at the same time, alliances between rent-seeking bureaucrats and privileged businesses may again increase the likelihood of an authoritarian outcome of regime transition (the 'bureaucratic authoritarianism' argument by O'Donnell 1973). Thus, there are more reasons to believe that regions with large bureaucracies should have a lower level of democracy.

### Age of bureaucrats

To measure the age of bureaucrats in the region, we apply two proxies: the share of bureaucrats younger than 30 years and the share of bureaucrats older than 50 years.[7] For bureaucrats and officials 30 years old or younger, most of their life and their entire professional career were spent after the collapse of the Soviet Union: the share of these bureaucrats varies between 19% and 35%, with an average share of 28%. Bureaucrats older than 50 years started their career before the dissolution of the USSR; the share of these officials varies between 14% and 25%, with on average 21%. There are, again, several effects associated with the age of bureaucrats. First, older bureaucracies are likely to contain a larger number of officials who spent a substantial portion of their life in the Soviet Union and were socialized there. It is likely that these officials are less inclined to support democratic values. As a result, they are likely to be more supportive of attempts of a regional governor to establish himself as a single power center in the region. Furthermore, older bureaucrats typically have limited career options outside the public sector – the Russian labor market strongly discriminates against older age cohorts. Thus, keeping their position is more important for them, and they are more likely to accept any orders of the regional governors for this reason. Younger bureaucrats, on the contrary, have not been subjected to Soviet socialization and, in addition, have larger job market options and therefore are less dependent on complying with every requirement of the regional governor (again, recall that we assume that the governors are power maximizing and thus potentially want to establish an autocracy).

Summing up, our expectation is that if the share of older bureaucrats is larger and the share of younger bureaucrats is smaller, autocratic consolidation in the region should be more likely. Interestingly, while both variables we discuss are negatively and significantly correlated (with the correlation coefficient being −0.470), as one would expect, there are also regions where both the share of bureaucrats above 50 years and the share of bureaucrats below 50 years are large. St. Petersburg stands out in particular in this respect, having a very low share of bureaucrats between 30 and 50 years and a high share of both young and old public officials. This type of bureaucracy may have unpredictable effects for democratization and, generally, may face substantial difficulties in its functioning: whether older and younger bureaucrats will be able to communicate with each other is questionable.

*Tenure of bureaucrats*

Tenure of the bureaucrats is captured, similarly, by the share of bureaucrats who have spent less than 1 year in the civil service (between 5% and 10% in different regions) and by the share of bureaucrats who have spent more than 15 years in the civil service (between 19% and 36%). Obviously, tenure is strongly correlated with age, and many explanations discussed earlier for the hypothetical effect of age would also apply for the effect of tenure. However, there is also an additional effect associated with tenure specifically – socialization into public service. Bureaucrats who have spent a longer period of time working in the public administration have probably internalized the values and norms of the civil service. There is a large literature (e.g., Ryavec 2003; Gel'man 2010b) pointing out the poor practices and dominance of informal relations in the Russian civil service. Thus, it is reasonable to assume that a bureaucrat with a stronger civil service socialization will be more compliant to any requirements of the governor, and, as a result, the political leadership would find it much easier to mobilize bureaucracy, for example, in order to pressure private business or manipulate electoral outcomes. We, of course, do not assume that every governor is interested in pressuring business – on the contrary, Yakovlev (2011) provides evidence of informal coalitions, which were established in several Russian regions between the regional elites and the regional businesses to promote economic growth. We merely imply that a governor with a bureaucracy more compliant to his needs *could* use it to pressure business *if this goal becomes necessary to promote his power.* If bureaucracy is less compliant, the option is absent – and therefore the governor is more constrained in the choices he could make.

There are two further effects of longer tenure. First, tenure is associated with accumulation of civil service–specific human capital, which again makes a decision to leave civil service particularly costly. Second, as any socialization, socialization into the civil service is likely to be associated with much stronger in-group feeling, which would make bureaucrats unwilling to openly criticize their counterparts or to protest illegal actions of their superiors. This, again, simplifies autocratic consolidation. As a result, we predict tenure to have a significant and negative effect on the democracy score.

### Education of bureaucrats

Finally, education is measured by the share of bureaucrats with a university degree. In generally, the higher level of education is also associated with higher probability to establish democracy, as the literature review in chapter 2 argues. The indicator varies between 74% and 95%, but there are only a handful of regions where the share of bureaucrats with a tertiary education is below 80% (this list, however, is highly heterogeneous: it includes Chukotka, one of the most distant Russian regions in the Far East; Sverdlovskaya Oblast with the capital of Ekaterinburg, one of the largest industrial centers of Russia; Perm Krai in the Ural Mountains, again a major industrial center; and Leningradskaya Oblast, the region surrounding St. Petersburg and known to be ruled by an extremely corrupt local regime; see Libman and Obydenkova 2014a). Education is likely to have two effects on the behavior of the public service. First, low education again increases compliance of bureaucrats with all sorts of informal practices (probably coming from the lack of understanding of legal norms). Second, however, deficit of human capital is likely to make bureaucracy a less effective information-collecting instrument. While the first effect should reduce the likelihood of establishing a relatively democratic regime in the region, the second effect should strengthen the likelihood of democratization, making regional governors less powerful. Thus, our predictions for this variable are ambiguous.

## 4.4   Results of the agency perspective

In Table 4.3, we bring the hypothetical effects of the agency of bureaucrats to a test. We run the baseline specification of our regressions, extracted from Table 4.1, but add characteristics of the regional bureaucracy one by one. We do indeed find significant and strong effects of some of them. First, we find a significant and negative effect of the size of bureaucracy on the level of democracy. Regions with larger bureaucracies tend to be more authoritarian. This is in line with the hypotheses we have suggested in the previous section. We acknowledge that the regression may be plagued by reverse causality: it is possible that more democratic regimes, which are to greater extent under public control preventing rent-seeking, are forced to establish smaller bureaucracies. But first, in Russia the size of the bureaucracy in a region is to a large extent determined by the federal

Table 4.3 The role of bureaucratic agency: dependent variable: Carnegie index of democracy, 2001–2010, OLS

| | (1) | (2) | (3) | (4) | (5) | (6) |
|---|---|---|---|---|---|---|
| Income per capita | -0.001 | -0.001 | -0.001 | -0.001 | -0.001 | -0.001 |
| | (0.001) | (0.001) | (0.001) | (0.001) | (0.001) | (0.001) |
| Urbanization | 0.141* | 0.202** | 0.203** | 0.195** | 0.194** | 0.164* |
| | (0.082) | (0.083) | (0.080) | (0.079) | (0.076) | (0.087) |
| Economic openness | 0.022 | 0.022 | 0.023 | 0.024 | 0.025 | 0.015 |
| | (0.019) | (0.019) | (0.019) | (0.017) | (0.019) | (0.020) |
| Education | -14.612 | -8.257 | 2.012 | -9.308 | -7.48 | 7.939 |
| | (17.415) | (18.044) | (18.071) | (17.945) | (17.221) | (18.445) |
| Natural resources | -0.005 | -0.011 | -0.015 | -0.005 | -0.021 | 0.011 |
| | (0.053) | (0.052) | (0.053) | (0.050) | (0.052) | (0.051) |
| Share of ethnic Russians | 6.601** | 5.749* | 8.120** | 6.106** | 8.303** | 6.528** |
| | (2.932) | (3.138) | (3.340) | (3.044) | (3.233) | (3.036) |
| Size of bureaucracy per capita | -2.479** | | | | | |
| | (1.214) | | | | | |
| Share of young bureaucrats (< 30 years) | | 0.239 | | | | |
| | | (0.193) | | | | |
| Share of older bureaucrats (> 50 years) | | | -0.447 | | | |
| | | | (0.275) | | | |
| Share of bureaucrats with short tenure (< 1 year) | | | | 0.851** | | |
| | | | | (0.425) | | |
| Share of bureaucrats with longer tenure (> 15 years) | | | | | -0.363** | |
| | | | | | (0.166) | |
| Share of bureaucrats with a university degree | | | | | | -0.224 |
| | | | | | | (0.203) |
| Constant | 19.945*** | 7.635 | 19.483*** | 8.611 | 23.646*** | 32.697* |
| | (4.740) | (7.042) | (5.834) | (5.325) | (6.714) | (19.265) |
| Observations | 79 | 79 | 79 | 79 | 79 | 79 |
| R-squared | 0.393 | 0.372 | 0.382 | 0.391 | 0.401 | 0.37 |

Note: see Table 4.1.

Source: Computed by authors using the data of Rosstat, Russian Census 2010 and Moscow Carnegie Center.

government (since many bureaucrats work not for the regional administration, but for the federal agencies), and in this case regional democracy should have no effect (one could imagine that the appointments in security services are influenced by the willingness of the federal government to undermine regional democracy or to contain strong regional autocrats, who could become rivals of the government in Moscow; but for civil public service this type of logic is unlikely). Second, as the discussion of the next section will show, the size (and many characteristics) of bureaucracy in Russia turns out to be highly path-dependent and influenced by the historical specificity of the regions.

The second effect we find is associated with the influence of bureaucratic tenure. In regions where the set of bureaucrats with a longer period of service is smaller or where the set of bureaucrats with a shorter period of service is larger (i.e., average tenure is shorter), the level of democracy is higher. This effect, again, is in line with the theoretical predictions. The problem of reverse causality is unlikely for the same reasons as discussed earlier (furthermore, it is not clear at all why more democratic regimes should be willing to replace public officials more frequently – it is indeed the case that political officials change more often in democracy, but bureaucrats, on the contrary, typically enjoy higher protection).[8]

For the age of bureaucrats and the education of bureaucrats we find no significant effects. As far as age is concerned, the reason is that probably the behavior of bureaucrats is to a much greater extent influenced by their socialization within the bureaucratic hierarchy and not by the general experience they collect throughout their life – if the regional bureaucracy is old, but includes a large number of individuals who have only recently joined the public service, it does not exhibit the negative characteristics described earlier. For education, most likely, the lack of effect is driven by the low variation of this variable: in most Russian regions, the majority of bureaucrats have obtained a university education; it is also often a requirement for many bureaucratic positions.

Summing up, the effects of the composition of bureaucracy, which have previously been neglected in the literature, seem to strongly influence regime transition in Russian regions. The effects are not only significant, but also quantitatively large. Increasing the share of bureaucrats with a short tenure in the total set of bureaucrats in the region by 1 percentage point results in almost 1 percentage point increase of the level of democracy. Thus, increasing the share of bureaucrats with a short tenure from a hypothetical level of 0% to 30% would be sufficient to ensure that *ceteris paribus* a region with the lowest level of democracy in our sample would become a region with the highest level of democracy.

## 4.5   Summary

The main results of this chapter can be summarized as follows. On the one hand, we find that structural factors have a substantial effect on the level of democracy; in particular, higher urbanization and larger share of ethnic Russians increase the level of democracy in the regions of Russia; non-Islamic regions are more democratic than Islamic ones. Other structural variables have no effect; a novel result of our investigation, differentiating it from previous studies, is that we find no influence of the geographic distance from Moscow on the level of democracy in the regions.

More importantly, we also confirm that agency matters, looking at the characteristics of the regional bureaucracy. We find that regions with larger bureaucracies and regions where more officials have a longer tenure are also less democratic. In contrast shorter tenure and smaller size of bureaucracy seem to be associated with a higher level of democracy. In the remaining part of the book, we will investigate how differences of regions in terms of the composition of bureaucracy influence the role other factors (the focus of individual chapters) play in terms of democratization or how democratization affects individual characteristics of the regions (again, discussed in separate chapters). Building upon the results of the previous sections, we will look in particular at the size and the tenure of bureaucrats, and we will disregard age and education, which turned out to be insignificant (this focus is also necessary to keep the size of the book tractable).

## Notes

1 In Russia, where secondary education is still guaranteed to the absolute majority of the population, looking at the variation in secondary schooling is less reasonable.
2 This difference in the Russian statistics is due to the fact that the elderly population is computed based on the retirement age, which varies for men and for women.
3 For example, the central government may find it more difficult to recruit competent and loyal bureaucrats to be sent there.
4 Certainly, low mobility in modern Russia limits substantially the outflow of population from remote regions, even if their industry was originally based on temporary workers from the rest of Russia ('*vakhtovyi metod*'); however, for us the important factor for the development of democracy is not the objective probability of out-migration but rather the expectations (and the associated culture), which may be more resilient.
5 We distinguish between internal (domestic) and external (international) geographic distances, according to the previous literature on the importance of both. External (international) geography is important, including, for example, distance to democratic and/or autocratic outsiders – Brussels, Helsinki or Central Asian states or China (where geographic distance becomes important for external influence, as the following chapters will demonstrate).

6 Disapproval of the quality of public service was, for example, one of the factors behind the Progressive movement in the United States in the early 20th century.

7 All data for the age, tenure and education of the bureaucrats are extracted from the Rosstat official statistics for the year 2008.

8 We have to acknowledge that even the most advanced regions of Russia can be described as nascent democracies at best. There is a large literature on excessive populism typical for these regimes; it could result in large turnover of both bureaucrats and politicians. However, the general arguments against reverse causality presented here are not affected by this limitation.

# 5    Historical legacies

The role of history as a determinant of contemporary political and social events has recently received substantial attention in political science scholarship. Chapter 2 provided a brief overview of a number of studies, engaging the problem of historical legacies in political development. Obviously, heterogeneity of Russian regions did not emerge only in the 1990s, when different regions of Russia entered the process of regime transition – different parts of Russia were characterized by different social and political histories, which could reflect the contemporary political variation. Following the general literature on historical legacies in post-Communist countries, it is reasonable to divide these legacies into pre-Communist and Communist ones. Pre-Communist legacies could be associated, for instance, with the political experience of the region before it became part of the Russian Empire or the USSR, the level of human development of Russian regions of the Tsarist era or the internal colonization of Russia (Lankina 2012; Etkind 2011). Communist legacies are linked to how different regions were governed in the USSR: since Russia is the country with the longest experience of Communist rule in the Eastern bloc, it stands to reason that the Communist legacies should be particularly pronounced. Thus, in this chapter we concentrate on the legacies of the Communist period.

During the Communist era, all Russian regions were ruled in the same way: there were no differences in local acts or regulations (even if the laws were set at the local level, they typically copied each other according to a common blueprint), and the omnipresent hierarchy of the Soviets, of the Communist Party and of the security agencies spread throughout the entire country. In reality, however, even during Communist rule there were some subtle differences between Russian regions. First, in the ethnic regions elites often enjoyed a de facto higher level of independence, which they exchanged for loyalist rhetoric; it, in fact, became the foundation of both national-level autocracies in newly independent Central Asian states and Azerbaijan and sub-national authoritarian regimes in many ethnic republics of modern Russia (Furman 2010). Second, there were differences in governance of agricultural and industrial regions, which, according to Gel'man et al. (2004), affected institutional and political choices made at the early stage of transition. Third, the extent to which Communist structures actually penetrated the entire society also differed. We will, in line with our previous work (Libman and Obydenkova 2013, 2015; Obydenkova and Libman 2015b), concentrate on the third factor and look at the differences across Russian regions in terms of the *membership of the Communist Party of the Soviet Union (CPSU)* in the 1970s.

This chapter investigates how differences in CPSU membership affected the level of sub-national democracy in Russia in the period from 2001–2010 – in other words, a decade after the fall of the Soviet Union. To prevent any confusion, we look at the share of CPSU members in the sub-national regions of the Russian Soviet Federative Socialist Republic (RSFSR) – in other words, what is to become the modern Russian Federation. Variation of CPSU membership across Soviet republics is less interesting for our analysis. In order to measure CPSU membership, we extract the data from the official reports of the Soviet party congresses; our key explanatory variable is the share of CPSU members in the adult population of the region in 1976, the middle of the Era of Stagnation under Leonid Brezhnev.

## 5.1 Computing the CPSU membership share in the Soviet era

Before proceeding to the discussion of the theory and the results, it is reasonable to briefly look at the way our key explanatory variable is computed. The official Soviet statistics did not report any information on the size of the regional party organizations; the information was provided on a regular basis for the party organizations of the Soviet republics only (these data were also analyzed by Western observers; see Rigby 1976). However, there is an indirect way to compute the size of the CPSU party organization in the Russian regions. The Communist Party was governed by regular congresses, which assembled representatives of all party organizations. The actual power of a congress was negligible, so it mostly served as a formal institution (unlike Politburo, where the actual decisions were made). The congress was de jure elected by party organizations, with one delegate representing a fixed number of party members. The candidates for these 'elections' were of course predetermined (except for the short period at the end of the Perestroika). The full minutes of the congresses were published, including the full list of delegates, also mentioning the region they were elected from. Thus, one can compute the share of CPSU members in these regions as follows: count the number of the congress members from a certain region, multiply it by the number of Communists a candidate was elected from and divide by the regional adult population (from the Soviet statistics).

Because congresses were purely formal, there was no incentive for regional party organizations to manipulate their representation (the rules of elections were also strictly monitored – a manipulation of this sort was hardly possible); therefore, the data can be treated as reliable. There are still some limitations the data face. First, some of the congress members were elected from the military; since in the USSR (as in the present-day Russia) location of individual troops was classified, these candidates were not listed according to the regions they represent, but merely as members of the military party organizations. However, if our goal is to investigate long-term effects of CPSU membership, excluding the military makes sense: its members are stationed in the region only temporarily and rarely interact with the regional population (if they decide to resign and stay in the region of their service, as military veterans they will be counted as part of the regional party organization). Second, the data is based on individual congresses and may therefore reflect only the specific features of a particular year. In this chapter, as mentioned above, the 25th congress (1976) is used. However, we also computed the regional CPSU membership according to the data of the subsequent congresses and party conferences. The obtained indicators are highly correlated with the original one (the correlation coefficient is close to 99%). Thus, the regional allocation of CPSU members remained stable in the long run, at least during the Stagnation and the early Perestroika periods.

## 5.2   The nature of the CPSU legacy

The Communist Party was probably one of the most important institutions in the Soviet Union. Membership in the party served as a precondition for obtaining any relevant position in the political or military hierarchy, literally any administrative position or a number of ideologically important jobs (like journalists). The rules of party admission changed throughout Soviet history, but the CPSU has always been quite restrictive in admitting applicants to its ranks (with the only exceptions the workers and the military). Informal quotas existed for different social groups, enterprises and regions. Still, the variation of regions in terms of CPSU membership was substantial – in Checheno-Ingushetiya in 1976 only 6% of the adult population belonged to the CPSU; in Moscow this number exceeded 15%.

The legacy of the CPSU could hypothetically be associated either with *institutions* or with *attitudes and behavior* (LaPorte and Lussier 2011; Pop-Eleches and Tucker 2011, 2014). Institutional legacy would imply the persistence of the Communist Party as an organization or, at least, the survival of some particular features of governance, which could be more likely in the regions with a large share of CPSU membership in the past. The persistence of a strong and powerful party with a clearly anti-democratic ideology would indeed be able to undermine the democratization process. The CPSU was officially prohibited in Russia in November 1991 (this decision was partially revised by the Constitutional Court in 1992); there are several Communist parties in Russia, which claim some sort of continuity to the CPSU (with the Communist Party of the Russian Federation [CPRF] as the most powerful entity; in 1993, the Union of Communist Parties SKP-KPSS was set up, which CPRF belongs to and which considers itself the official successor of the CPSU). However, CPRF or any other new Communist organization did not inherit the membership and the organizational structure of the CPSU; they had to be created anew (and often had a very different leadership than the CPSU, so it is unlikely that there is a direct institutional legacy here).[1] Even in terms of voting patterns, there is no correlation between CPSU membership and the votes cast for the CPRF. Thus, direct institutional continuity is unlikely to give us a valid explanation for possible lasting CPSU legacies.

Indirectly, institutional legacy could be associated with the survival of *nomenklatura* networks. This legacy, to some extent, is at the border between an institutional one and a behavioral one – the existence of *nomenklatura* networks also changes the behavior of politicians and bureaucrats. Former Communists could probably maintain stronger ties with each other, helping each other in the new environment and ensuring political and economic control. If the share of CPSU members was larger, the roots of the *nomenklatura* networks could also have been stronger, and, as a result, the old informal connections could persist. And if the politics and economy of the region were still controlled by a closed circle with caste-like membership, it clearly increased the likelihood of a non-democratic outcome of regime transition by encapsulating regional politics and limiting the extent of competition. There exists a large literature on *nomenklatura* legacies in Russian regions, which in particular focuses on the composition of regional elites (Kryshtanovskaya and White 1996; Hughes 1997; Rivera 2000; Gaman-Golutvina 2008; Moses 2008). However, we have to stress that CPSU membership and being part of the *nomenklatura* were *not* identical; a large number of Communists, although occupying important positions, were not part of the ruling networks, and many CPSU members did not have any ruling positions at all. Voslenskiy (1991), in his seminal book on the *nomenklatura*, clearly distinguishes between CPSU members and a narrower group of *nomenklatura* leaders.

Behavioral and attitudinal legacies of the CPSU would imply that members of the CPSU were in some sense *different* from the rest of the population in terms of their norms and behavioral practices; these differences should have persisted in the behavior of the former Communists after the fall of the USSR and, possibly, affected the behavior of other groups to a greater extent if the share of former CPSU members was larger. But what was the main difference between CPSU members and other Soviet citizens in the 1970s? The literature allows us to distinguish between three options.

- First, since the CPSU members were subjected to extreme indoctrination and pressure by the Communist party (Mickiewicz 1971) and were also very carefully selected, it is reasonable to assume that they were also more loyal ideologically to the existing regime. This argument has been investigated in a number of papers utilizing public opinion surveys and other empirical methods (Remington 1988; Hill 1991; Gibson et al. 1992; White 1994; Bahry et al. 1997), but the available empirical evidence is ambiguous: while some studies indeed confirm stronger ideological loyalty of CPSU members, others find no effect or ambiguous effects.

- Second, an even more likely explanation from the point of view of the literature could be the following: since the CPSU was a necessary step in a political or economic career, it could have attracted people with stronger career motivation regardless of their ideological commitment. Since in the 1970s to 1980s the overall belief in the Communist ideology in the USSR was relatively weak, most of these career-oriented members had to 'play along' and participate in the existing rituals of the Communist party, without actually believing in them (Unger 1981; Harris 1986; Glazov 1988; Shlapentokh 1989; Titma et al. 2004). It implies that the CPSU members selected themselves based on a higher level of opportunism and compliance to the existing norms, whatever they are. Certainly, some level of opportunism was generally needed in the Soviet Union, since all Soviet citizens had to participate in some sort of rituals associated with the Communist ideology, but the CPSU members voluntarily made a commitment to a much greater and active level of participation, which they were willing to exchange for a successful career.

- Third, and finally, CPSU membership was, to some extent, the only legal form of political activism in the Soviet Union. Communists were typically better informed and were able to participate in political decisions to a greater extent than other people (Hough 1976a; Bahry and Silver 1990; Marks 2004; Brader and Tucker 2008). It is also important to notice that in the late Soviet era the government actually accepted some level of commitment to particular rules in areas not crucial from a security or ideology point of view, which also made some form of political activism possible.

The implications of these values for the development of democracy vary. The ideological commitment, clearly, makes democratization less likely: the ideology of the CPSU was hardly compatible with a democratic society. Opportunistic behavior as such does not imply any inclination to supporting or rejecting democracy, but in the post-Soviet environment it de facto made the consolidation of an authoritarian regime more likely since the degree of stability of political regimes was very low: thus, if the regional governor could rely on a more opportunistic and compliant population, it was easier for him to consolidate his rule. Finally, political activism reduces the likelihood of autocratic consolidation since it increases the willingness of the population to participate in politics. Note, however, that political activism may be combined with political opportunism or with ideological commitment – in the latter case it even strengthens the negative implications for democratization (not only are former Communists rejecting democratic values, but they are also willing to actively oppose them), and in the former case the implications for democracy are unclear. Summing up, the sentiment of former CPSU members should, generally speaking, be anti-democratic, with the exception of the case when they are characterized by higher political activism and at the same time do *not* feature a higher level of ideological loyalty or opportunistic behavior.

However, even if we have reasons to expect the CPSU members to oppose democratization or at least to behave in a way simplifying autocratic consolidation (opportunism), why do we expect the values of a very small group (mostly less than 10% of the adult population of the region), which is also declining in its size over time,[2] to impact the process of regime transition in any serious way? Why should we expect former CPSU members to be a particularly important group in this regard – as opposed to other social groups? To start with, it is reasonable that particular behavioral traits of the former CPSU members as we have already discussed are unlikely to have disappeared after the collapse of the USSR – the ideological loyalty should have made the CPSU members more resilient to the overall erosion of the Soviet political values, and opportunism and political activism are very deep characteristics related to life experience and are unlikely to change depending on the political situation. Furthermore, former CPSU members could have affected broader segments of the society, making them accept their values and principles. The literature on value diffusion suggests the existence of two mechanisms: vertical and horizontal transmission. Vertical transmission is associated with transmission of values over generations within families or within other institutions of socialization (especially educational facilities) (Jennings and Niemi 1968; Zuckerman 2005; Jennings et al. 2009; Bisin and Verdier 2010). Horizontal diffusion suggests that the values of CPSU members are transmitted within the same generational group through casual interaction (Becker et al. 2015). Three mechanisms could have created a suitable environment for horizontal diffusion:

- First, if the CPSU members were indeed politically more active in the past, this activism should increase their social reputation while making a judgment about political issues – and, as a result, support horizontal value transmission.
- Second, a large literature (Gerber 2000; Geischecker and Haisken-DeNew 2004) suggests that the CPSU members were relatively more successful in adapting to the new market environment than the average citizen. It may be related to self-selection into the party (which, in addition to ideological loyalty, could also have tried to take abilities of possible members into account – but Egorov and Sonin (2011), as mentioned, suggest that merit-based selection is unlikely to survive in a non-democratic regime) or, more likely, with the persistence of informal connections (possibly, of the *nomenklatura* networks), which were observed not only in Russia, but also in other post-Socialist countries (Backhaus 2008). Life success of the former CPSU members could have also strengthened horizontal diffusion (e.g., peer effects, see Saez-Marti and Sjogren 2008).
- Third, the impact of former CPSU members and the development of an autocratic regime may be mutually reinforcing. If the regional authoritarianism becomes more pronounced, the norms and values of its supporters (i.e., former CPSU members) also gain in terms of popularity – and this, in turn, supports the horizontal spread of values.

If the values and behavioral patterns of former CPSU members spread throughout the entire population, it makes it either more supportive of non-democratic governments (ideological commitment; note that these governments should not necessarily be the Communist ones – the public may decide to support any populist authoritarian regime using some elements of the Soviet rhetoric or referring to the Soviet nostalgia) or more opportunistic and unwilling to actively engage in politics, especially if it implies certain risk (opportunistic behavior of the former CPSU members). However, it is also possible that the persistence of CPSU values and norms is not related to their impact on the entire population: the Communist norms may survive primarily either in the regional elites or in the regional bureaucracy. For these two groups, survival of Communist norms in regions with large CPSU membership in the past is even more likely since at the onset of the transformation a large portion of bureaucracy and regional elites consisted of (former) Communists. Then bureaucrats and elites are likely to recruit new members based on their personal connections or on similarity of political and social attitudes: for former Communists other former Communists are more likely to fit these criteria, and, as a result, if there are a sufficient number of other former party members in the population, they will be recruited. Furthermore, the public, if the share of former CPSU members is high, is also likely to be more supportive of the persistence of the old cadre in the elites and in the bureaucracy. Finally, a large share of former Communists could strengthen the in-group cohesion of the bureaucracy, improving its loyalty to political decisions and reducing willingness to criticize them, regardless of the content of these decisions (Druckman 1994; Brewer 1999; de Figueiredo and Elkins 2003).

In addition, at least for Russia, another channel of persistence of Communist values and of vertical and horizontal value transmission may be important: the education system. Post-Soviet Russia exhibited very strong continuities in terms of staff employed in teaching positions in the educational sector at all levels – schools, colleges and universities. In many cases, former CPSU members continued to hold key positions in the Russian academic sector, wielding major influence on the content of scholarly debate and teaching. This influence is particularly heavy in the social sciences and humanities, where in the Soviet Union the share of CPSU members was disproportionally high and in many cases party membership was an informal prerequisite due to the Soviet leadership's perception of the 'ideological nature' of the disciplines. Importantly, in modern Russia, a selected assortment of social sciences classes is mandatory *in all teaching programs for all disciplines and at all levels*; for example, engineers and students of medicine and sciences must pass courses in philosophy, just as do students of humanities, economic theory and the social sciences. Despite formal changes in curricula, these subjects were taught by the same individuals throughout the 1990s and 2000s as previously, and there was some overt resistance to changing the curricula and attempts to keep old content under new labels (Kovzik and Watts 2001; Zweynert 2007). Based on this finding, we conjecture that regions with a higher percentage of Communists had a larger portion of their population subjected to ideological indoctrination through the educational sector.

The following is a striking example. In the late 1990s, Moscow State University offered a class with a seemingly neutral title on 'Major World Religions and Cultures' as part of the mandatory curriculum for the humanities. However, this name was actually a substitute for the course 'Scientific Atheism and Marxism-Leninism'. While the title was different, the content was based on the famous Communist interpretation of religion 'as the opiate of the people' (a famous slogan of Soviet Union during its existence), and to pass this course, students were required to state this exact view in the exam. Another course, 'Modern Philosophy of the 20th Century', was merely a new title for the course '[Marxist] Dialectic and Historical Materialism'. The essays of Vladimir Lenin made up about 70% of the reading for this course, and the rest were the writings of highly trained scholars of Leninism. Students were expected to cite the collected work of Lenin to successfully pass the exam. These curricula persisted even in the Russian capital, which was characterized by a much greater openness toward Western ideas and higher standards of living, and at one of the oldest and most prestigious universities. Provincial universities and colleges with very low-salaried lecturers and limited resources for transformation would be even more susceptible to these problems.

Summing up, the institutional CPSU legacy could be associated with either (a) survival of the Communist party (as mentioned, we did not observe it in Russia) or (b) survival of *nomenklatura* networks. Attitudinal and behavioral CPSU legacy could result from differences in the values of the CPSU members being (a) more loyal to the regime; (b) more opportunistic; or (c) more active politically and would assume that the former Communists had a major impact on (a) formation of the values of the elites; (b) formation of the values of the bureaucracy; (c) formation of public opinion; or (d) content of university curricula and dynamics of tertiary education. Vertical and horizontal norm diffusion would make the norms, originally accepted only by the Communists in each of these four environments, accepted to a greater extent by other members of the group (politicians, bureaucrats, etc.) and survive over time. In what follows, we attempt to deal with the available empirical evidence regarding the possible CPSU legacies. Most of the arguments we have collected suggest that a higher share of the CPSU members in the region in the past should be associated with *lower* levels of democratization.

## 5.3    Empirical results

In order to test the effects of the CPSU legacies empirically, we use the standard regressions we developed in the previous chapter and add the share of CPSU members in 1976 to the set of controls. The regression we estimate includes fewer regions than the baseline because for some regions (which did not exist in the USSR as separate entities and were parts of higher-ranked political units – Adygeia, Chukotka, Evreyskaya Oblast, Karachaevo-Cherkessia and Khakassia, as well as Leningrad Oblast and the City of St. Petersburg, which formed a single region) no data on the size of the regional party organization is available.[3] Furthermore, we run a regression excluding the City of Moscow – a clear outlier with a very high share of CPSU members (probably due to the special status of the union capital and the location of the government and party central institutions). The results are reported in Table 5.1 and clearly confirm our expectations. We find a significant and strong effect of CPSU membership on contemporary

*Table 5.1* The impact of CPSU legacies on the level of democratization: dependent variable: Carnegie index of democracy, 2001–2010, OLS

|  | (1) | (2) |
|---|---|---|
| Income per capita | 0.001 | 0.001* |
|  | (0.001) | (0.001) |
| Urbanization | 0.258*** | 0.235*** |
|  | (0.072) | (0.074) |
| Economic openness | 0.025 | 0.026 |
|  | (0.030) | (0.028) |
| Education | −20.398 | −16.476 |
|  | (17.054) | (17.148) |
| Natural resources | −0.078 | −0.100 |
|  | (0.055) | (0.065) |
| Share of ethnic Russians | 6.380** | 6.073** |
|  | (2.760) | (2.794) |
| Share of CPSU members, 1976 | −1.459*** | −1.287*** |
|  | (0.458) | (0.465) |
| Constant | 21.250*** | 19.109*** |
|  | (4.816) | (4.805) |
| City of Moscow included | Yes | No |
| Observations | 71 | 70 |
| R-squared | 0.497 | 0.509 |

Note: see Table 4.1.

Source: Computed by authors using the data of Rosstat, Russian Census 2010, Soviet statistics, CPSU party congress minutes 1976 and Mosco.w Carnegie Center.

democratization in Russia: regions with a larger share of CPSU members had a lower level of democracy.

Which factors could influence the persistence of the CPSU legacies from the large catalogue developed in the previous section? In a previous paper, we use the data for the period from 2000–2004 to investigate this issue (Libman and Obydenkova 2015), looking at the composition of the elites and public attitudes. As for elites (which we study using the large set of biographies of the members of regional elites published by ISANT 2003), we find no evidence that in regions with a larger share of former CPSU members a larger fraction of elites had background in the Soviet *nomenklatura* or even were older. A striking example is Kaliningrad. This region had an extremely high share of CPSU members in the population in the Soviet era (which is not surprising: Kaliningrad was populated after World War II by military veterans, who either joined the party at the front lines of the war or had easier access to it) but a very young elite with a very small fraction of former CPSU members in the period from 2000–2004. In terms of the preferences of the public, we find that in regions with a larger share of CPSU members, the public opinion surveys show lower willingness of the population to participate in any protest actions *ceteris paribus* the level of approval of the government – this is consistent with the picture of opportunistic behavior inherited from the Communist past. At this stage, however, caution is required – a large number of influential studies (McAllister and White 1994; White and McAllister 1996, 2004; Colton 2000; Hutcheson 2004) using different samples find highly heterogeneous and partly insignificant effects of the Communist past on political convictions of individuals in post-Soviet Russia.

The previous work did not investigate the effect of the CPSU legacy on the educational system. To correct this omission, we perform a tentative test of this effect in this chapter. Specifically, we use the age composition of the lecturers at public universities in the region (state-owned educational sector is dominant in Russia) as the dependent variable.[4] We specifically looked at the share of lecturers older than 60 years and the share of lectures younger than 40 years (the first group spent the biggest part of its career in the USSR and is quite numerous in Russia; the second group spent its entire academic career after graduation in post-Soviet Russia). We control for the level of income (2000–2006), which could affect the ability to hire new professors and their salaries; distance from Moscow (which affects the attractiveness of the region for possible applicants for academic positions); and the total number of students enrolled in the public universities (larger number of students may make the need to hire more professors more acute). We find, in line with what we expect, that in regions with higher CPSU penetration the share of elderly lecturers is higher than in the rest of Russia. The share of young lecturers is not affected by CPSU legacies. If we control for the share of elderly population in the regional population, results for the share of elderly lecturers do not change. It is plausible to assume that if the share of older lecturers is higher, it should strengthen the persistence of the Communist legacies in the composition of the curricula.

In Libman and Obydenkova (2015) we find a very strong and significant effect of CPSU membership on the composition of regional bureaucracy: the average bureaucrat in a region with large CPSU membership in the past is older than in a region with a smaller CPSU membership. It seems to fit the logic of opportunistic behavior of former CPSU members as well: if the norms of opportunism and compliance spread through the regional bureaucracy, it makes it a much more convenient tool in the hands of a governor willing to establish a regional authoritarian regime. The effect of the CPSU legacies on the composition of the bureaucracy is, in fact, the most robust and substantial one can establish. In the data for the period from 2001–2010, used in this book, we also find correlation between some features of the bureaucracy and the CPSU legacy. In particular, the correlation coefficient between the CPSU membership share and the share of bureaucrats older than 50 years is positive (0.462) and highly significant. There is also a positive and significant correlation between the share of bureaucrats with long tenure and the size of bureaucracy, on the one hand, and the share of CPSU members in the 1970s, on the other, but only if we drop the City of Moscow. It is reasonable – as mentioned, Moscow was a clear outlier in terms of CPSU membership and also differs from the rest of the country in terms of the size of bureaucracy (due to its functions as the federal capital). Thus, the variables negatively affecting the level of democracy are positively correlated with the CPSU legacies of the past – suggesting that bureaucratic continuity indeed is an important channel enabling the effect of historical legacies of the Communist era on regional democracy in contemporary Russia.

## 5.4  Non-linearity

The effect of the CPSU legacies may, however, be more complex than the simple linear regression analysis shows. It is possible to hypothesize that different arguments we provided in the previous sections explained the behavior of CPSU members in different regions of Russia. To account for the heterogeneity of the CPSU membership effect on the level of democracy, we depart from the standard parametric analysis and use a semi-parametric approach. Specifically, we run the baseline specification from Table 4.1, excluding the share of CPSU members from the set of controls. Then we compute the residuals, or the differences between the level of democracy one would obtain from the baseline regression and the actual level of democracy. Finally, we apply non-parametric local polynomial smoothing, plotting the share of CPSU members against the value of the residuals. The picture shows how the otherwise *unexplained* portion of the variation of the level of democracy is influenced by the variation in the share of CPSU members in the Soviet era. The results are reported in Figure 5.1.

For the majority of regions, where the share of CPSU members did not exceed 10%, the effect is clearly negative and almost linear (although it weakens and becomes almost negligible for the regions with 8%–9% of CPSU members, i.e., close to the average for the Soviet Russia). For the regions with a large share of CPSU members, the effect is significant and positive. The group of regions for which the CPSU membership share exceeded 10% is extremely small: it includes the City of Moscow, Tver, Magadan, Kaliningrad, Kaluga, Kostroma and Kamchatka. Four of these regions are in Central Russia (with Tver, Kaluga and Kostroma being close neighbors of the City of Moscow); two are in the Far East, where the high share of CPSU members was driven by the large construction projects

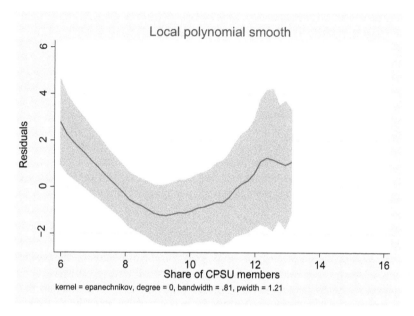

*Figure 5.1* Local polynomial smooth, effect of CPSU membership share in 1976 on the unexplained variation in the levels of democracy

Source: Computed by authors using the data of Rosstat, Russian Census 2010, Soviet statistics, CPSU party congress minutes 1976 and Moscow Carnegie Center.

implemented by the USSR but may to some extent be simply a function of the low population of these regions; and one in the West – the Kaliningrad region. The confidence bands for regions with large CPSU membership are very large and allow for both high and low levels of democratization.

Thus, there seems to be a difference in the way CPSU legacy affects regions with extremely high shares of CPSU membership in the past. There are two possible explanations for this effect. First, it is possible that very large CPSU organizations were more heterogeneous. Garcelon (1997) shows that a large portion of the democratic movement in the Perestroika era actually originated from the party ranks; possibly, large organizations gave greater opportunities for the development of these alternative points of view. The CPSU was merciless in its attempts to prevent factionalism, but, possibly, it was more successful in the regions with smaller party organizations, where monitoring the party members is easier. Second, large party organizations in the early days of Perestroika could have provided greater opportunities for emerging political activism and discussions, which could have improved the conditions for democratization. Small party organizations could have felt more isolated and thus put greater effort to control the unity of their ranks. However, given the small number of regions with very large CPSU membership, it is possible that the effect we see is driven by particular region-specific variables. More detailed investigation of these particular case studies goes beyond the objective of our book.

## 5.5 Bureaucratic agency

As mentioned, bureaucratic continuity is probably one of the main channels allowing the CPSU legacy to persist. However, an interesting question in the context of this book is whether we can establish some variation in the effect of the *structural factor* (i.e., the CPSU legacy) depending on the *agency factors*. Stated otherwise, does the effect of the CPSU legacies change depending on the bureaucratic behavior? The approach we are going to use in this chapter will be replicated in each subsequent chapter of this book; we have to acknowledge, however, that for the particular variable we look at now, the approach should be used with certain caveats, as outlined in the following.

To start with, we take two characteristics of bureaucracy which, according to chapter 4, have an influence on the level of democracy: size of bureaucracy and tenure of the bureaucrats. Then we split all regions according to the *median* of each of the characteristics (for tenure we look at both proxies – share of bureaucrats with short tenure and share of bureaucrats with long tenure – separately) and replicate our regressions for each of the sub-samples. The decision to use the median and not the mean is driven by the fact that we want to make sure that the size of each of the sub-samples is roughly the same; otherwise we would find it difficult comparing results across sub-samples due to the variation in the degrees of freedom. Thus, we can show how the same structural factor influences democratization depending on the bureaucratic agency factor.

Table 5.2 reports the main results of our analysis. The findings are straightforward: the CPSU legacy effect is significant for regions with *short bureaucratic tenure* and with *small bureaucracies*. Otherwise it is insignificant. The finding is unusual, in particular if we relate it to the previously presented arguments – we claimed that it is bureaucratic continuity which results in the continuous effect of legacies, but it turns out that precisely the regions with short tenure (i.e., lower continuity of bureaucracy) drive our results. However, we believe that the correct interpretation of our findings is the following. For regions with *long tenure* and *large bureaucracy*, level of democracy is low anyway (see chapter 4), and also the share of CPSU members in the 1970s is high (as discussed earlier). The *variation* in terms of the CPSU legacy across these regions does not add a substantial effect to this overall low level of democracy. For the regions with *short tenure* and

Table 5.2 The impact of CPSU legacies on the level of democratization conditional on bureaucratic legacy; dependent variable: Carnegie index of democracy, 2001–2010, OLS

| | (1) | (2) | (3) | (4) | (5) | (6) |
|---|---|---|---|---|---|---|
| Income per capita | 0.000 | 0.002*** | 0.000 | 0.002** | 0.001 | 0.001 |
| | (0.001) | (0.001) | (0.001) | (0.001) | (0.001) | (0.001) |
| Urbanization | 0.263* | 0.208** | 0.460*** | 0.091 | 0.219* | 0.291*** |
| | (0.142) | (0.096) | (0.087) | (0.112) | (0.123) | (0.080) |
| Economic openness | 0.069*** | −0.104*** | −0.046 | 0.037 | 0.022 | 0.002 |
| | (0.020) | (0.033) | (0.043) | (0.034) | (0.028) | (0.041) |
| Education | −38.467 | −2.770 | 1.540 | −40.509 | −31.801 | −9.619 |
| | (27.589) | (19.937) | (21.106) | (26.465) | (42.339) | (18.586) |
| Natural resources | −0.020 | −0.068 | −0.046 | −0.127 | 0.035 | −0.064 |
| | (0.092) | (0.099) | (0.048) | (0.100) | (0.100) | (0.051) |
| Share of ethnic Russians | 4.555 | 10.567*** | 9.278*** | 5.031 | 1.911 | 10.547*** |
| | (3.993) | (3.077) | (2.932) | (4.032) | (5.902) | (3.077) |
| Share of CPSU members, 1976 | −0.804 | −2.609*** | −2.199*** | −0.591 | 0.132 | −2.116*** |
| | (0.810) | (0.507) | (0.512) | (0.842) | (0.922) | (0.560) |
| Constant | 21.005*** | 27.030*** | 9.958 | 26.135*** | 15.653 | 20.858*** |
| | (6.212) | (6.086) | (6.050) | (6.012) | (10.225) | (5.013) |
| Size of bureaucracy | Above median | Below median | | | | |
| Share of bureaucrats with short tenure | | | Above median | Below median | | |
| Share of bureaucrats with long tenure | | | | | Above median | Below median |
| Observations | 34 | 36 | 32 | 32 | 35 | 35 |
| R-squared | 0.515 | 0.653 | 0.782 | 0.459 | 0.377 | 0.768 |

Note: see Table 4.1.

Source: Computed by authors using the data of Rosstat, Russian Census 2010, Soviet statistics, CPSU party congress minutes 1976 and Moscow Carnegie Center.

*small bureaucracy*, CPSU membership in the 1970s is also typically small, but the *variation* of this membership is substantial enough to have an effect on the level of democracy for this sub-sample.

If this interpretation holds, another important remark can be made. While bureaucratic continuity is clearly important for the Communist legacies, it is not the only channel of legacy persistence. In particular in regions where bureaucracies are weak and their continuity to the Soviet past is limited, other channels may become especially important. For example, one could hypothesize that in these regions the bureaucratic control over public behavior is weaker, and, as a result, public attitudes matter to a greater extent. Anyway, the results suggest that the persistence of the Communist legacies is a complex phenomenon which is driven by different factors depending on various contemporary characteristics of the regions (for a more detailed discussion of the interplay of current and historical factors see Mendelski and Libman 2014).

## 5.6   Summary

Historical legacies of Communism seem to have an important impact on the level of democratization in the Russian regions, along with the contemporary factors investigated in the previous chapter. This chapter looked in particular at the legacies of the Communist era and focused on how penetration of CPSU membership ('communist party saturation', as this characteristic is referred to by Hough 1976a) influenced the level of democracy. We find a robust and persistent negative effect of CPSU membership in the 1970s on contemporary democratization in Russia. There are several explanations for this effect: the impact of the values of the former Communists on the behavior of the public, legacies of the past in the education system and persistence of old Soviet bureaucracy. At the same time, we find that the negative effect of the CPSU legacy is actually driven by regions with small bureaucracies and with short bureaucratic tenure. We also show that the negative effect of the CPSU legacy is absent for the regions with very high CPSU membership rates in the past. This somewhat counter-intuitive fact has been addressed through the combined analysis of pre-Soviet legacies of Tsarist Russia and CPSU membership during the Communist and within the literature on human capital and its historical persistence over the century (Lankina et al. 2015). The regions with highly educated populations over Tsarist Russia became the regions with the highest CPSU membership. This nexus of two historical periods and co-existence of two different historical legacies and their survival explains the absence of a strong negative impact of the highest share of CPSU members on the level of democratization. That is, this potentially strong negative impact had been moderated by the legacy of the previous Tsarist regime.

## Notes

1 Furthermore, CPRF officially styles itself as a successor of the Communist Party of the RSFSR (1990–1991), which was formed by the conservative circles in the CPSU and was to some extent in the opposition to the Gorbachev government and the 'central CPSU', so even here the continuity is not clear. CP RSFSR was also prohibited in August 1991.

2 In 1990 the average age of a CPSU member was 56 years; it means that by 2010 the average CPSU member was 76 years old, with the average male life expectancy in Russia in 2010 being equal to 69 years; i.e., a large portion of the former CPSU members should be retired or dead by the end of the first decade of the 2000s.

3 Another region for which a similar problem could have occurred was Checheno-Ingushetiya, which was split into Chechnya and Ingushetiya after 1991. As mentioned, following the general consensus in the literature, we exclude Chechnya from our data. For Ingushetiya we assume that the CPSU membership share was the same as for the entire Checheno-Ingushetiya; this assumption is plausible given the cultural and historical similarities of the Chechens and the Ingushs and the similar economic and social level of development of the territories belonging to these two ethnicities; for St. Petersburg and Leningrad Oblast, for example, there are strong differences in the level of development, which makes such a generic assumption questionable.

4 The variable is available for 2007.

# 6   External factors

In chapter 2 we have discussed the growing attention to the contribution of external factors to regime transition world-wide and, in particular, in the post-Soviet space. Growing political, social and economic interdependence of countries is likely to strengthen the role external influences (both democratic and anti-democratic) play in the context of regime transition. The investigation of this book, however, looks at a somewhat different context than most studies of external factors – our attention is at the sub-national level of regime transition. It creates two challenges: one theoretical and one empirical. Theoretically, the question is about how strong the 'penetration' of the external factors can be: Are they able to reach the processes happening at the regional level and not merely change the developments in the capital cities? Empirically, how do we capture the impact of external factors at the sub-national level?

## 6.1   External factors at the sub-national level

There are, hypothetically, four circumstances under which external factors could influence the sub-national level of regime transition. First, it is likely to happen if, economically and socially, the parts of the country which encounter the strongest external influence are different from the capital city or central regions, where national politics is decided. Some studies analyzed the emergence of sub-national regions not only as actors in national politics but also in international politics (Keating 1995). This became an especially important topic within the development of the European Union and the encouragement for the sub-national authorities to develop paradiplomatic activities on the part of both national policy-makers, as well within European regionalism, in particular the Committee of the Regions (Keating 1988, 2002). However, the foreign contacts between sub-national regions and foreign actors are not an exclusively European phenomenon. Thus, in Mexico, for example, the northern states have hosted massive foreign direct investments from the United States, which makes them a much more suitable gateway for external influences than other parts of the country, including, possibly, Mexico City (Sandler 1997). In China, Shanghai is a more important gateway for international trade than Beijing.

Russia is, from the point of view of this mechanism, a rather complex case. On the one hand, unlike China or Mexico, it has a highly centralized economy: most of the trade flows are organized through the capital cities, and the economic value added is produced by a handful of resource regions. None of the Russian regions (even those which potentially could have obtained this role – like Kaliningrad or St. Petersburg in the West or Primorsky Krai in the East) have really developed into 'gateway regions' with very strong connections to foreign partners. On the other hand, Russia is a huge country, and the international economic and social ties of its regions vary a lot. Whether this variation is sufficient to generate effects strong enough to influence regime transition remains to be seen.

Second, in some cases foreign actors consciously target particular territories attempting to stimulate democratization (or, possibly, to promote consolidation of authoritarian regimes there). It can happen, for example, because of particular ethnicities inhabiting certain parts of the country; because of geographic location of these territories; or because of historical connections (Obydenkova 2007, 2006b). For example, European attempts to promote democratization in Karelia, a northern Russian region at the border of Finland, have been more substantial than one could otherwise expect for a region of the same economic and political importance in Russia – because Karelia is now one of two Russian regions sharing a common border with the EU and because of particular interest of Finland in this region (Obydenkova 2006a). Another effect is associated with Finland's position in terms of issuing visas for Russian citizens – there is evidence that the Finish consulate in St. Petersburg, serving citizens of the Russian northwestern regions, is substantially more open than other consulates, which creates larger opportunities for cross-border travel.

Third, external factors could play an important role in affecting transition at the sub-national level in case some of the regions are more active in developing their foreign policy and international economic relations than others. Paradiplomacy has been an important issue for many Russian regions in the 1990s (Obydenkova 2006a; 2008), when they have attempted to strengthen their status vis-à-vis the central government by directly establishing political ties to countries and regions outside Russian borders. While outright paradiplomatic activity has been important only for a handful of regions (like Tatarstan or Bashkortostan), almost all Russian regions put substantial effort in developing their international economic ties to foster growth. It is reasonable to hypothesize that the way these ties were developed affected the trajectories of regime transition – for example, by influencing norms and values of regional elites, which, to some extent, could learn from their foreign partners (Obydenkova 2012). In the 2000s, Putin's administration did not prohibit this effort, but rather tried to put it under central control: sub-national external economic policy became part of the coordinated central economic policy, and contacts between sub-national regions of Russia and other countries became heavily supervised and coordinated by the Ministry of Foreign Affairs (Alexeev 2000; Vardomsky 2009).

Fourth, there is also an indirect channel one has to take into account – external factors could influence transition at the sub-national level indirectly by affecting political development at the national level. In fact, external changes frequently cause the central government to change its attitude toward economic, political and social processes happening in the regions. While in many cases the impact of this channel is the strongest (indeed, many sub-national political changes in Russia in the last two and a half decades have been driven by reaction on federal politics – from the abolition of the Soviets in 1993 to numerous changes in the election or appointment processes for regional governors in 1996, 2004 and 2012), for us it is less interesting since it is unlikely to explain the *variation* of democratization paths in the regions, which is the topic of this book.

The role of external factors at the sub-national level is, however, generally limited by another important force – the impact of the federal government. Unless the federal center is extremely weak, international economic ties of the regions and their foreign contacts happen within the framework of the federal law, which also specifies, for example, rules for the travel of foreign nationals, regimes of border crossing in border regions, investment regimes, rules for information exchange and so forth. In the Soviet Union, for example, central control over national borders was so encompassing that even border regions could hardly experience any form of external influences on their politics (to the extent sub-national political variation existed in the USSR – we have reviewed this topic in the chapter 5). The 1990s, of course, were a period when regions had substantial opportunities to violate the rules and regulations set by the federal government (partly by forging informal alliances with federal bureaucrats working in the region, e.g., customs or emigration officials). In the 2000s, however, the autonomy of the regions in this respect diminished dramatically. Putin, on the one hand, generally considered strong and uncontrolled regions a major challenge for his administration, potentially leading to the collapse of Russia (see his first major public interview in Gevorkyan et al. 2000), and, on the other hand, considered foreign policy and international economic relations an issue to be determined at the highest level possible. Thus, the ability of the regional governments and regional societies to deal with foreign counterparts was subjected to high level of control, which was gaining strength over time.

Summing up, while the geographical size and heterogeneity of Russia make it a suitable case for various external influences, a high level of economic centralization (which persisted throughout its post-Soviet history) and of political centralization (which is an outcome of Putin's policy since 2000) should substantially weaken the role of external influences. If external influences are present at the sub-national level in Russia, however, they most likely are related to *linkages* and not to *leverages* in the terminology of Levitsky and Way (2006), described in chapter 2. There is, in fact, almost no evidence that external actors (both democratic and autocratic) actively used their resources to pressure individual sub-national governments in Russia, even if they had such an opportunity. If the impact did happen, it should have been related to informal ties between people and elites through trade, investments, cultural and information exchange and so on, which could have been facilitated by the foreign governments in some regions (through joint projects, simplified visa regime, etc.) as opposed to the average treatment of Russian regions. There is only one rather special case, when the West indeed used informal restrictive measures against some of the Russian regions – the Northern Caucasus. On the one hand, the Western countries have been mostly critical to the Kadyrov administration and, generally, Russian policy in Chechnya, citing numerous human rights violations in the region, and, as a result, were relatively slow in developing ties to these regions. On the other hand, security concerns resulted in more complicated visa issuance practices for people living in the Northern Caucasus, effectively restricting the ties between these regions and the West. However, for Northern Caucasus other factors (the war in Chechnya and the continuous Islamist insurgency, substantial attention of the central government and growing xenophobia in the ethnically Russian regions), certainly, had a much stronger impact than any external factors.

## 6.2    Measuring external influences

In order to investigate external influences, we need to agree on a particular way of measuring them. Here the approach of the literature is ambiguous; it is driven by the highly heterogeneous nature of external factors, which could potentially influence regime transition. In this chapter we concentrate on an approach which has been widely used in the literature and measure the intensity of external influences by the geographical distance between the Russian regions and the respective foreign countries. This approach is particularly suitable to measure the effect of linkages. Regions located closer to the foreign countries should exhibit more intensive economic and social ties to them – for example, shorter distances facilitate travel. Furthermore, proximity should also affect the self-perception of the regional population, which is more likely to take the policies of the foreign actor, if successful, as a yardstick. In a highly influential paper, Lankina and Getachew (2006) have shown that geographic proximity to Europe did support democratization in Russian regions. The literature typically looks at either distance to Brussels or distance to Helsinki – we opted for the former, without any loss of generality of our results.

However, our goal is to introduce heterogeneous external influences into the analysis. A huge literature has thus far investigated the role of external democratic factors, mostly associated with the activity of the EU and the United States; for Russia the European Union and other European organizations (like the Council of Europe) are particularly important. However, recently attention was drawn to the role of non-democratic countries, which could potentially promote fellow non-democratic regimes. Examples of these countries include Russia itself, but also China, Iran, Saudi Arabia and Venezuela (Allison 2008; Ambrosio 2009; Tolstrup 2009; Corrales 2009; Cameron and Orenstein 2012; Kamrava 2012; Baracani and Di Quirico 2013; Bader 2015; Obydenkova and Libman 2015a). The literature on the autocratic external actors is in its infancy, particularly because the specific mechanisms and goals of these actors have rarely been explored. The evidence is even more limited regarding the impact of autocratic external actors at the sub-national level.

Hypothetically, the impact of autocratic external actors could, as in the case of democratic external actors, be divided into intentional and unintentional (Obydenkova and Libman 2015a; for discussion of typologies of external influences see Vachudova 2005; Jacoby 2006; Levitsky and Way 2006, as well as chapter 2). Intentional influence is associated with conscious promotion of authoritarian regimes. The existing literature identifies five reasons why intentional autocracy promotion could happen. First, it could be an outcome of ideological convictions of a regime, trying to create similar political systems in other regions or countries it could influence (Owen 2010). Second, it could be driven by rent-seeking considerations – an alliance with an autocratic regime could simplify rent-seeking as opposed to the interaction with a democracy, which is more committed to producing public goods (Bader et al. 2010). Third, autocracy promotion could result from concerns about possible diffusion of democracy – for example, spill-over effects of revolutions happening abroad (Owen 2005; Lada 2013). Fourth, authoritarian regimes could strengthen autocracies abroad due to geopolitical concerns – in this case the only reason why autocracies are supported is that their international political options are more limited, and they are more likely to ally themselves with other autocracies (Obydenkova and

Libman 2014; Babayan and Risse 2015). Fifth, one could observe simple imitation of the policy of democratic regimes.

All these five motives are likely to be relatively weak if the target of autocracy promotion is a sub-national regime. Sub-national democratization is highly unlikely to be strong enough to spill over to another country (it will, in fact, have hard time surviving in the country where it is happening because of the pressure of the central government; see Diaz-Cayeros et al. 2003). Ideological motives also rarely have an impact on dealings with sub-national regimes – they are typically insufficiently important from this perspective. In the same way, if the autocracy is simply imitating democracies and their democracy promotion, it will probably focus at the national level. Sub-national regions could matter from the geopolitical point of view – in this case the so-called 'pockets of autocracy' (Tolstrup 2015) could emerge, when a foreign power supports a de facto independent separatist authoritarian enclave in another country. While Russia itself has used this tool frequently in the post-Soviet space, there is no evidence that this instrument was ever used against Russia (separatist enclaves like Chechnya never had organized support from another state). Thus, essentially, support to a fellow authoritarian regime is likely to be associated with rent-seeking opportunities – for example, joint exploration of resources. In this case, the main tool a non-democratic external actor has is associated with structuring trade deals and investments in a way that gives more power to the incumbent – this will be discussed in the next section.

In addition, there may be unintentional aspects of autocracy promotion. Interacting with a foreign government, regional elites may, as mentioned, internalize its norms and values and learn its practices – this is especially likely to happen if regional politicians deal with national-level ones, since the latter have an informally stronger position in these negotiations. As a result, tools used abroad can be copied by a sub-national regime.

There is, however, an important difference in this respect between unintentional aspects of democracy promotion and of autocracy promotion. Democracies typically present extremely attractive role models for the entire population, especially if there is intensive interaction at the social and economic level – this is, probably, one of the reasons for the soft power of EU democracy promotion. Autocracies occasionally also have a certain level of normative power, but it functions only if they are built on a clear and appealing ideology. In the modern world, ideological autocracies are rather exception than rule. In many cases their ideologies are extremely specific (e.g., Saudi Arabia or Iran) and hardly appealing outside a particular cultural context. In Russia, potentially, only Islamic regions could perceive these ideologies, but the Russian government (and the regional elites) put enormous effort into preventing anything resembling Islamism to develop.

In some cases, the soft power is based on economic success – for example, this may be the reason for attraction of the Chinese model (Gill and Huang 2006). In Russia, however, proponents of the 'Beijing consensus' are typically to be found in Moscow and not in the actual border regions to China – there regional elites and the population are rather concerned about the possible inflow of Chinese emigrants and growing Chinese influence (for critical discussion see Sullivan and Renz 2010); furthermore, institutional (Communist rule) and cultural issues make China a difficult example to accept for the Russian public. As a result, it is unlikely that unintentional *non-democratic influences* will affect the general public – unlike unintentional *democratic influences*. The effects of the autocratic external actors are more likely to be relevant for the *elites*. But, if that is the case, geographic proximity (which in the previous literature was actively used precisely to capture all sorts of unintentional effects due to social interactions) may fail to capture external influences – elites are more mobile than the general population, and geography is less important for their interplay. Therefore, our prior expectations for geographical proximity to an external actor to have an impact are stronger for proximity to Brussels than for proximity to non-democratic actors.

Still, we include in our analysis the potential impact of several external non-democracies. There are no reasons to expect Iran or Saudi Arabia to have any significant impact at the sub-national level in Russia – ties to these countries are closely monitored by the center. China may play a certain role, but only in the Far East – and, again, it is subject to extremely detailed monitoring by the central government, which makes it less likely to manifest itself at the sub-national level (one could hypothetically observe Chinese influences at the national level, but it is outside the scope of this book). Thus, the most suitable candidates for influencing sub-national regime transition are *authoritarian post-Soviet countries*. There are three reasons to look at this group of states. First, many of them managed to become consolidated autocracies earlier than Russia did. Second, borders within the post-Soviet space are still very porous, and interaction is extremely intensive (Coppieters 1996), which may increase the strength of particular influences. Third, the Russian government until recently paid less attention to interaction at the sub-national level with the post-Soviet countries than with countries outside the former Soviet Union, and therefore sub-national governments may have enjoyed larger opportunities.

We will, in particular, look at four sources of external influences. First, we include in our regressions distance to Minsk to capture the possible influence of Belarus. Belarus has been classified as 'not free' by Freedom House since 1996, consistently having a score of 6 or lower in terms of both political rights and civil liberties. At the same time, Belarus maintained a relatively high level of economic prosperity, to a large extent based on

Russian subsidies, combined by a consolidated autocratic regime (Obydenkova 2010). This could make Belarus an attractive country to copy not only for the regional elites, but also for the regional population – Belarus did not implement any market reforms and positions itself as a country preserving a social system lost in the 'capitalist' transformation in Russia. It is hard to interpret the position of Belarusian president Alexander Lukashenka as a coherent ideology, but still, it appears that the regime attempts to describe itself (in its own eyes, but also in the eyes of the Russian public) as a 'better Russia', free from many problems Russia itself encountered in the 1990s. In addition, Lukashenka has traditionally been very active in Russian internal politics and frequently (in spite of disapproval from Moscow) interacted with individual governors. In the 1990s, some believed him to have aspirations toward the leadership in Russia itself (or in a new Russia-Belarus Union) (Libman 2011); these aspirations clearly disappeared after Putin came to power, but the influence of the Belarus model could still remain substantial. Finally, Belarus is also culturally very close to Russia (with Russian being the most frequently spoken language, even surpassing the official Belarusian; see Zaprudski 2007).

We also look at distances to three other capitals – Astana (Kazakhstan), Baku (Azerbaijan) and Tashkent (Uzbekistan). All three are stable autocracies (Kazakhstan is classified by Freedom House as 'not free' since 1994, although it has somewhat higher scores than Belarus; Azerbaijan is classified as 'not free' since 1993 (with the exception of 1997–2002, when it was borderline 'partially free'); and Uzbekistan is classified as 'not free' since 1992 and is ruled by strong regimes of Nursultan Nazarbayev, Heydar and Ilham Aliev and Islam Karimov. Kazakhstan has strong economic ties to many Siberian regions; Uzbekistan maintains important connections to a number of Russian regions, being a major cotton producer; and Azerbaijan shares a number of ethnic minorities with the Russian Northern Caucasus (Markedonov 2006) and has experienced very high growth rates over the last decade due to its very large oil reserves. As such, all three countries could have an impact on regime transition – although in this case, unlike Belarus, an ideologically driven intentional impact is very unlikely, as well as any influence on public sentiment – more likely are the interactions at the elite level based on rent-seeking coalitions, as well as unintentional learning effects.

## 6.3   Results

Table 6.1 summarizes the findings of our analysis. We present five new specifications, where we add to each one of the measures of geographic distance we have presented here. Adding all geographical distances at once is not reasonable due to substantial multicollinearity problems. Note that if the geographical distance is *large*, the region is located farther away from

*Table 6.1* The impact of external factors on the level of democratization; dependent variable: Carnegie index of democracy, 2001–2010, OLS

| | (1) | (2) | (3) | (4) | (5) |
|---|---|---|---|---|---|
| Income per capita | −0.000 (0.001) | −0.000 (0.001) | −0.000 (0.001) | −0.000 (0.001) | −0.000 (0.001) |
| Urbanization | 0.183** (0.084) | 0.185** (0.085) | 0.178** (0.075) | 0.188** (0.079) | 0.183** (0.084) |
| Economic openness | 0.022 (0.020) | 0.023 (0.019) | 0.023 (0.020) | 0.023 (0.020) | 0.022 (0.020) |
| Education | −4.907 (18.335) | −6.971 (18.368) | −4.477 (16.674) | −8.321 (16.965) | −4.767 (18.362) |
| Natural resources | −0.004 (0.052) | −0.005 (0.052) | −0.014 (0.055) | −0.012 (0.055) | −0.004 (0.052) |
| Share of ethnic Russians | 6.497** (3.052) | 6.695** (3.038) | 6.768** (2.842) | 6.892** (2.930) | 6.513** (3.049) |
| Distance to Minsk | 0.000 (0.000) | | | | |
| Distance to Baku | | 0.000 (0.000) | | | |
| Distance to Astana | | | −0.001** (0.001) | | |
| Distance to Tashkent | | | | −0.001* (0.001) | |
| Distance to Brussels | | | | | 0.000 (0.000) |
| Constant | 13.932*** (4.999) | 14.157*** (4.866) | 15.494*** (4.597) | 15.737*** (4.672) | 14.046*** (5.137) |
| Observations | 79 | 79 | 79 | 79 | 79 |
| R-squared | 0.359 | 0.363 | 0.404 | 0.392 | 0.359 |

Note: see Table 4.1.

Source: Computed by authors using the data of Rosstat, Russian Census 2010, various Internet sources (for distances) and Moscow Carnegie Center.

the potential source of external influences and therefore the effect should be *weaker*. Thus, for democratic external influences, smaller distance to Brussels should be associated with higher level of democracy, and the beta coefficient should be negative; for autocratic external influences, on the opposite, the beta coefficient should be positive.

The results are unambiguous. Of five new variables, three are insignificant: there is no correlation between the level of democracy and distances to Minsk, to Baku and to Brussels. Two of the variables are significant and negative: if the regional capital is closer to Tashkent or to Astana (i.e., distance is smaller), the level of democracy we find in this region is, *ceteris paribus* other factors, even higher than elsewhere! This clearly contradicts the idea of an anti-democratic external influence associated with proximity to Central Asian countries. To investigate the effects further, we again use a semi-parametric approach: estimate the baseline regressions without the distance measures, compute the residuals and use a non-parametric polynomial smoothing approach linking residuals to the distance measures. All results are presented in Figure 6.1. One can clearly see that there is no consistent

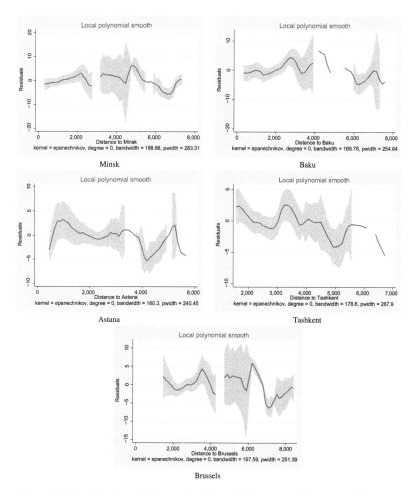

*Figure 6.1* Local polynomial smooth, effect of the external factors on the unexplained variation in the levels of democracy

Source: Computed by authors using the data of Rosstat, Russian Census 2010, various Internet sources (for distances) and Moscow Carnegie Center.

pattern of the effect of distance to various capitals on the level of democratization; the effects for Astana and Tashkent appear to be driven just by a handful of outliers. Thus, our general conclusion is that geographic proximity to democratic and non-democratic countries does not influence the level of democracy.

We also run a modification of regressions (2) – (4), where we introduced an interaction term between the distance to Baku (Tashkent or Astana) and the share of ethnic Russians in the region. It is possible that the learning effects are particularly strong between these countries and the Russian ethnic regions, where the ethnic elites may feel closer to other non-Russian nations (also because they may share common religion – Islam – and common historical connections – nomadic past for some of the Siberian ethnicities and for Kazakhstan). The interaction term is, however, always insignificant.

The result for non-democratic countries is in line with our hypotheses: since the effects are more likely to be driven by elite interaction, distance should not matter. What is more puzzling, however, is the lack of effect of proximity to Europe. It not only contradicts our hypotheses, but also a number of insightful studies cited earlier, which, using the data for 2000–2004, convincingly show that distance to Europe actually increases the level of democratization in Russian regions. Our study, however, uses the data for 2001–2010 – in other words, it investigates a different time frame than the previous research. This could provide a possible explanation for the differences in the effects.

First, we may document the results of centralization and particular policies chosen by the Putin administration. In 2005 Russia experienced a major step toward centralization, after free elections of governors in individual regions were replaced by appointment by the federal president. Over time, as mentioned in chapter 3, the central government gradually replaced the strongest regional governors and presidents, which – what is particularly important for us – were also the most active in terms of paradiplomacy and developing external economic ties. At the same time, the central government substantially restricted opportunities for the civil society to cooperate with foreign partners. While economic and cultural linkages were mostly able to develop as in the past, the center put substantial effort into isolating regional political life from any external influences. For example, in 2006 individuals with a foreign residence permit or a double citizenship were prohibited to run as candidates for public office at any level. Therefore, at the political level (including regional administrations), ties to foreign partners were severed, restricted or put under federal control; at the social level ties persisted, but barriers were created to prevent these social and economic connections from influencing politics.

Second, in the 2000s the Western countries also gradually decreased their interest toward promoting democracy in Russian regions. Partly it was associated with disappointment from the previous effort of the 1990s, which, evidently, had little impact; partly it was driven by the shifting attention of the European countries and societies in general, with the post-Soviet world becoming less important and China turning into the main focus of attention. At the same time, economic ties between Russian regions and Western countries (especially the EU) blossomed – a growing Russian consumer goods market resulted in a massive shift of production facilities to the Russian regions (for example, most of the automotive companies organized their production in Russia). This shift, however, followed the same logic as described earlier: purely economic focus and clear exclusion of any political dimension and dialogue with civil society. While even in this case foreign investments could support democratization (for example, through slow and gradual change of values of the regional population), effects would take decades to manifest themselves – in the short run, however, inflow of Western capital could have even cemented non-democratic regimes in Russian regions (Stoner-Weiss 2000).

## 6.4 Summary

The results of this chapter seem to be straightforward. External influences, both by democratic and autocratic external actors, measured by the geographic proximity, have no significant impact on the democratization processes in Russian regions. The situation changed in this respect from the early 2000s, in which the previous literature suggested that geographic proximity to Europe supported the democratization process. Most likely, the lack of any effects in our paper reflects the process of centralization, which became particularly pronounced in the second half of the first decade of the 2000s. The limited liberalization of 2012, when elections of regional governors were reinstated (Moses 2014), is unlikely to change the outcome, since the central government remained in control of the regions, both politically and economically.

As mentioned, our analysis so far was based primarily on a single proxy – geographic distance. While there are good reasons to use it, and it is also compatible with a part of the literature, other variables may provide different insights in how external factors influence the Russian regions. It may matter in particular for autocracy promotion, which is associated to a very large extent with the interaction across elites. In particular, as chapter 2 suggests, we may look at a specific mechanism of external influence – the presence of a 'limiting factor'. The next chapter explores this mechanism in greater detail.

# 7 Limiting factor

The logic of the limiting factor, presented in chapter 2, is potentially an important aspect of the regime transition process. To reiterate, the idea of the limiting factor can be, simplified, presented as follows: there exists a unique factor or source of economic growth which is relevant for the regional (or national) economy both at the micro level (i.e., key companies require access to this resource) and at the macro level (i.e., the regional economy as a whole cannot function without having access to this resource). Switching from this resource to an alternative is very difficult due to geographical location (restricting access to alternative markets), existing international treaties or, in particular, technological complementarities. Finally, the access to this resource is controlled by the regional (or national) government – either, again, because of the existing norms and laws or because the actor controlling the resource is willing to deal only within the official political framework. In this case, the incumbent is likely to use her control over the resource to silence potential opposition from the business community and to transform economic control into political control.

Chapter 2 outlined numerous forms and shapes in which limiting factors can be present in the modern world. In this chapter we investigate a particular aspect of the limiting factor logic, which one can observe in case of the Russian regions. Generally, for Russian sub-national regimes, a limiting factor is a very attractive way of establishing political control. Russian regions have no independent police or security force and, under Putin, lost any way of influencing federal police forces operating on their territory (Petrov 2005).[1] Under these conditions, they need a different instrument to establish political control – and transforming economic control into political control is often the easiest approach regional governors can use (McMann 2006; Nureev 2010). The Russian economy is still strongly influenced by Soviet patterns of production, which were based on creating supply chains where each producer had no alternatives but to cooperate with a given supplier – this, of course, is a fruitful ground for the emergence of the limiting factor logic. In this chapter, we will investigate a particular form of these Soviet economic ties, which is also relatively easy to measure – the role of *post-Soviet trade* as a limiting factor in Russian regions.

## 7.1  Post-Soviet trade as a limiting factor

Economic ties between Russian regions and other post-Soviet countries can be traced back to the Russian Empire and its industrialization process of the 19th through early 20th centuries. They were substantially strengthened by the Soviet planned economy. The Communist bloc exhibited different forms of organization of the planned economies: some countries allowed certain economic freedom to individual enterprises; some (like China) created multiple isolated economies based on self-sufficiency in different regions. The USSR integrated the entire economic space into a system of supply chains, which was supposed to act like a single factory following the general plan; the system was created without any regard for the official administrative borders of the Soviet republics (see also Alampiev 1963 on the relation between Soviet economic planning and the official territorial division of the USSR). Even more, in the Brezhnev era, Soviet planning frequently focused on the so-called 'territorial production complexes' (*territorial'noproizvodstvennye kompleksy, TPK*), which were frequently designed to include enterprises from different regions (Pertzik 1984).

The Soviet economy evolved in isolation from the global economy, which resulted into substantial specificity of the industrial standards and production patterns used by individual companies – as a result, as mentioned, it was often very difficult to find a substitute for the established Soviet supplier without needing to completely change the entire equipment. An excellent example, which we discuss in Libman and Obydenkova (2014b), is the cotton supply from Central Asia to Russian textile enterprises. Russian textile producers had their entire equipment adjusted to work with cotton, which has a particular length of fiber – this cotton can be found only in Central Asia. At the same time, in the Central Asian republics (particularly Uzbekistan), cotton was cultivated for decades to fit the machinery of Russian textile producers. As a result, simply switching to buying cotton from China or India for Russia (or simply switching to selling cotton elsewhere for Uzbekistan) was not an option after the collapse of the USSR.

The dissolution of the Soviet Union and the emergence of new borders have certainly created major obstacles for the continuation of these economic connections between the newly independent states. To some extent, the ties were disrupted already within the new national borders – the old Soviet coordination mechanisms (the central planning by *Gosplan*) ceased to exist, and the new mechanisms of market coordination still needed time to develop (the so-called disorganization argument in the economics literature; see Blanchard and Kremer 1997). However, the disorganization across new national borders was of course much stronger and contributed to the extent of economic decline of the post-Soviet countries in the 1990s. Still, economic ties in many cases persisted and were revived and developed in the 2000s, when economic growth in Russia started. In fact, part of the paradiplomatic and external economic activities we have discussed in the previous chapter was associated precisely with reviving trade connections between post-Soviet countries. Certainly, the Russian economy of the 2000s differed substantially from the Soviet economy in the sense that new production lines were installed and new connections to the West were created. However, the old Soviet technological complementarities also persisted to a very large extent, at least in some of the Russian regions.

Summing up, post-Soviet trade fits at least one of the criteria of the limiting factor: the switching costs from these trade dependencies are extremely difficult. However, one can show that other criteria of a limiting factor are satisfied as well. First, we can test whether trade with post-Soviet countries contributes to economic growth of Russian regions. For this purpose, we used the standard growth regression (presented in greater detail in the next chapter, when we proceed to discussing implications of sub-national democratization in Russia for economic growth in the Russian regions) for the period from 2001–2010 and re-estimate it adding the share of the trade with post-Soviet countries to the set of covariates (we will describe the details on how the variable was computed in what follows). We find a strong and significant positive effect of the post-Soviet trade share on economic growth in Russian regions. Thus, again, a further condition for a limiting factor is satisfied.

Second, post-Soviet trade is frequently organized in a way different from the free market transactions standard international trade analysis implies. In many post-Soviet countries (Uzbekistan or Belarus), the government controls foreign trade, and therefore any trade transaction requires a 'political backing', which is typically done through the interaction of the regional governor with state-owned enterprises and politicians of the trade partner. Even if no state control over foreign trade of this scope exists (e.g., in case of Ukraine), still, the risks of cross-border trade in the post-Soviet world (given the generally low level of contract enforcement in these countries, as well as the general lack of intergovernmental cooperation; Kubicek 2009; Wirminghaus 2012) require political involvement to protect the assets from expropriation and the deal from unilateral predatory actions. Governors of the Russian regions, as mentioned, were heavily involved in this process. In many cases lack of political support makes trade deals impossible. Again, a further condition for a limiting factor is satisfied.

It is important to stress that while in econometric analysis and in the subsequent discussion we talk about 'post-Soviet trade' in general, the limiting factor logic emerges because of dominance of particular transactions with a *single* supplier or customer (or with a very small group of suppliers or customers) – in other words, the monopolistic or oligopolistic structure of markets. However, the Soviet industrial organization precisely resulted in the creation of internal oligopolies and monopolies, which after the collapse of the USSR turned into oligopolies and monopolies in international trade. Identifying individual transactions and supplies empirically is impossible due to the lack of data, but, generally, post-Soviet trade is more likely to be done by monopolies than other trade flows of Russian regions.

## 7.2    Measuring post-Soviet trade

In order to measure the dependence of the region on post-Soviet trade, we compute the share of the trade turnover (exports plus imports) made with post-Soviet countries in the total trade turnover with all partners. Since our baseline regression already includes the general trade openness measure (share of trade turnover with all partners in GDP), this additional variable captures how important the post-Soviet countries are in the regional trade flows *ceteris paribus* the overall foreign trade. 'Post-Soviet' countries are defined in the official Russian statistics (which is the source of our information) as members of the Commonwealth of Independent States (CIS). It means, first, that we do not include the Baltic countries in our analysis. While many of the old Soviet dependencies also persisted in relation to the Baltic states (e.g. the role of Baltic harbors for Russian exports), having focused on EU integration, Lithuania, Estonia and Latvia, of course, went much further in terms of restructuring their economies and becoming independent of the old Soviet ties.

Furthermore, we do not include Georgia after it left the CIS in 2009. Since Georgia is included for the 2001–2008 period, this omission should not play a big role in our analysis. Third, since 2009 Russian official statistics reports trade with Abkhazia and Southern Ossetia (which are recognized as independent states by Russia) separately, this trade does not, however, count as trade with CIS states (Abkhazia and Southern Ossetia are not members of the CIS). The role of these two territories in trade flows is negligible. Finally, the most serious omission is that the Russian statistics do not seem to fully account for trade with Belarus, which is part of the Union State of Russia and Belarus and does not have functioning trade borders. We acknowledge this limitation but have to point out that previous research (EDB 2013) has shown that trade with Belarus does not contribute to economic growth in Russian regions – the effects mostly come from trade with

Central Asia, which is fully accounted for in our data. It may be related to the fact that Belarusian exports to Russia are mostly associated with (heavily subsidized) machine building, which is less important than the import of resources from Central Asia.

Our data include only official trade. In the post-Soviet world, unofficial trade ties are extremely important for some of the regions (e.g., Central Asia or most 'frozen conflicts' regions), but, according to the existing assessments (Libman and Vinokurov 2011), its role for Russia is rather limited (although some small-scale informal trade is definitively present in the border regions of Russia). Furthermore, informal trade is by definition organized unofficially, without any involvement of the government, and, thus, does not satisfy the criteria of the limiting factor presented in chapter 2.

As a final remark, we have to notice that the introduction of post-Soviet trade in our analysis can be viewed not only within the limiting factor logic, but also from the point of view of the discussion of external influences. Teorell (2010) suggests that trade with autocracies could hypothetically have a different impact on the regime transition process than trade with democracies (although he finds no evidence for this conjecture using cross-country data). Most of the post-Soviet countries Russia trades with are consolidated non-democracies, and trade interaction could serve as a bridge for transmitting ideas and learning processes of the regional elites (which, as described, are systematically involved in the trade negotiations). Furthermore, the preference for political backing of trade negotiations from the side of the post-Soviet countries is to a certain extent an outcome of their political systems – in Uzbekistan, for example, the authoritarian rule and de facto planned economy are strongly linked to each other. Still, our data also include trade with Ukraine during the Orange Revolution era (2005–2009). Hence, the interpretation of our findings in line with the limiting factor theory seems to require fewer assumptions on our side and, thus, should be preferred.[2] We will, however, also explicitly use a specification, which should alleviate concerns regarding the interpretation of our findings.

## 7.3  Results

Table 7.1 presents the results of the econometric estimations. Specifically, we run three regressions. In column (1) we proceed as in chapters 5 and 6: adding share of post-Soviet trade to other covariates of our baseline regression. In columns (2) and (3), in addition, we also control for geographic distances to Central Asian capitals – Astana and Tashkent. The idea of the specifications (2) and (3) is to differentiate the possible 'limiting factor' effect from the 'external influences' effect associated with geographic proximity, which have been discussed in the previous section. Thus, we consider

*Table 7.1* The impact of the limiting factor on the level of democratization; dependent variable: Carnegie index of democracy, 2001–2010, OLS

|  | *(1)* | *(2)* | *(3)* |
|---|---|---|---|
| Income per capita | 0.000 | 0.000 | 0.000 |
|  | (0.001) | (0.001) | (0.001) |
| Urbanization | 0.173** | 0.165** | 0.150** |
|  | (0.080) | (0.067) | (0.061) |
| Economic openness | 0.017 | 0.008 | 0.007 |
|  | (0.019) | (0.020) | (0.019) |
| Education | −0.466 | −3.493 | 2.705 |
|  | (18.052) | (15.865) | (15.680) |
| Natural resources | −0.003 | −0.009 | −0.012 |
|  | (0.052) | (0.055) | (0.055) |
| Share of ethnic Russians | 7.226** | 8.597*** | 8.387*** |
|  | (3.168) | (3.126) | (3.065) |
| Share of post-Soviet trade | −0.046 | −0.098** | −0.099** |
|  | (0.039) | (0.039) | (0.038) |
| Distance to Tashkent |  | −0.002*** |  |
|  |  | (0.001) |  |
| Distance to Astana |  |  | −0.002*** |
|  |  |  | (0.001) |
| Constant | 14.648*** | 19.462*** | 18.881*** |
|  | (4.965) | (4.460) | (4.215) |
| Observations | 79 | 79 | 79 |
| R-squared | 0.371 | 0.438 | 0.452 |

Note: see Table 4.1.

Source: Computed by authors using the data of Rosstat, Russian Census 2010, various Internet sources (for distances) and Moscow Carnegie Center.

(2) and (3) as preferred specifications. We look only at distance to Central Asia because, as mentioned, previous research has shown that it was trade with Central Asian countries which particularly boosted economic growth in Russia – so, if we find any limiting factor effects, they should be linked to this region (see EDB 2013).

The results of the estimations look as follows. In specification (1), the share of post-Soviet trade has a negative sign but is insignificant. In specifications (2) and (3), the variable is significant and has a negative sign – thus, in our preferred specifications, we indeed find that *trade with post-Soviet countries reduces the likelihood of democratization in Russian regions*. We also checked whether this 'jump in significance' of the regression coefficients could be driven by multicollinearity and computed the variance inflation factors (VIFs) for specifications (2) and (3). However, the VIFs, which are acknowledged to serve as proxies for multicollinearity, are in both cases very low (the VIF for the distances to Tashkent/Astana is 1.67 and 1.40, respectively, and the VIF for post-Soviet trade controlling for respective distances is 1.63 and 1.58) and substantially below the threshold, which is typically considered to be problematic in terms of multicollinearity.

In order to understand the differences between specifications, we also again applied the semi-parametric approach – exactly in the same way as in the previous chapters. The results are presented in Figure 7.1. If we control for the distance to Tashkent (controlling for Astana yields very similar results), one can see that the effect is mostly negative throughout the possible reach of the values of the post-Soviet trade share actually observed among the Russian regions. If we don't control for geographic distances, the effect of post-Soviet trade is different for regions with very a high level of trade dependence (here we do observe a negative and significant effect) and for most other regions (where no significant effect at all is observed). The last result is, in fact, reasonable given the logic of the limiting factor. As mentioned, a limiting factor should affect, in particular, regions where switching costs are prohibitive. It is reasonable to hypothesize that it happens only after a certain threshold of trade dependence and affects only regions with very high levels of post-Soviet trade. If the trade share is beyond this threshold, regions can easily switch to other trade partners, and therefore the limiting factor logic does not apply.

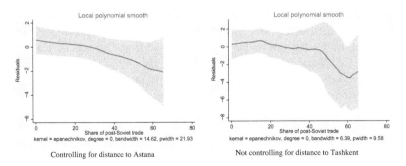

*Figure 7.1* Local polynomial smooth, effect of the limiting factor on the unexplained variation in the levels of democracy

Source: Computed by authors using the data of Rosstat, Russian Census 2010, various Internet sources (for distances) and Moscow Carnegie Center.

Our results therefore strongly confirm the presence of a limiting factor associated with dependence on post-Soviet trade. If Russian regions exhibit larger trade with the post-Soviet countries, they are also characterized by lower levels of democracy. The mechanism seems to be the following. In the early 2000s, economic growth set on in Russia, making further development of the Russian industry possible (in the 1990s, production in Russia was mostly economically unattractive, with the exception of resource industries; Gaddy and Ickes 2002 describe Russia of that era as a 'virtual economy'). However, in order to benefit from this growth (e.g., growing consumer demand), Russian companies depended on access to crucial resources and supplies, which often had to be supplied from other post-Soviet countries. The business from these countries, however, either was under governmental control (and as such unable to engage in business transactions without explicit permission of the political leadership) or was concerned about risky involvement with foreign customers. It is not surprising that during this period regional governors actively engaged in reestablishing links between the companies of their region and producers from other post-Soviet countries. However, as a result, regional governors obtained control over a crucial factor, which guaranteed that they could enjoy the support of the industry. This support was used to transform economic control into political control – particularly over regional legislatures and over media. In the regions where access to a single resource controlled by the governors was less crucial (for example, because the regional economy was sufficiently diversified), the ability of governors to gain economic power and to transfer it into political power was limited, resulting in a higher likelihood of a democratic outcome of regime transition.

In Libman and Obydenkova (2014b), we provide a particular example of how the logic of the limiting factor works, looking at the region of Ivanovo in Central Russia. Ivanovo is a region for which the influence of the limiting factor is particularly easy to trace: it is the traditional 'textiles capital' of Russia, which depends on the supply of cotton from Uzbekistan. Cotton export in Uzbekistan is organized through three state-owned companies, and literally any more or less significant deal in this area is implemented only if the regional governor personally participates in the negotiations. In the 1990s, Russian textiles, as the entire Russian economy, experienced a deep crisis: consumer demand was low and was mostly covered by cheap 'shuttle imports' from Turkey and China. Thus, in the 1990s, Ivanovo, which also experienced a stronger economic decline than the average Russian region, remained relatively democratic: governors were weak and regularly lost their positions.

The situation changed in 2000, when the new governor, Vladimir Tikhonov, came to power (beating his predecessor in relatively competitive elections). Economic growth again revived the textiles industry of Ivanovo, which at that moment also experienced the process of consolidation, with the development of a small number of powerful business groups ('textile oligarchs'). Tikhonov used his control over cotton negotiations[3] to establish control over the regional parliament, where, using the support of the textile industry, he set up a new parliamentary group, which ultimately forced Tikhonov's rival, Vladimir Grishin, to resign from the position of the assembly's chairman. As a result, Tikhonov successfully used the limiting factor to consolidate his regime, which lasted until 2005 (when he was forced to resign under extreme pressure from Moscow).

## 7.4 Bureaucratic agency

For the mechanism we described, the behavior of bureaucrats seems to be crucial. While the highest echelon of regional politics also frequently engaged in conducting trade negotiations, in many cases the regional governments were represented by bureaucrats. Bureaucrats also played an important role by controlling access to the limiting factor. Therefore, if the region has higher bureaucratic capacity (i.e., the governor can organize control over access to the limiting factor) and loyalty (i.e., bureaucrats are willing to support the governor in this endeavor), autocratic consolidation in this region is more likely. This is what we intend to test by looking at the agency of the bureaucracy. For this purpose, we apply the same approach as in chapter 5: we split the sample into several groups, depending on the characteristics of the regional bureaucracy, and check which group is actually determining the outcomes we reported earlier: significant and negative effect of the trade with post-Soviet countries on democratization.

Table 7.2 reports the main findings of our analysis. Again, we look at the sub-samples according to the size of the bureaucracy and the length of the bureaucratic tenure. First, we find that the effect of post-Soviet trade is significant only in regions where the size of the bureaucracy is above the median. As mentioned in chapter 4, larger bureaucracy can be seen as an indicator of stronger state capacity; therefore, if the bureaucracy is large enough, it may be easier for the governor to establish control over the access to the limiting factor (for example, having sufficient bureaucratic manpower to supervise the negotiations, to analyze the market situation, etc.). In regions where the bureaucracy is small, governors may fail to effectively control trade negotiations with the foreign partners, even if these partners are interested in the involvement of the governor in the negotiations.

Second, the effect is significant only for regions where the share of bureaucrats with a very long tenure is above the median. Bureaucrats with longer tenure, generally, are more likely to have experienced stronger socialization

Table 7.2 The impact of the limiting factor on the level of democratization conditional on bureaucratic legacy; dependent variable: Carnegie index of democracy, 2001–2010, OLS

| | (1) | (2) | (3) | (4) | (5) | (6) |
|---|---|---|---|---|---|---|
| Income per capita | 0.000 (0.001) | 0.000 (0.001) | −0.001* (0.001) | 0.003*** (0.001) | 0.001 (0.001) | −0.001 (0.001) |
| Urbanization | 0.088 (0.085) | 0.185* (0.091) | 0.201** (0.087) | 0.01 (0.088) | 0.141 (0.090) | 0.177** (0.077) |
| Economic openness | 0.019 (0.025) | −0.005 (0.032) | 0.025 (0.030) | 0.015 (0.031) | 0.02 (0.027) | 0.015 (0.041) |
| Education | 25.051 (24.802) | −13.289 (30.691) | 1.004 (21.575) | 11.675 (26.181) | 6.235 (32.672) | −7.687 (18.437) |
| Natural resources | 0.043 (0.080) | −0.101 (0.098) | 0.048 (0.068) | −0.145 (0.095) | 0.01 (0.088) | 0.008 (0.041) |
| Share of ethnic Russians | 10.618** (4.296) | 8.746** (4.204) | 10.945** (4.373) | 7.997* (4.018) | 5.836 (6.295) | 12.761*** (3.813) |
| Distance to Astana | −0.002** (0.001) | −0.002 (0.001) | −0.002** (0.001) | −0.003*** (0.001) | −0.002** (0.001) | −0.002*** (0.001) |
| Share of post-Soviet trade | −0.125** (0.052) | −0.078 (0.065) | −0.148 (0.088) | −0.065 (0.043) | −0.073* (0.042) | −0.128 (0.092) |
| Constant | 16.421*** (5.509) | 21.143*** (6.926) | 18.572** (7.120) | 18.055*** (6.443) | 15.699 (9.925) | 20.007*** (5.043) |
| Size of bureaucracy | Above median | Below median | | | | |

| | | | Above median | Below median | Above median | Below median |
|---|---|---|---|---|---|---|
| Share of bureaucrats with short tenure | | | | | | |
| Share of bureaucrats with long tenure | | | | | | |
| Observations | 39 | 39 | 37 | 35 | 39 | 39 |
| R-squared | 0.482 | 0.498 | 0.637 | 0.517 | 0.429 | 0.652 |

Note: see Table 4.1.

Source: Computed by authors using the data of Rosstat, Russian Census 2010, various Internet sources (for distances) and Moscow Carnegie Center.

within the civil service, which in Russia (since Russian bureaucracy is not independent of the political class) implies higher readiness to follow any requests set by the political leadership – otherwise bureaucrats have little chances of survival in the administrative hierarchy. They are probably also more used to informal practices flourishing in the Russian public administration, which of course are very important for successful control over the limiting factor (where governors use not their de jure authority but rather their informal dominant position in negotiations). Besides, as discussed in chapter 5, regions where bureaucracy is characterized by longer tenure are also typically characterized by stronger CPSU legacies, which also make bureaucracies more compliant. As a result, in these regions governors should find it easier to use bureaucracy to restrict access to the limiting factor to business groups potentially 'causing trouble' by, for example, financing opposition groups or attempting to directly influence politics outside the scope of the governor's control. Thus, again, the findings confirm the general logic of the limiting factor presented earlier.

## 7.5   Summary

This chapter provides evidence on a particular type of limiting factor and its ability to influence political development in the Russian regions –trade with post-Soviet countries. We found that Russian regions which are more dependent on trade with the post-Soviet world are also less democratic. Our findings concerning bureaucratic agency also confirm that we look at the effect of the limiting factor: regions with larger and more loyal bureaucracies were particularly likely to exhibit the effects we describe. We have to stress that post-Soviet trade is merely one of the types of limiting factor which could play a role in the context of our study. Natural resources, potentially, could also serve as limiting factors, but they are mostly under control of the central government and large oil, gas and mining corporations, which often are able to counter-balance the pressure of the governors (the situation is different with smaller region-level business, like the textile companies in the case of Ivanovo, as we discussed). However, we leave the identification and the examination of other limiting factors for further research.

## Notes

1 In the 1990s, regional governments had the co-determination right on appointments of the heads of police on their territory and contributed to financing police; thus, although the police function as such was exercised by the federal government, sub-national regimes had a way to influence police decisions. Under Putin, financing of all security agencies was centralized; appointments were made without any consideration of regional governors; and, finally, a system of rotations was

installed preventing informal alliances between local heads of police and other security agencies and local political elites (Schultz et al. 2014).

2 Running separate regressions for trade with individual post-Soviet countries is impossible due to the lack of data.

3 It is worth noticing that Tikhonov himself came from the textiles industry, being a director of a large textile plant, Shuiskie Sitsy, since 1988.

# Part II

# Consequences of democratization

# 8 Economic effects

After discussing the causes of democratization in Russia and singling out the major factors driving the variation of sub-national political regimes, we proceed to the analysis of consequences of democratization – and start with one of the most studied variables in both political science and (in particular) economics, looking at the effects of democratization on economic growth and economic liberalization (note that throughout this chapter we use the concept of 'economic liberalization' very broadly to describe the overall quality of economic institutions like contract enforcement, property rights protection, regulatory pressure on business, etc., in line with de Haan et al. 2006).

The literature on how democracy and democratization should affect economic growth is immense (e.g., Sirowy and Inkeles 1990; Przeworski and Limongi 1993; Helliwell 1994; Tavares and Wacziarg 2001; Fidrmuc 2003; Papaioannou and Siourouins 2008; Rodrik and Wacziarg 2005; Doucouliagos and Ulubasoglu 2008) and contains numerous contradictory arguments and results (see also our discussion in chapter 2). On the one hand, there is an established tradition considering growth effects of democratization with utmost skepticism: democracies are more prone to populist policies, resulting in overproduction of public goods and excessive taxation; they are more likely to engage in redistribution and may fail to maintain efficient macroeconomic policy, leading to high inflation. Furthermore, democracies lack the ability to implement necessary economic reforms, failing to achieve the required consensus in the society. A 'benevolent dictator' (a metaphor well established in economics, e.g., Olters 2001) would be able to overcome these obstacles. On the other hand, autocracies fail to produce public goods necessary for economic development (e.g., education or health care), focusing instead of military spending (Adsera et al. 2003; Deacon 2009; Albalate et al. 2012), and often behave in a predatory manner, violating property rights and creating unbearable conditions for private business. In addition, non-democratic regimes may be concerned about growth due to 'backward links' to political regimes, which are discussed in the political science modernization literature (Preworski et al. 2000; Boix and Stokes 2003; Acemoglu and Robinson 2006b; Shen 2007; see also chapter 4). This chapter aims to contribute to these debates through studying the interconnection between different levels of democracy and economic consequences investigating *non-linear effects* of democracy on growth.

Economic liberalization is also a well-studied topic in the economics literature (Giavazzi and Tabellini 2005; Aixala and Fabro 2009; Guiliano et al. 2013). Numerous papers have addressed the 'chicken-and-egg' question of whether economic liberalization precedes or follows political liberalization, as chapter 2 outlines. But the general link between democracy and economic institutions is also questionable. On the one hand, as mentioned, populism may make dirigist policies more attractive for the government – indeed, in many cases, especially in poorer countries, politicians are willing to support punctualist interventions in economic processes. Furthermore, autocracy is often better able to discipline street-level bureaucrats, imposing very high punishments for corruption (Obydenkova and Libman 2015b). On the other hand, again, non-democracy may have little interest in promoting rule of law, even only in the economic sphere, and may use its unconstrained power for rent-seeking. Again, we intend to investigate this issue using the sample of Russian regions and focusing on possible non-linearities of effects of democracy.

## 8.1   Economic growth and sub-national democracy

Although the general literature on growth and democracy is, as mentioned, very large, the set of studies investigating growth implications of sub-national political regimes is extremely limited (Besley and Burgess 2002; Hiskey 2005). It is partly driven by the challenges already presented in chapter 3: the lack of reliable information on sub-national democracy, which in this case is paired with the lack of reliable information on the economic dynamics of sub-national regions. Still, before proceeding to the empirical part of our investigation, we need to clarify a further concern: which mechanisms could make sub-national democracy relevant for economic growth. Regional governments have limited instruments of economic policy at their disposal (even in the most decentralized federations); in addition, their policy measures are frequently counteracted by the interventions of the federal administration. Therefore, why should sub-national democracy matter?

Hypothetically, it is possible to distinguish across four channels which would create the effects of sub-national political regimes on economic growth. First, sub-national governments could differ in terms of providing public goods, including, for example, education and health-care services or infrastructure. This channel, however, is likely to be relatively less important for Russia, first, because for many public goods the federal government plays a more important role than the sub-national administrations, and second, because the federal government determines standards of public goods provision (e.g., for education and health care, which are to a large extent a regional responsibility), with which the regional governments have to comply. In a centralized federation like Russia, where fiscal revenue is mostly accumulated at the central level and regions are to a large extent financed through transfers, provision of public goods should play a subordinate role. What is possible, however, is that the implementation of federal directives in terms of public goods provision varies from region to region – for example, while some governors may accept a purely formalistic approach complying with the federal standards regardless of the actual implications, other regional leaders may take a more responsible approach, taking the needs of the regional economy into account.

Second, regional governors may affect the business environment and economic regulations in the region – in this case, economic growth is influenced by economic liberalization. Again, officially sub-national governments have little room for maneuver in this respect in Russia since most standards are set at the federal level. Here, however, the issue of implementation becomes especially important. The literature acknowledges that the implementation of federal norms varies from region to region (Lambert-Mogiliansky et al. 2007; Gimpelson et al. 2010; Granville 2010; Plekhanov and Isakova 2011; Beazer 2011; Bruno et al. 2013; Yakovlev and Zhuravskaya 2013), and the ability of the federal government to control the implementation of its directives is limited because of the standard principal-agent problems in the bureaucratic hierarchy. It is possible that the extent to which particular rules are implemented in some regions and not implemented in others depends on the specifics of sub-national political regimes.

Third, probably the most important channel is associated with sub-national economic assistance to selected companies closely affiliated with the regional governments. This assistance could take the form of direct subsidies (as far as the federal budgetary law permits them) but is very often associated with indirect help – for example, advantages by public procurement auctions, selective application of regulatory norms, informal pressure on competitors and so forth. Russian regional governments are still strongly connected to the regional business community and frequently use the economic instruments at their disposal to support or to discourage some companies. Sub-national regimes matter in this respect in two instances. First, the decisions of local governments are often driven by rent-seeking considerations (Cai and Treisman 2004). Second, as we have already pointed out while discussing the causes of democratization, control over regional economies is crucial for authoritarian consolidation in the regions. This control, however, can be achieved either through selective application of regulations (as discussed in the following) or through coalitions with local companies. Therefore, an unintended consequence of the application of particular tools for autocratic consolidation is that these tools matter for economic growth.

Fourth, regional political regime could matter in terms of redistribution. In the 1990s, several regional governments (in particular, the City of Moscow and Tatarstan) have engaged in substantial redistribution programs (fueled by the revenues they had at the moment) compensating for the shortcomings of the federal redistribution. The decision to use these redistribution mechanisms, again, depends upon the political regimes – governors may be forced to engage in redistribution to satisfy the requirements of the regional population or use redistributive schemes to silence potential public disapproval. In the first decade of the 2000s, the period we study in this book, the role of these redistribution programs diminished substantially given both reallocation of fiscal revenue to the central level (De Silva et al. 2009) and expansion of central fiscal spending, particularly visible in case of the so-called mega-projects – large construction and development projects implemented by the Putin administration (Mueller 2011). Thus, while we have to acknowledge this channel, we do not expect it to play a major role.

Summing up, economic growth effects of sub-national political regimes in Russia should be associated with, first, selective application of the federal law, and second, informal coalitions between governors and business, which should be particularly likely for certain political regimes. Two other effects (redistribution and provision of regional public goods) should play a lower role. Other typically mentioned factors of growth effects of autocracies (macroeconomic policy, military spending, etc.) are probably mostly irrelevant in the Russian context since these functions are controlled by the federal government.

## 8.2    Non-linear effects

Given the complexity and the heterogeneity of findings of the literature dealing with the economic growth effects of democratization, we decided to use an approach which allows for greater variation of possible effects to be taken into account – we explicitly allow the effects to be non-linear. The existing literature has indeed partly followed this approach, in both parametric and non-parametric econometric analysis. In the parametric analysis (which will be, in our case, confirmed by the non-parametric estimations), two settings are typically discussed: the $U$-shaped effect of democracy on economic growth and the inverse $U$-shaped effect of democracy on economic growth. The first assumes that regimes which are closer to 'pure' democratic or non-democratic types perform better economically than 'intermediate' regimes. We have to stress, of course, that in Russia we do not have 'pure' democracies among the regions – even the most democratic sub-national governments are at best examples of what would be described as 'hybrid' regimes in the cross-country literature (Levitsky and Way 2010). However, the arguments of the literature suggesting the $U$-shaped effects of democracy on growth still apply, as we will show. The second argument is, of course, the opposite one – 'intermediate' regimes perform better than 'pure' regimes.

Historically, the inverse $U$-shaped effects argument has been suggested earlier and can be traced back to Barro (1996). His influential article, basically, is built on a rather simple premise: 'intermediate' regimes combine advantages of democracies (limited rent-seeking) and autocracies (limited populism). Wu (2004) describes these regimes as able to solve what he calls the 'Madison dilemma', in other words, the trade-off between rent-seeking by the government and rent-seeking (through redistribution) by the population. The arguments of the $U$-shaped effects literature are more complex and include four branches of the literature.

First, $U$-shaped effects can be driven by the considerations of regime survival (Acemoglu and Robinson 2006a; Gates et al. 2006). In autocracies, governments are inclined to introduce economic reforms if they consider them to be beneficial in terms of rent generation. In democracies, reforms are introduced if there is a public demand for them. 'Intermediate' cases, however, face a difficult dilemma while introducing reforms: on the one hand, the electoral considerations are less important (so 'democratic' pressure for reforms is weak), but, on the other hand, the risks associated with reforms (e.g., changing balance of power in the elites) are higher than for stable autocracies, and therefore, an 'autocratic' motive for reforms is not pursued as it is extremely risky.

Second, in the intermediate regimes, inefficient economic institutions can actually be preferred as a tool of political control. Autocracies can ensure their control over society through direct pressure (repressions, censoring, etc.). Democracies have no need to use such instruments. 'Intermediate' regimes are limited in terms of their ability to use repression but also do not want to comply with the demands of the public. So they can consciously design economic institutions to be inefficient and nontransparent in order to have an opportunity to pressure the economic actors and to ensure they do not support the opposition. Darden (2001, 2008) describes this mechanism in the 'blackmail state' theory: institutions are inefficient, forcing business to violate the law for survival, but these violations can be used to blackmail the private companies into supporting the government. But, as a result, the economic environment is unfriendly for economic growth.

Third, the inverse *U*-shaped effect of democracy on growth can be driven by the differences in the set of veto players. In autocracies, the number of veto players is small, so it is easy to implement economic reforms. In democracies, there are numerous veto players, but there is also substantial public pressure. In the 'intermediate' regimes, however, the number of veto players is large (so that coordination of their decisions is complicated), but the public pressure is low – and, as a result, policy is much more prone to be an outcome of a rent-seeking compromise. We have to point out though that a large number of veto players is not necessarily detrimental for economic policy – on the contrary, a large number of veto players can be seen as a sign of stability of economic policy, which may outweigh for private actors any benefits of economic reforms. The arguments based on the number of actors are discussed, among others, by Mohtadi and Roe (2003).

Fourth, the effect can be driven by the transparency of the regimes. Typically, business is attracted to environments where the political decision-making logic is clear – which is the case in both democratic systems (which operate according to the rule of law) and, to some extent, in non-democracies, where the decisions are made by a handful of people. 'Intermediate' regimes are typically characterized by much more complex decision-making patterns, with numerous players involved, but in a highly nontransparent way, which may be more difficult to grasp for business. In this case, even attractive economic institutions may fail to provide long-term reassurances to business whether the system will function in this way in the long run. The literature documents that both actual risk of predation (Petrova and Bates 2012) and perception of this risk (Kenyon and Naoi 2007) are lower in autocracies and in democracies than in the intermediate regimes.

Again, we need to re-assess these arguments taking into account that we study sub-national economic policies. The general argument of the *U*-shaped effects theory seems to hold for sub-national politics as well, although, as mentioned, the key problem of democratization – the populist redistribution effects – are less important for Russia since they are out of the control of regional governors. However, there are other forms of populism which can be pursued at the sub-national level: for example, business can be pressured into making 'voluntary contributions' to local budgets and to off-budget organizations controlled by governors, or politicians can try to gain popularity using the general critical attitude of Russians to private property and to markets supporting the more protectionist behavior of the bureaucrats.

As for the inverse *U*-shaped effects, the argument of regime survival is probably less relevant for Russia, since in the period from 2004–2010, regional governors were appointed; there is a consensus in the literature that economic performance had no influence on the way regional politicians were evaluated by the center (we will discuss a version of this argument in what follows, however). The argument concerning the number of veto players applies to Russian regions – in more autocratic regimes, the decisions are ultimately made by a single person (the dominant governor), which, on the one hand, creates risks for companies, but on the other hand, if access to the regional leader is present, makes some sort of commitments of regional politics possible; in the 'intermediate' cases, multiple veto players prevent any economic decision to be made or lead to extreme rent-seeking pressure ('decentralized corruption' argument by Shleifer and Vishny 1993). The argument associated with informal institutions and their abuse by the 'intermediate' regimes is reasonable for Russian regions as well, since in Russia, as mentioned, informal practices (implementation of the law) are precisely the main tool at the disposal of the regional governors. This, of course, implies that there is an effect of political regimes on economic liberalization as well – we will explicitly test for it in what follows; furthermore, regimes which are closer to the corners of the political spectrum in Russia may also use informal institutions as a source of power given the centralized nature of Russian federalism. Finally, the argument associated with clarity of decision-making is definitively applicable at the sub-national as well as at the national level.

## 8.3 Empirical approach and results

The empirical approach we use is fairly standard for growth econometrics. We run a cross-sectional regression; as the dependent variable we use the average annual growth rate of the real (inflation-corrected) GDP of the region from 2001–2010. The set of controls includes the standard covariates of the growth literature (on growth econometrics see Durlauf et al. 2005). We control for the GDP level of the year 2000 (which is necessary because regions with smaller initial GDP are more likely to show higher growth rates due to the base effects); investment rate (computed as total investments to GDP); economic openness; education; and natural resource rent. All variables are computed as in the previous chapters. Moreover, we run two sets of regressions. The first includes all observations from our data. The second excludes four outliers, which are problematic from the point of view of growth rates: Kalmykia (an ethnic republic in the Volga region); Ingushetia (again an ethnic republic in the Northern Caucasus); and Chukotka (an autonomous okrug in the Far East). For all three regions, enormous erratic year-to-year variation of the GDP growth rates was observed, which indicates either strong abnormalities in the growth rates (they could be determined by the fact that in the 1990s and early 2000s these regions were used as 'internal tax havens' for tax optimization by large Russian companies) or problems with growth statistics. We also exclude the City of Moscow – this region is the location of the headquarters of multiple Russian multi-regional corporations, and therefore its growth data may inaccurately include growth performance of other territories (Libman 2012).

For each sub-sample we estimate three specifications. First, we run a regression excluding any political variables. Here, as expected, investment rate is strongly and positively correlated with GDP growth. It is hardly surprising; in fact, this is precisely the result one expects to receive from the standard economic theory (another variable from the growth theory – population growth – is not relevant for us due to, on the one hand, a short time frame of our analysis, and, on the other hand, low population growth rates in most Russian regions, which are unlikely to have an effect on economic performance). Other variables are insignificant; most notably, natural resources have no significant effect on economic growth. We will investigate this variable in greater detail in the chapters to follow; here it is sufficient to indicate that while the research for the early 2000s typically finds a significant and positive effect of natural resources on sub-national growth (Libman 2013a; Ahrend 2012), studies using later periods (Alexeev and Chernyavskiy 2014, 2015) also establish insignificant effects, most likely driven by resource revenue centralization. Second, we add the democracy variable. Third, to deal with possible non-linearity, we extend the specification by adding the square of the democracy variable.

The results are the following (see Table 8.1). If we keep three outliners, democracy and democracy squared are insignificant. This is, however, not our preferred specification since, as mentioned, we have reasons to doubt the quality of growth data for these regions. If we exclude three outliers, our findings are, first, that if we simply add the linear democracy indicator, it has a significant and negative coefficient, but, second, if we also add the squared democracy indicator, we indeed find evidence of a non-linear $U$-shaped effect. This is also what the semi-parametric analysis shows (Figure 8.1), performed similarly to the previous chapters: we run baseline regressions (1) and (4), predict residuals (for the respective samples used in this regressions) and estimate a non-parametric regression of these residuals on democracy score. In fact, we find evidence of a $U$-shaped effect for both regressions with and without outliers. Semi-parametric regressions also show that the minimum of the parabola is actually located within the sample of the observed democracy values, which makes the effect not merely non-linear, but also unambiguously non-monotonic.

Our results, therefore, suggest that regimes with 'higher' and 'lower' democracy scores both have better economic growth performance than 'intermediate' regimes. This is, as mentioned, likely to be explained by, first, the number of veto players and the dependence on the public pressure while implementing necessary economic reforms and, second, the willingness of the regional government to use the low quality of economic institutions as

*Table 8.1* The impact of political regimes on economic growth, dependent variable: average real GDP growth rate, 2001–2010, OLS

| | (1) | (2) | (3) | (4) | (5) | (6) |
|---|---|---|---|---|---|---|
| GDP of the year 2000 | 0.000 (0.000) | 0.000 (0.000) | 0.000 (0.000) | 0.000 (0.000) | 0.000 (0.000) | 0.000 (0.000) |
| Economic openness | 0.007 (0.009) | 0.008 (0.010) | 0.007 (0.010) | 0.005 (0.008) | 0.009 (0.009) | 0.011 (0.009) |
| Education | 5.281 (6.138) | 5.185 (6.176) | 4.207 (5.668) | 7.072 (4.962) | 7.253 (4.830) | 5.969 (4.225) |
| Natural resources | −0.016 (0.017) | −0.016 (0.016) | −0.017 (0.016) | −0.033* (0.017) | −0.035** (0.017) | −0.032* (0.016) |
| Investments | 15.035*** (5.338) | 14.731*** (5.265) | 14.796*** (5.314) | 17.666*** (4.675) | 17.245*** (4.890) | 18.073*** (4.759) |
| Democracy | | −0.021 (0.046) | −0.459 (0.379) | | −0.064* (0.036) | −0.849*** (0.274) |
| Democracy squared | | | 0.007 (0.006) | | | 0.013*** (0.004) |
| Constant | −0.236 (1.867) | 0.458 (2.059) | 7.104 (5.976) | −1.09 (1.417) | 0.720 (1.950) | 12.606*** (4.261) |
| Outliers | Included | Included | Included | Excluded | Excluded | Excluded |
| Observations | 79 | 79 | 79 | 75 | 75 | 75 |
| R-squared | 0.217 | 0.22 | 0.239 | 0.335 | 0.358 | 0.411 |

Note: see Table 4.1.

Source: Computed by authors using the data of Rosstat, Russian Census 2010 and Moscow Carnegie Center.

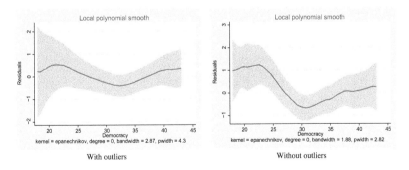

Figure 8.1 Local polynomial smooth, effect of democracy on the unexplained variation in economic growth

Source: Computed by authors using the data of Rosstat, Russian Census 2010 and Moscow Carnegie Center.

a pressure tool against business and as an instrument of political control. The last argument, as mentioned, is empirically testable, and this is what we intend to do in the next section.

## 8.4    Economic liberalization and sub-national democracy

Measuring economic liberalization and, more generally, the quality of economic institutions at the sub-national level is a very difficult task. We use the approach which has been introduced in the literature by the previous studies (Alexeev and Chernyavskiy 2015) and apply as the dependent variable an *index of economic risk*, which was developed by RA Expert – a reputable Russian investment rating agency. We use the indicator for the period from 2009–2010. The index is based on expert opinion assessments and attempts to capture the risk of business activity in individual provinces of Russia from different angles. High values indicate that the risk level is higher. The best results have been achieved by the Belgorod region, for which substantial anecdotal evidence of effective economic policies is present. The worst result is achieved by Ingushetia, which is, in fact, an outlier in terms of the RA Expert index. Interestingly, as Figure 8.2 shows, there is almost no

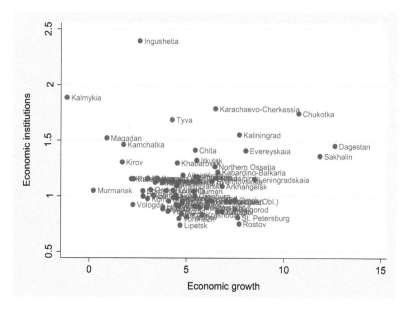

*Figure 8.2* Correlation between economic growth and economic institutions (RA Expert)

Source: Computed by authors using the data of Rosstat and RA Expert.

correlation between the economic growth and the quality of economic institutions; we will discuss this observation in what follows while attempting to interpret our results.

The regression we estimate (see Table 8.2) includes the following controls. First, we control for the share of ethnic Russians: it is possible that regions with a low share of ethnically Russian population differ in terms of the culture of economic policy or that they are to a larger extent closed to outside investors, which could reflect itself in the rating. Indeed, we see a clear negative correlation between the proxy of investment risk and the share of ethnic Russians: if the share of ethnic Russians is higher, investment risk is lower. Second, we control for education quality: implementation of better economic institutions is easier in regions with higher quality of human capital. Third, we control for the natural resources, which can discourage the government to invest effort into improving the quality of economic institutions and instead concentrate on predatory behavior. We also add democracy and democracy squared to the set of control variables. Given the very high level of the index of economic liberalization for Ingushetia, we estimate our regressions with and without this outlier.

*Table 8.2* The impact of political regimes on economic institutions, dependent variable: RA Expert Investment Risk 2010, OLS

|  | (1) | (2) | (3) | (4) |
|---|---|---|---|---|
| Education | −0.264 | −0.245 | −0.295 | −0.283 |
|  | (0.423) | (0.421) | (0.466) | (0.456) |
| Natural resources | 0.001 | 0.001 | 0.001 | 0.002 |
|  | (0.002) | (0.002) | (0.001) | (0.002) |
| Share of ethnic | −0.590*** | −0.576*** | −0.468*** | −0.378*** |
| Russians | (0.180) | (0.178) | (0.151) | (0.142) |
| Democracy |  | −0.001 | −0.097* | −0.062 |
|  |  | (0.005) | (0.052) | (0.043) |
| Democracy squared |  |  | 0.002* | 0.001 |
|  |  |  | (0.001) | (0.001) |
| Constant | 1.628*** | 1.646*** | 3.013*** | 2.377*** |
|  | (0.193) | (0.228) | (0.839) | (0.676) |
| Outliers | Included | Included | Included | Excluded |
| Observations | 79 | 79 | 79 | 78 |
| R-squared | 0.291 | 0.292 | 0.344 | 0.237 |

Note: see Table 4.1.

Source: Computed by authors using the data of Rosstat, Russian Census 2010, RA Expert and Moscow Carnegie Center.

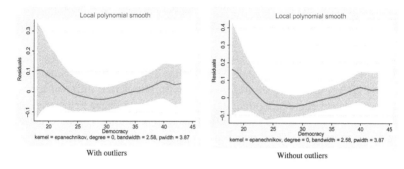

*Figure 8.3* Local polynomial smooth, effect of democracy on the unexplained variation in the quality of economic institutions (RA Expert)

Source: Computed by authors using the data of Rosstat, Russian Census 2010, RA Expert and
Moscow Carnegie Center.

The findings are puzzling. For the full sample, we again observe a non-
linear effect, which is, however, very different from what one would expect
from the growth analysis: 'intermediate' regions in terms of democratization have *lower* investment risk than high-democracy and low-democracy
regions. This result, however, becomes statistically insignificant if we drop
just one region – Ingushetia. In the semi-parametric analysis, however (see
Figure 8.3), we find a non-linear effect with and without the outlier. The
results are in any way striking as they are clearly incompatible with our
original hypothesis: 'intermediate' regimes have low quality of economic
institutions (because they use it as a tool to consolidate their power) and, as
a result, exhibit lower growth rates.

There are two possible sets of explanations one could suggest. On the
one hand, it is possible that the 'intermediate' regimes have lower growth
rates *in spite of* their effort to improve economic institutions – that is, other
factors dominate the quality of institutions (this may explain why we find
almost no unconditional correlation between institutional quality and economic growth). 'Intermediate' regimes may be more capable of improving
the quality of economic institutions following Barro's logic: they are less
inclined to the purely informal predatory approach of outright autocracies,
where the entire business landscape is controlled by the local governors,
but they also are not influenced by the need to satisfy public demands for
populism. On the other hand, there are also particular risks associated with
'intermediate' regimes, which may be perceived as more important.

First, these regions may be, as mentioned, perceived as relatively intransparent by the business actors – and because in Russia implementation of any
regulation is always questionable, it may be enough to reduce the business

activity. Second, while we have argued that the general argument of Acemoglu and Robinson (2006a) based on the survival of regimes is less applicable for Russia, a variation of this argument is still possible: political regime may influence the expectations business has regarding the longevity of the regional governor, which is, as mentioned, determined by the likelihood of federal interventions. If the region is controlled by a powerful autocrat, federal intervention is, although possible, still relatively more costly for the center – and therefore regional business may perceive the existing institutional environment as more robust and persistent. In relatively democratic regions, the power of the governor either faces stronger constraints (by other segments of the elite, stronger regional parliament, etc.), so that political change is less important and the continuity of economic policy can be sustained even under the new governor, or, again, the federal government is less likely to replace the regional leaders, at least in a way entirely ignoring the preferences of the regional population. As a result, in both democratic and autocratic regions, business could assume that the current political situation will be stable, as will the economic institutions it creates. 'Intermediate' regimes may be perceived as unstable – and, even if they offer higher-quality economic institutions, it would not be enough for the business to compensate for the risks associated with sudden power change (which, as Libman et al. 2012 show, is likely to be associated with an increase in predatory behavior of the new governor).

There is, however, an alternative interpretation, which questions our basic assumption: high-quality economic institutions are not always good for economic growth. For the Russian case, however, a large literature argues that the relation between business activity and economic institutions is more complex – under certain conditions Russian business actually prefers a low quality of economic institutions (e.g., Hellman 1998; Sonin 2003; Polishchuk and Savvateev 2004). In particular, it can be driven by learning effects: Russian companies in the 1990s formed in an environment of extremely bad economic institutions and intransparent regulations; therefore, they find it easier to operate in this environment than in a formally superior institutional environment, where they have to adjust and to adapt to new rules. Large companies may also prefer bad institutions because they give them higher power, which they use as a competitive advantage. The discussion as to how robust this 'demand for bad institutions' was in the 2000s is ongoing: while some papers convincingly show that during this period business was still interested in 'playing by the old rules' of the Russian economy as it emerged in the 1990s, others claim that there was a stronger interest of business to adapt to new rules and to create a transparent and efficient market environment (see discussion in Havrylyshin 2007). More detailed investigation of this argument is beyond the framework of this book.

## 8.5   Bureaucratic agency

As in the first part of the book, in the second part we investigate how bureaucratic agency modifies the effects of structure; in this case, we look at how growth effects of democracy change depending on the characteristics of bureaucracy – again, concentrating at the size of the bureaucracy and tenure of the bureaucrats. Table 8.3 reports our main findings. The effects of democracy on growth seem to persist regardless of the tenure; they do, however, change depending on the size of the bureaucracy. We find the non-linear effect we described only for regions with a large bureaucracy. If the bureaucracy is small, increasing the level of democracy has a straightforward negative effect on economic growth. It means that while positive growth effects of authoritarian regimes can be realized by regions with either small or large bureaucratic capacity, to realize positive effects of democratic regimes, the regions should have large bureaucratic capacity – otherwise economic growth will simply decrease.

As mentioned, we believe that the main advantage business extracts from working in an authoritarian region is that it perceives its political system as more predictable and less exposed to risks from outside the region (especially federal interventions). It is independent of the size of bureaucracy and is rather determined by the strength of the governor in relation to the federal center. In democratic regions, we argued that the predictability is based on the strength of the regional political system, which precludes a newly appointed governor to engage in unrestricted rent-seeking and stops the federal government from appointing a leader without taking regional preferences into account. Possibly, the existence of a stronger bureaucracy is perceived by the business as an additional factor binding economic policy and regulation in regions with more democratic regimes, even if the center decides to replace the regional governor. Therefore, if bureaucracy is small and has limited capacity, democratic regions cannot alleviate concerns of private business regarding a possible policy change in the near future.

## 8.6   Summary

This chapter provided new insights into the consequences of democratization in regards to economic growth. More specifically, it has demonstrated that political regimes of Russian regions have had significant influence on their economic development. We found evidence of non-linear effects of regional democracy on both economic growth and the quality of economic institutions. Specifically, regions with 'intermediate' political regimes perform worse than outright 'autocracies' and 'democracies'. It is not matched by the effects of political regimes on economic liberalization: here we find the opposite effect, which is, however, not robust and is basically driven by the

Table 8.3 The impact of political regimes on economic growth conditional on bureaucratic agency, dependent variable: average real GDP growth rate, 2001–2010, OLS, outliers excluded

| | (1) | (2) | (3) | (4) | (5) | (6) |
|---|---|---|---|---|---|---|
| GDP of the year 2000 | 0.000 | 0.000 | 0.000 | 0.000 | 0.000 | 0.000 |
| | (0.000) | (0.000) | (0.000) | (0.000) | (0.000) | (0.000) |
| Economic openness | 0.010 | 0.009 | 0.018* | 0.003 | -0.001 | 0.067*** |
| | (0.012) | (0.018) | (0.010) | (0.011) | (0.012) | (0.020) |
| Education | -5.885 | 11.417** | 12.153** | 1.013 | 13.614 | -1.159 |
| | (9.013) | (4.971) | (4.825) | (6.727) | (9.065) | (5.144) |
| Natural resources | -0.030 | -0.019 | -0.007 | -0.057*** | -0.028 | -0.031 |
| | (0.019) | (0.026) | (0.031) | (0.017) | (0.034) | (0.020) |
| Investments | 20.243*** | 14.442 | 13.491** | 32.391*** | 22.099*** | 12.835** |
| | (5.333) | (9.731) | (5.330) | (8.734) | (7.419) | (6.157) |
| Democracy | -1.021* | -0.561* | -0.747*** | -1.504*** | -0.807 | -0.749** |
| | (0.524) | (0.310) | (0.235) | (0.524) | (0.828) | (0.279) |
| Democracy squared | 0.017* | 0.007 | 0.011*** | 0.023** | 0.013 | 0.010** |
| | (0.009) | (0.005) | (0.004) | (0.009) | (0.014) | (0.005) |
| Constant | 15.826** | 9.107* | 10.199*** | 21.434** | 8.91 | 14.317*** |
| | (7.527) | (5.021) | (3.587) | (7.876) | (13.823) | (3.646) |
| Size of bureaucracy | Above median | Below median | | | | |
| Share of bureaucrats with short tenure | | | Above median | Below median | | |
| Share of bureaucrats with long tenure | | | | | Above median | Below median |
| Observations | 37 | 37 | 34 | 34 | 39 | 35 |
| R-squared | 0.551 | 0.389 | 0.509 | 0.596 | 0.451 | 0.555 |

Note: see Table 4.1.

Source: Computed by authors using the data of Rosstat, Russian Census 2010 and Moscow Carnegie Center.

inclusion of one single region into the sample. We hypothesized that the results are driven by differences in the level of uncertainty in different types of regimes (according to the literature review in chapter 2). These differences are driven by different appointment policies the federal government is likely to pursue with respect to regional governors, as well as different consequences of appointments of new governors in terms of the possibility of change of economic policy in the region. The analysis of the role of agency provided for some unexpected results as well. Results from the analysis of bureaucratic agency can be explained in line with the aforementioned interpretation – the uncertainty with respect of economic policy and the need to perform well in front of the central government.

To sum up, the theoretical conclusions implied by the empirical results is that in Russia political stability was more important for growth than reforms and liberalization. In a country which experienced massive turmoil in the 1990s and where business operates based on a 'pessimistic consensus' (Oleinik 2005), the results can be foreseen from an economist perspective. However, it is the first, by now, analysis in a laboratory-like setting of the sub-national level, when controlled for national-related factors, that traced the impact of democratization for economic development. We also highlight that while analyzing political stability in sub-national regimes, it is insufficient to look at the standard arguments regarding political stability in democracies and autocracies at the national level (e.g., Feng 1997; Obinger 2000; Blanco and Grier 2009); one also has to incorporate the role of the federal government into analysis.

# 9 Life satisfaction, well-being and happiness

The analysis of economic growth, which we have presented in the previous chapter, is, while important, still not sufficient to evaluate the consequences of democratization for the population. The literature on the consequences of democratization emphasizes the importance of such issues as life satisfaction and well-being. Both concepts have subjective and objective measurement. The objective side can be easily measured by such life experience as having regular trips abroad, having a car and the like. The subjective aspects is more difficult to capture but not impossible. This chapter focuses on the consequences of democratization for the population and asks a straightforward question of whether or not the people feel satisfied and happy about their lives, as well as employs some other measurements that allow us to make more objective observations on the level of life satisfaction.

*Subjective well-being*, or (a term more frequently used by economists) *happiness*, can be consistently measured using public opinion surveys (Frey and Stutzer 2002). Subjective well-being can deviate from formal economic indicators for three reasons. First, as mentioned, there may be statistical inaccuracies in the official data. Second, the Easterlin paradox (Easterlin 1974, 1995; Easterlin et al. 2010) argues that higher income does not necessarily generate higher happiness levels, since people assess their well-being focusing on relative rather than absolute income. The idea of the Easterlin paradox (or Easterlin effect) is based on an empirical observation: growth of income does not necessarily generate the corresponding growth of happiness of the subjects. The explanation Easterlin suggested is as follows: subjects, when evaluating their happiness, do not consider their income in isolation (i.e., what they could afford to buy for the money they earned), but rather compared it with the earnings of others. If the former increased to the same extent as their own earnings, or even grew at a faster rate, happiness did not increase. Third, subjective well-being can also be directly affected by democracy, as the large literature on the so-called 'procedural utility of democracy' suggests (Frey and Stutzer 2000a, 2000b). While happiness as subjective well-being is important, the chapter looks also at the more objective variable – life satisfaction and other more objective measurements of the well-being and health of the population (through statistics on, for example, such issues as vodka consumption by the population). This chapter will investigate satisfaction, happiness and well-being in greater detail looking at Russian regions.

## 9.1 Democracy, satisfaction and happiness

The impact of democratic political systems on life satisfaction and happiness has been a topic for scholarly investigation at both the cross-national level (Dorn et al. 2007), as well as looking at the sub-national level in Switzerland (Frey and Stutzer 2000a, 2000b; Dorn et al. 2008). Some studies also discussed the effect of political freedom for Eastern European transition countries, but the conclusions for this sub-group are more heterogeneous (Hayo and Seifert 2003; Hayo 2007; Guriev and Zhuravskaya 2009). Somewhat simplified, there are two reasons why democracy could improve life satisfaction and happiness *ceteris paribus* income people receive. First, a large literature (Frey et al. 2004; Stutzer and Frey 2006) suggests that people 'extract utility' from participating in political decision-making even if they cannot, in the ultimate account, influence the results of this decision-making. Through participating in various forms of joint political and social action, as well as the opportunity to exercise the freedom of speech and action and to demonstrate openly their opinions in various forms (such as, for example, demonstrations, protests, referendums, elections), people feel more fulfilled and significant in the society, which provides for a vision of the more useful life (and explains utility as an aspect of happiness). This is precisely what is called procedural utility: its source is not a particular policy, but a procedure by which the policy is reached. The key element of procedural utility is the *feeling* of involvement, which strongly separates democratic decision-making from the authoritarian system, which often alienates people from politics, making them feel like passive participants facing uncontrollable and costly decisions from the high level. The strongest evidence for procedural utility has been obtained, however, not from democratic systems in general, but from direct democracy – the referendum-based system of political decision-making existing in the Swiss cantons. Second, democracy is typically associated with higher levels of personal freedoms and civil rights, which again should improve both life satisfaction and happiness for a given level of income (for a critical analysis see Veenhoven 2003).

There are, however, also reasons to be skeptical about the positive effect of democratization on life satisfaction and happiness especially in post-Socialist countries including Russia. First, the ability of representative democracy of the post-Soviet style to really generate procedural utility is questionable. The political culture and knowledge of Russians is mostly very low and still strongly influenced by Soviet stereotypes and modern pass media that is highly controlled by the central government (especially the television, see Mickiewicz 2008). Given this historical legacy and modern situation, the people may simply perceive democracy as much more uncontrollable, chaotic and driven by hidden forces (the last perception can also be encouraged by very strong fears of Western conspiracies associated with democratization, which exist in Russian society; see Oushakine 2009; Ortmann and Heathershaw 2012). On the contrary, the Soviet system actually tried to limit the feeling of alienation of the population by involving it into numerous political activities (through the party system, the Communist Youth Union and the almost mandatory political education system) and developing a sense of unity based on the shared ideology of Communism. These activities, of course, were only nominal and highly ritualized, and the alienation between the Soviet population and the ruling class was substantial, but in retrospect modern Russians could find the less clear democratic system a greater problem. Second, in Russia democracy is strongly linked in public perception with 'liberal' economic reforms; whether this link is justified is questionable (in fact, our sub-national data do not support it), but many Russians view it this way and also connect economic reforms with instability, the empowerment of the elite and the emergence of 'new rich Russians', paralleled by the increasing poverty of some social layers, increasing the socio-economic divide in the society (in sharp contrast to the Soviet idea of equality). As a result, they may also have negative feelings toward democratization. If that is the case, democratization should actually lead to lower levels of life satisfaction and happiness.

## 9.2   Measuring satisfaction, well-being, and happiness

In order to measure the level of life satisfaction, well-being and happiness in Russian regions, we apply data from three surveys. Unfortunately, all three surveys were implemented in 2013 – in other words, three years after the democracy indicator for Russian regions was measured. We acknowledge this as a limitation, but, unfortunately, no systematic earlier data are available. The first indicator is an *index of social well-being (indeks sotsial'nogo samochustviya)* published by the Foundation for Civil Society Development (FCSD). FCSD is an NGO (non-governmental organization) specializing, among other things, on investigating the political and social situation in the regions. While the FCSD is believed to be rather close to the Russian government, the data for the index were extracted from a large public opinion survey, *Georating*, which is conducted by the Public Opinion Foundation (FOM), a reputable polling agency. The survey is particularly important for us since it uses representative samples in each region – in other words, data are representative not only for the Russian Federation in general, but also for each of its constituent units. Therefore, with all the usual caveats regarding empirical measurement (Frey and Stutzer 2002), the data can be considered as relatively reliable. The data of the surveys are available for almost all regions with very few exceptions.

## *Satisfaction and well-being*

The FCSD index is measured from 1 to 100, with 100 being the highest level of satisfaction with life. The index was constructed based on responses to four key questions: (a) whether respondents are generally satisfied or unsatisfied with the situation in their respective region; (b) whether respondents believe that the situation is improving or deteriorating; (c) whether respondents observe dissatisfaction of people surrounding them with the regional government; and (d) whether people consider the possibility of personally participating in protest actions. These four questions were used to classify regions into four groups according to well-being. This group of the question is mainly constructed to capture the opinion of the population and *satisfaction as an opinion (perception)*. To complement for the subjective aspect of these questions, a few further questions were added to capture the *objective* facts to create a more complete picture of the *actual* well-being of the population, based on *facts* and not on opinion about the facts (perception). Within each group, further selection was based on responses to four other questions that reflect more: (a) whether respondents have taken a loan, driven a car or traveled abroad recently (in Russia these activities are indicative of higher personal wealth); (b) whether they consider their material well-being as very good, good, average, bad or very bad; (c) whether they think their material well-being has improved or deteriorated; and (d) whether they faced situations which would make them willing to participate in protest actions.

Of the four basic questions, two are clearly related to **objective** well-being. Two other questions are somewhat more problematic, since the responses to them may also be driven by the perception of personal risks associated with criticizing or directly opposing regional governors, which themselves can be determined by the specifics of the regional political system. Supporting questions partly refer to a purely material aspect of well-being, which would be helpful if our goal were merely to correct measurement errors in the official statistics, but is problematic if we also want to test the procedural utility theory.

## Happiness

Therefore, we also used two other indicators which focus specifically on narrowly defined subjective well-being (or happiness). Therefore, we use data from another FOM survey, where respondents in different regions of Russia were asked the following question: 'Generally speaking, do you consider yourself a rather happy person or a rather unhappy person?' Thus, we obtain two dependent variables: the share of respondents describing themselves as happy and the share of respondents describing themselves as unhappy. All three indicators we use in this chapter are significantly correlated with each other, although the correlation coefficients do not exceed 0.55 in absolute terms. The FCSD index is positively correlated with the share of happy individuals in the regions and negatively correlated with the share of those who consider themselves as not happy. The share of happy individuals is negatively correlated with the share of not happy individuals (it is not trivial because the third option, 'Cannot respond to the question', was also present). The share of happy individuals in Russia is close to 73%, with the highest level of happiness achieved in Tyva (86%) and the lowest in Kursk region (56%). The highest share of those who consider themselves unhappy is observed in Ivanovo region (26%); and the lowest indicator is in Tyva (6%). The result is striking since Tyva is among the 10 poorest regions according to official income data – it is, however, also fairly isolated from the rest of the country due to its remote geographic location, the predominance of non-Russian ethnic population (a lower share of ethnic Russians in our sample is observed only in Dagestan and Ingushetia) and the specifics of its historical path.[1]

## Vodka consumption

In addition to the discussion of survey-based proxies of happiness and well-being, which mostly follow the existing happiness research, we also decided to look at a further variable which may play a crucial role in the Russian context – we investigated how democratization affects the *alcohol consumption* in Russian regions, focusing in particular on *vodka consumption per capita.* Vodka consumption is a good reflection of life (un)satisfaction, (un)happiness and well-being as public health. Thus, we use this unique variable to account for these three aspects all together. It stands out as a variable relevant for Russia due to historical reasons. More narrowly, it is an indirect proxy of life satisfaction. The psychological literature (Murphy et al. 2005) confirms that alcohol consumption increases as a reaction to growing life dissatisfaction, probably as an attempt to find a substitute to the disappointing reality. However, alcohol consumption in Russia is a major risk factor for public health. There exists a large literature discussing the disastrous implications of alcohol dependence for shorter lifespan and higher mortality in Russia (Walberg et al. 1998; Rehm and Gmel 2007; Leon et al. 2007; Denisova 2010), and consumption of vodka could be seen as particularly problematic in this respect. Hypothetically, we could also acknowledge that the consumption of vodka is influenced by the ability to control the market of alcohol and to enforce the existing regulations (for example, aiming at limiting alcohol consumption by youth) – we will provide an indirect test of these conjectures in what follows.

## 9.3    Empirical analysis and results

To investigate the impact of democratization on subjective well-being, we again run a cross-sectional regression, controlling for the following variables. First, we control for income per capita – our goal is, as mentioned, to establish the effect of democracy on happiness *ceteris paribus* income. Second, we add economic openness – exposure to the global world could affect the cultural specifics of the regional population and exacerbate the Easterlin effects – if people in the region 'measure' their well-being upon the well-being of their trade partners, they are more likely to show dissatisfaction with their environment. Third, again to deal with possible 'yardstick effects' and cultural specifics, we also control for the share of ethnic Russians. Fourth, we introduce proxies for crime rates and health-care system quality in the region – number of registered crimes per capita and number of doctors per capita – to deal with possible effects of public goods production on happiness. Fifth, finally, we control for education level, which could play a decisive role from the point of view of the Easterlin effects, but also can be seen as a proxy for the quality of public good education.

The results, which are reported in Table 9.1, are unambiguous – we find no significant effect of democracy on subjective well-being. Thus, for the Russian case, procedural value of democracy cannot be confirmed. Our interpretation is that, probably, for Russia, where we even the most 'democratic' regions are still lacking substantial elements of a stable democratic system of the Western style, the extent of alienation of the population from politics is high even in relatively democratic regions. Furthermore, the effect of sub-national regimes on civil rights and personal freedoms, which again could potentially be associated with an increase in happiness, is strong for the

Table 9.1 The impact of political regimes on subjective well-being and happiness, OLS

| Dep. var. | (1) FCSD index | (2) FCSD index | (3) Happiness | (4) Happiness | (5) Un-happiness | (6) Un-happiness |
|---|---|---|---|---|---|---|
| Income per capita | 0.002** (0.001) | 0.002** (0.001) | 0.001** (0.001) | 0.001** (0.001) | -0.001*** (0.000) | -0.001*** (0.000) |
| Economic openness | 0.08 (0.051) | 0.086* (0.051) | 0.054* (0.028) | 0.055* (0.028) | -0.022 (0.016) | -0.018 (0.016) |
| Education | -14.99 (28.425) | -13.649 (28.477) | -31.448 (19.477) | -31.097 (19.788) | 2.443 (13.055) | 3.455 (13.152) |
| Healthcare system | -0.104 (0.113) | -0.097 (0.116) | -0.094 (0.079) | -0.093 (0.081) | 0.03 (0.052) | 0.035 (0.052) |
| Crime | 0.002 (0.002) | 0.002 (0.002) | -0.002* (0.001) | -0.002 (0.001) | 0.001 (0.001) | 0.001 (0.001) |
| Share of ethnic Russians | -16.807*** (4.120) | -15.658*** (4.401) | -10.333*** (3.212) | -10.032*** (3.444) | 6.360*** (2.189) | 7.226*** (2.262) |
| Democracy | | -0.156 (0.227) | | -0.041 (0.150) | | -0.118 (0.103) |
| Constant | 65.559*** (6.388) | 67.526*** (7.569) | 90.106*** (5.380) | 90.620*** (5.621) | 11.859*** (3.233) | 13.342*** (3.710) |
| Observations | 77 | 77 | 77 | 77 | 77 | 77 |
| R-squared | 0.259 | 0.265 | 0.246 | 0.247 | 0.284 | 0.299 |

Note: see Table 4.1.

Source: Computed by authors using the data of Rosstat, Russian Census 2010, FOM, FCSD and Moscow Carnegie Center.

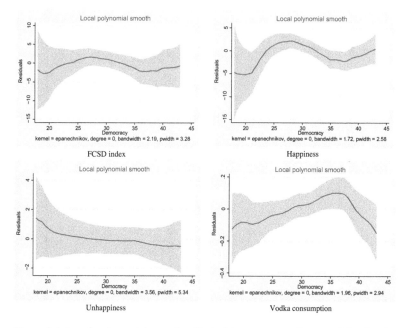

*Figure 9.1* Local polynomial smooth, effect of democracy on the unexplained variation in well-being characteristics

Source: Computed by authors using the data of Rosstat, Russian Census 2010, FOM, FCSD and Moscow Carnegie Center.

national level of analysis but much weaker for the sub-national level, at least in Russia, where direct repressions (using police or paramilitary organizations) are absent even in most authoritarian regions. If we use a semi-parametric approach (along the lines presented earlier), for two of three indicators there is obviously no effect of democracy on well-being; there is some weak evidence of non-linearity of effect of democracy on the share of those who claim to be happy according to the FOM survey, but the effect is not robust (see Figure 9.1).

Most other covariates we have added are insignificant. Interestingly, we observe a significant and positive correlation between economic openness and happiness. Possibly, regions with greater exposure to international trade are also better at supplying their population with high-quality goods. Furthermore, Russians may value international openness as such, which would increase their well-being (a result which looks particularly important given the political developments of 2014). Income and well-being are significantly and positively correlated (again, we have to notice that while this correlation holds for the sample in general, there are also important outliers – like Tyva). Thus, strictly speaking, we do not confirm the Easterlin paradox logic in our dataset.

## 9.4 Vodka consumption

Let us now proceed to the discussion of our last proxy –vodka consumption. We compute the per capita vodka consumption based on official sources (for the year 2010, given the availability of data) and regress it on both linear and squared terms of democracy. We also add several further control variables. We control for income per capita – it is likely to determine consumption habits in general and the resources available for alcohol purchases. We also add the share of ethnic Russians, since different cultures in Russia may have different standards regarding alcohol consumption. We control for economic openness, which could be associated with import of different consumption habits from abroad (weakening the position vodka has in the traditional Russian context). We also control for health-care system and crime rate: while a more advanced health-care system could reduce vodka consumption (being able to effectively inform the population about the risks, at least to a certain extent possible in the Russian cultural context), higher crime rates are likely to encourage vodka consumption (for example, because of illegal sales of alcohol[2] or because of the development of criminal sub-culture). Finally, we add education to the set of controls, which potentially could also be associated with better knowledge about the consequences of alcohol consumption and the spread of social norms of the educated class limiting the consumption of alcohol (again, to a certain extent possible). We also perform semi-parametric analysis, with results presented in Figure 9.1 and confirming the findings of the parametric econometrics.

Most covariates have the predicted sign and significance (see Table 9.2). Crime rate has a positive and significant effect; so does income (again, probably reflecting larger resources the public has). Education has a negative and significant effect. What is more important for us is that we find evidence of an inverse *U*-shaped effect of democracy on vodka consumption: higher levels of democracy and autocracy are associated with lower vodka consumption than the intermediate levels. It is possible that the intermediate regimes are associated with the highest level of alienation of the public from politics (autocracies function according to the old decision-making patterns well known to Russians, and democracies offer larger opportunities for political participation). Furthermore, intermediate regimes may be perceived as less stable (as the discussion of the previous chapter shows), which increases the level of personal uncertainty and (possibly in response) of vodka consumption.

*Table 9.2* The impact of political regimes on vodka consumption, dependent variable: vodka consumption per capita, 2010, OLS

|  | (1) | (2) | (3) |
|---|---|---|---|
| Income per capita | 0.000*** | 0.000*** | 0.000*** |
|  | (0.000) | (0.000) | (0.000) |
| Economic openness | 0.001 | 0.001 | 0.001 |
|  | (0.002) | (0.002) | (0.001) |
| Education | −1.669** | −1.915** | −2.090** |
|  | (0.719) | (0.769) | (0.799) |
| Healthcare system | −0.001 | −0.001 | −0.000 |
|  | (0.003) | (0.003) | (0.003) |
| Crime | 0.000*** | 0.000*** | 0.000*** |
|  | (0.000) | (0.000) | (0.000) |
| Share of ethnic Russians | −0.077 | −0.158 | −0.283* |
|  | (0.157) | (0.172) | (0.161) |
| Democracy |  | 0.009 | 0.115** |
|  |  | (0.007) | (0.049) |
| Democracy squared |  |  | −0.002** |
|  |  |  | (0.001) |
| Constant | 0.623** | 0.535** | −0.975 |
|  | (0.243) | (0.233) | (0.733) |
| Observations | 79 | 79 | 79 |
| R-squared | 0.481 | 0.498 | 0.539 |

Note: see Table 4.1.

Source: Computed by authors using the data of Rosstat, Russian Census 2010 and Moscow Carnegie Center.

In the next step, we again look at bureaucratic agency, using precisely the same approach as in previous chapters (see Table 9.3). Our main finding is that the effect we described is driven by regions with small bureaucracies – in other words, limited bureaucratic capacity. This is important to deal with the already mentioned possibility that the effects we observe are driven by the extent of governmental control over the markets of alcohol. Our results suggest that in this case the crucial difference is not between more democratic and less democratic regions, but across regions with different state capacity. If it is sufficiently high, probably, control is strong in both more and less democratic regions, and it weakens the effects of political regimes we described on vodka consumption. In case bureaucracy is weaker, the effects of political regimes play a larger role.

Table 9.3 The impact of political regimes on vodka consumption conditional on bureaucratic agency, dependent variable: vodka consumption per capita, 2010, OLS

| | (1) | (2) | (3) | (4) | (5) | (6) |
|---|---|---|---|---|---|---|
| Income per capita | 0.000*** | 0.000 | 0.000*** | 0.000** | 0.000* | 0.000*** |
| | (0.000) | (0.000) | (0.000) | (0.000) | (0.000) | (0.000) |
| Economic openness | 0.001 | 0.001 | 0.004** | 0.001 | 0.003* | −0.004 |
| | (0.001) | (0.002) | (0.002) | (0.002) | (0.001) | (0.003) |
| Education | −0.844 | −0.073 | −2.355** | −2.922* | −3.131* | −0.486 |
| | (1.656) | (1.528) | (0.995) | (1.550) | (1.707) | (1.139) |
| Healthcare system | 0.001 | −0.006 | 0.000 | 0.002 | 0.001 | −0.003 |
| | (0.005) | (0.005) | (0.004) | (0.004) | (0.004) | (0.005) |
| Crime | 0.000** | 0.000*** | 0.000 | 0.000*** | 0.000** | 0.000*** |
| | (0.000) | (0.000) | (0.000) | (0.000) | (0.000) | (0.000) |
| Share of ethnic Russians | −0.119 | −0.518** | −0.054 | −0.536** | −0.534*** | −0.433 |
| | (0.267) | (0.229) | (0.246) | (0.198) | (0.157) | (0.277) |
| Democracy | −0.036 | 0.207*** | 0.091* | 0.198** | 0.036 | 0.077 |
| | (0.084) | (0.067) | (0.049) | (0.076) | (0.085) | (0.063) |
| Democracy squared | 0.001 | −0.003*** | −0.001* | −0.003** | 0.000 | −0.001 |
| | (0.001) | (0.001) | (0.001) | (0.001) | (0.001) | (0.001) |
| Constant | 0.808 | −2.571** | −0.69 | −2.075* | 0.577 | −0.859 |
| | (1.186) | (1.064) | (0.660) | (1.054) | (1.444) | (0.880) |
| Size of bureaucracy | Above median | Below median | | | | |
| Share of bureaucrats with short tenure | | | Above median | Below median | | |
| Share of bureaucrats with long tenure | | | | | Above median | Below median |
| Observations | 39 | 39 | 37 | 35 | 39 | 39 |
| R-squared | 0.556 | 0.479 | 0.631 | 0.676 | 0.539 | 0.663 |

Note: see Table 4.1.

Source: Computed by authors using the data of Rosstat, Russian Census 2010 and Moscow Carnegie Center.

## 9.5   Summary

To the best of our knowledge, this is the first analysis that focuses on the consequences of democracy with regard to these three variables in one setting. Our findings provide a mixed picture of the effects of political regimes on well-being. On the one hand, there is no evidence that the survey-based happiness indicators are in any way influenced by the level of democracy. On the other hand, we find that vodka consumption per capita – a very important indicator in the Russian context – is higher in regions with 'intermediate' regimes and lower in more democratic and more autocratic regions. It implies that intermediate regimes, in addition to facing lower growth rates (as discussed in the previous chapter), also encounter higher health risks due to more widespread consumption of alcohol.

### Notes

1 Tyva was controlled by the Qing dynasty of China from the mid-18th century until 1912; became Russian protectorate in 1914; was declared an independent republic allied with Soviet Russia in 1921; and became part of Russia in 1944. Thus, among all Russian regions except Kaliningrad (former German Koenigsberg, which was, after World War II, populated anew by Russian colonists), it has the shortest period of stay within the Russian state.
2 In Russia the market for alcohol is heavily regulated. One has to notice that illicit production of alcohol (*samogon*) is probably not included in the data we use.

# 10 Public policy and natural resources

As mentioned in chapter 8, our main results describing the effects of sub-national regime variation on economic growth were determined by political stability and not by the actual policy choice of different regimes. In this chapter, however, we investigate the consequences of sub-national regimes for public policy. In particular, our focus will be on natural resources and the way governments deal with them. The focus on natural resources is important for the Russian context for obvious reasons – Russia is extremely rich in terms of both mineral and non-mineral resources, and therefore it is hardly possible to discuss the development of Russian politics and economy without taking this aspect into account. We will, in particular, look at the problem from two angles. First, we look at the ability of sub-national governments to *use natural resources as drivers of economic growth*. From this perspective, we will look at mineral resources, which play the role of the key source of growth in Russia in the 2000s. Second, we look at the ability of the sub-national government to *replenish the exhaustible natural resources*. This question is, obviously, especially relevant for biological resources, and therefore we look at how sub-national governments in Russia preserve forests – again, one of the key resources Russia has at its disposal.

## 10.1  Mineral resources: theory

The literature on the economic effects of mineral resource endowment is extremely rich and is strongly related to the discussion of the (economic) resource curse: resource-rich regions (or countries) are characterized by lower growth rates (see a recent survey in van der Ploeg 2011). The first version of this argument in economics – the 'Dutch disease' literature – did not focus on institutions and rather described negative effects of resource richness as associated with reallocation of natural resources across different sectors (Corden and Neary 1982). More recent literature, however, incorporated institutions in the analysis. There is a consensus in economics that improvement in *economic institutions* – better protection of property rights and contract enforcement, less predatory regulation, etc. – can be a remedy against the resource curse (e.g. Tornell and Lane 1999; Mehlum et al. 2006; Brueckner 2010). The attitude toward *political institutions* – and especially democratization – is divided. On the one hand, authoritarian regimes with their low level of accountability are more likely to abuse resource rents, which would decrease the level of economic growth (Dunning 2005; Robinson et al. 2006; Bulte and Damania 2008; Cabrales and Hauk 2011). On the other hand, weak nascent democracies (which are typically found in developing countries) are prone to populism, and in a resource-rich economy, this populism would lead to political fixation on redistribution of resource rents and lack of necessary economic reforms (Eifert et al. 2002; Collier and Hoeffler 2009). Empirically, the conclusions are also highly contradictory.

The analysis of sub-national resource curse is, generally, a novel field, and most studies in this area have concentrated on purely economic effects or looked at the role of economic institutions (Johnson 2006; Papyrakis and Gerlagh 2007; Goldberg et al. 2008; Caselli and Michaels 2009; Corey 2009; James and Aadland 2010; James and James 2011; Michaels 2011; Borge et al. 2013; Papyrakis and Raveh 2014). Political institutions at the sub-national level are, as chapter 2 suggests, extremely difficult to measure, and therefore there is little evidence in terms of how sub-national democracy should affect the use of natural resources. Another problem is that resource rents – more than any other aspects of sub-national economy – attract the attention of the central government. Fights for redistribution of resource rents are relevant for many federations (e.g., Canada) and in some cases are important for de jure or de facto state collapse (e.g., Iraq in the 2000s). If the federal government is strong enough, it typically manages to establish control over natural resources, which are then redistributed across the entire country. This is, in fact, what we observe in Russia in the first decade of the 2000s. In the 1990s some natural resources (diamonds in Sakha, oil in Tatarstan or Bashkortostan or forests in Komi) were captured by the sub-national governments; other resources (natural gas) were controlled by federal state-owned companies (Gazprom); and yet other resources (oil in Siberia) were under mixed control of federal private and state-owned business.[1] In the 2000s Putin's government gradually reestablished federal control over resources by restoring control over large resource companies and changing the tax system, with a larger portion of resource rents attributed to the federal budget (on the history of Russian center-periphery relations in the oil sector see Bahry 2005; Kusznir 2008; Kryukov et al. 2011; Yenikeyeff 2014; Alexeev and Chernyavskiy 2015). This is, in fact, reflected in the most recent studies of natural resources and in our findings in chapter 8, which all show an insignificant growth effect of natural resources at the sub-national level: resource rents are simply channeled away from the regional economy.

However, regional governments still posses another instrument which could influence the ability of natural resources to affect economic growth. Sub-national governments in Russia have a much stronger influence on the non-resource sector and its ability to develop. Thus, sub-national governments can influence the ability of the resource sector to stimulate economic growth in the non-resource sector or the 'transmission' of resource growth into non-resource growth. Even though a substantial portion of resource revenue leaves the regions (either through federal taxation or through transfer pricing of resource companies), some of the rent remains in the region and is paid to the employees of resource companies. These rents are in turn either spent for consumption in the region (and thus promote the economic growth there through a spillover effect), invested in the region (for example, for construction purposes) or exported out of the region. In case the regional business environment is favorable, the consumer goods sector and retail will flourish, giving the region additional impulses for growth (Libman 2013b). If the business environment is, however, problematic, the resource rents will not generate further growth since a large portion will be de facto appropriated by regional bureaucrats or lost. The extent to which the non-resource sector can benefit from these resource sector spillovers can also be determined by the regional political regime – and factors like economic institutions and political stability associated with it (we have discussed these arguments in the previous chapters of this book).

## 10.2 Mineral resources: empirical model and results

Let us therefore proceed to empirical testing of the possible implications of sub-national political regimes for the ability of mineral resources to generate economic growth. For this purpose we use the same model as in chapter 8 in the analysis of sub-national economic growth, but with a certain modification: instead of regressing growth on democracy and democracy squared, we regress the economic growth measure on democracy and the interaction term between democracy and the natural resources.[2] The interaction term is the key variable of interest: it shows us how the resource effect on growth changes if the level of democracy increases. We analyze this change using the approach suggested by Brambor et al. (2006) by plotting the marginal effects of natural resource variable for different levels of democracy variable, as well as presenting the associated confidence intervals. Table 10.1 reports our main findings. Specification (1) uses the full sample; specification

*Table 10.1* The interplay of political regimes and mineral resource endowment as determinants of economic growth, dependent variable: average annual growth rate 2001–2010, OLS

|  | *(1)* | *(2)* | *(3)* |
|---|---|---|---|
| GDP of the year 2000 | 0.000 | 0.000 | 0.000** |
|  | (0.000) | (0.000) | (0.000) |
| Economic openness | 0.006 | 0.013 | 0.012 |
|  | (0.010) | (0.009) | (0.009) |
| Education | 4.707 | 8.072* | 7.152 |
|  | (6.272) | (4.778) | (4.752) |
| Natural resources | 0.039 | −0.179** | −0.213** |
|  | (0.107) | (0.084) | (0.086) |
| Investments | 15.092*** | 15.948*** | 15.840*** |
|  | (5.388) | (4.477) | (4.420) |
| Democracy | 0.002 | −0.114** | −0.145*** |
|  | (0.059) | (0.044) | (0.046) |
| Natural resources * Democracy | −0.002 | 0.005* | 0.006** |
|  | (0.003) | (0.003) | (0.003) |
| Constant | −0.15 | 2.247 | 3.137 |
|  | (2.245) | (2.024) | (2.055) |
| Outliers | Included | Excluded | Excluded |
| Tiumen region | Included | Included | Excluded |
| Observations | 79 | 75 | 74 |
| R-squared | 0.224 | 0.378 | 0.392 |

Note: see Table 4.1.

Source: Computed by authors using the data of Rosstat, Russian Census 2010 and Moscow Carnegie Center.

(2) excludes the outliers we have dropped in chapter 8 (and is therefore our preferred specification); specification (3) drops a further outlier – the region of Tiumen, which is the main oil and gas region of Russia and thus could benefit disproportionally from resource rents.

The results can be summarized as follows. For the full sample, democracy has no effects for growth (as expected, given the results of chapter 8), and the interaction term is also insignificant. For the samples excluding outliers, we find a significant and positive interaction term between resources and democracy. As Figure 10.1 suggests, this significant effect should be interpreted as follows. For regions with low and average levels

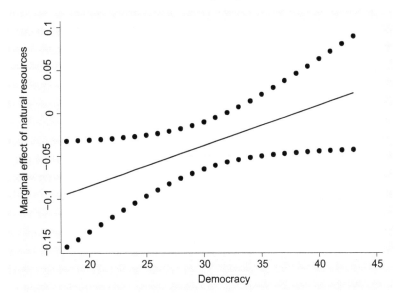

*Figure 10.1* Marginal effects of natural resources on growth conditional on level of democracy, 95% confidence intervals

Source: Computed by authors using the data of Rosstat, Russian Census 2010 and Moscow Carnegie Center.

of democracy (which, actually, cover the majority of our sample), we find no significant effect of natural resource rents on growth. For regions with high democracy levels (13 regions of our sample), growth effect of natural resources is significant and positive. Stated otherwise, natural resources contribute to growth only if democracy is high enough. We have to stress that most of these 'democratic' regions are actually resource poor, although some (Arkhangelsk, Karelia or Perm) have substantial resource rents. The resource-richest regions of Russia find themselves among those with democracy levels below the threshold.

The result is puzzling if we compare it to the previous literature. In our previous paper (Libman 2013a), which investigated the period from 2000–2006, we found that resources contributed to economic growth in Russia in *non-democratic regions*, but only under condition that they had relatively efficient bureaucracy. Why did the situation change in the second half of the first decade of the 2000s? (Recall that this is the period for which the resource data we use were collected.) The most likely explanation for our findings is, again, the change in the institutional design of

Russian federalism. In the early 2000s, sub-national regions were still ruled by elected governors (while elections were abolished in 2004, the number of appointed governors exceeded the number of governors who still came to power based on elections only in 2007). These governors enjoyed higher independence from Moscow and were less concerned about the reaction of the center in terms of their political career. On the other hand, although electoral manipulations were widespread already in the early 2000s, governors had to care about the support of the regional population to ensure reelection. As discussed in chapter 8, this concern could have triggered populist moves – and, indeed, this is the main reason why weak nascent democracy could exacerbate the economic resource curse. In the second half of the first decade of the 2000s, Russian regions were ruled by appointed governors, who had only one goal – to please the federal center. For the federal government, popularity of the regional governors was rather unimportant for reappointment decisions (Reisinger and Moraski 2012; Reuter and Robertson 2012; Rochlitz 2013), and therefore substantial incentives for rent-seeking emerged (Libman et al. 2012). We argue that in somewhat more democratic regions the opportunity for rent-seeking still remained lower due to the impact of multiple regional players (including stronger regional civil society).

Rent-seeking is, however, not the only problem non-democracies could create in the second half of the 2000s. One of the consequences of the excessive centralization of Russian federalism is the predominantly formalistic approach to exercising public policies. It is associated with excessive pressure of controlling organizations and entities which developed in Russia in the second half of the 2000s and focused exclusively on formal implementation of federal requirements. Therefore, in many cases regional governors were more concerned about literally fulfilling the request of the center and tried to limit their initiative (which would create risks of incorrect implementation of federal directives – this risk was more important for regional governors than the economic performance of their region). Again, democracy (which forces governors to take regional interests into account) is limiting this formalism.

Thus, we argue that in the first and in the second halves of the first decade of the 2000s regional governors faced different incentives. In the first half of the first decade of the 2000s elected governors were to some extent concerned about gaining support of the regional population. In Russia it implied massive redistribution and other populist moves, which were exacerbated by regional democracy. Therefore, non-democratic regions performed better. In the second half of the 2000s, appointed governors cared primarily about federal support, fulfilling federal requirements and rent-seeking, and this effect was limited through regional democracy. Therefore, relative to other regions of that period, democratic regions performed better. As mentioned, democracy has two contradictory effects in terms of public policy – on the one hand, it increases populism, but on the other hand, it contains rent-seeking and formalism of the elites. Changes of the federal policy made each of these aspects relatively more important, resulting into the outcome we observed. Notice, however, that the positive effect of democracy is present in very few regions with a very high level of democracy (as opposed to other regions of our sample). For most regions, resources had no effect on growth, which is consistent with the outcomes of the overall centralization trend the Russian economy faced.

## 10.3 Mineral resources: bureaucratic agency

The treatment of the non-resource sector depends not only on political regimes, but even to a greater extent on the behavior of bureaucracies; therefore bureaucratic agency, which has been a consistently discussed topic throughout this book, is also relevant for the analysis of public policies in resource sector. We perform the same analysis as in the previous chapters and report its results in Table 10.2. One can see that the positive effect is present only in regions with large bureaucracy and where bureaucratic tenure is relatively short.

The size of bureaucracy is, as mentioned, a proxy for the capacity of the regional bureaucracy. From this point of view, the result is reasonable: governments need not only to be democratic (and therefore less inclined to rent-seeking) to implement growth-enhancing public policies, but they also have sufficient governance capacity (Acemoglu et al. 2014 provides a recent discussion of a similar argument). This is precisely what we find. Note that we do not argue that larger bureaucracy as such is supporting economic growth – the empirical results in this respect, even for Russia, are, as mentioned earlier, heterogeneous. Our argument is that in order to improve public policy, one needs a *combination* of democracy and sufficient governance capacity. Since, as we have mentioned in chapter 4, most Russian regions with large bureaucracy also have lower democracy levels, this combination will be observed only in very few cases. The impact of tenure may be linked to the lack of socialization of bureaucrats into existing practices and routines of public service, which in Russia very often implies very high level of corruption – less entrenched bureaucracies are less affected by this problem.

Table 10.2 The interplay of political regimes and mineral resource endowment as determinants of economic growth conditional on bureaucratic agency, dependent variable: average real GDP growth rate, 2001–2010, OLS, outliers excluded

| | (1) | (2) | (3) | (4) | (5) | (6) |
|---|---|---|---|---|---|---|
| GDP of the year 2000 | 0.000 | 0.000 | 0.000 | 0.000 | 0.000 | 0.000 |
| | (0.000) | (0.000) | (0.000) | (0.000) | (0.000) | (0.000) |
| Economic openness | 0.014 | 0.01 | 0.024* | 0.003 | -0.003 | 0.079*** |
| | (0.012) | (0.018) | (0.012) | (0.013) | (0.012) | (0.019) |
| Education | -5.129 | 13.196** | 15.382*** | 0.861 | 17.616* | 1.820 |
| | (8.913) | (5.617) | (4.672) | (8.773) | (9.036) | (5.213) |
| Natural resources | -0.293** | -0.11 | -0.313** | -0.094 | -0.046 | -0.413*** |
| | (0.111) | (0.086) | (0.140) | (0.094) | (0.185) | (0.108) |
| Investments | 17.895*** | 13.514 | 10.101** | 32.992*** | 23.171*** | 8.833* |
| | (5.069) | (9.727) | (4.134) | (8.956) | (7.622) | (4.411) |
| Democracy | -0.129* | -0.117** | -0.117* | -0.164* | -0.027 | -0.268*** |
| | (0.071) | (0.047) | (0.058) | (0.080) | (0.071) | (0.057) |
| Natural resources * Democracy | 0.008** | 0.003 | 0.010** | 0.001 | 0.001 | 0.012*** |
| | (0.004) | (0.003) | (0.005) | (0.003) | (0.006) | (0.004) |
| Constant | 4.732 | 2.424 | 1.754 | 1.887 | -3.483 | 8.863*** |
| | (3.202) | (3.059) | (2.121) | (3.755) | (3.628) | (1.714) |
| Size of bureaucracy | Above median | Below median | | | | |
| Share of bureaucrats with short tenure | | | Above median | Below median | | |
| Share of bureaucrats with long tenure | | | | | Above median | Below median |
| Observations | 37 | 37 | 34 | 34 | 39 | 35 |
| R-squared | 0.55 | 0.37 | 0.547 | 0.531 | 0.427 | 0.638 |

Note: see Table 4.1.

Source: Computed by authors using the data of Rosstat, Russian Census 2010 and Moscow Carnegie Center.

## 10.4 Governance of the forest sector

The development in the forest sector was, to some extent, the opposite of what has happened in the Russian federal system in general and in the mineral resource sector in particular. Here the Russian Federation experienced a strong trend toward decentralization. The property rights on forests in Russia belong to the federal government (forests are legally not different from other natural resources in this respect). In the early 1990s, however, the de facto control over forests and decision-making over forest use were decentralized, originally to the municipal governments and, after several years, to the regional governments. Until 2004, Russia continued to centralize the authorities in forest governance; in 1997, in particular, it created a federal agency responsible for the monitoring of forests, reforestation and all other related activities. This trend, however, was broken in 2006, when a new Forest Code was passed (again, in apparent contradiction to the oil and gas sector, where regional share in the resource revenue continued to go down). The Forest Code transferred almost all authorities related to forest use and reforestation to regional governments. The federal government remained responsible for setting the basic rules of forest use and monitoring their implementation. In particular, regional governments received the right to allocate the forests to private forest users (businesses engaged in logging activities for profit), determine their environmental obligations and monitor them.

The reasons for this abnormal development are most likely associated with an attempt to strengthen the commercialization of forest use. Regional governments had stronger incentives to attract forest users and negotiate attractive conditions. At the same time, the federal government could reduce its financial obligations with respect to reforestation. Regions were still compensated for the additional costs they faced because of the new assignments through federal transfers, but the amount of these transfers was typically incomplete to effectively exercise all new functions. For us, it is important to notice that the regional governments received substantial autonomy in implementing the reforestation functions – thus, they were responsible for the replenishment of natural resources (on the evolution of the Russian forest sector see Torniainen et al. 2006, 2010; Torniainen and Saastamoinen 2007; Wendland et al. 2011; Ulybina 2014). Reforestation in Russia is either implemented by regional governments themselves or by businesses leasing forest areas in line with their agreements with the regional governments. Our previous work (Libman and Obydenkova 2014a) has shown that the effect of reforestation at the sub-national level was driven by two factors: the extent of federal support (through transfers) and the degree to which local non-governmental actors (forest users or civil society) were involved in forest governance. Wendland et al. (2014), looking at a different time frame (early 2000s), show that democratization is positively correlated with commercial logging activities. The implications of political regimes for reforestation, however, have not been studied thus far.

There are, hypothetically, two possible effects of democracy on reforestation, again driven by two different implications of democracy for public policy – stronger inclination to populism and weaker rent-seeking. Limited opportunities for rent-seeking should in general encourage reforestation, since otherwise the financial means accumulated for it will be misused. Populism could have different implications. On the one hand, it could again require the government to increase investments in reforestation to satisfy the public demand. Our previous work (Libman and Obydenkova 2014a), as well as the existing research on the generally very weak role of ecological thinking in Russia (Usacheva 2011), makes it questionable whether a populist government would indeed massively invest in reforestation from this perspective; however, a certain revival of civil society activism in Russian regions in the second half of the first decade of the 2000s was also associated with growing environmental activism (with the case of Khimki forest near Moscow, which was pivotal for the development of civil society and the opposition in Russia, being an excellent example). On the other hand, regional governments also have to deal with the informal rules of forest use, which have been established in the Russian regions over decades (and strengthened in the post-Soviet era, see CNSI 2005). These rules, in turn, oscillate between being based on rational forest use in some regions and allowing for excessive forest disturbance (e.g., by local population for non-commercial purposes) in others. Summing up, theoretically, we can expect both positive and negative effects of democracy with respect to reforestation activities, which will be put to the test in what follows.

## 10.5   Reforestation: empirical model and results

The empirical model we estimate in this section is based on Libman and Obydenkova (2014a) and, unlike other regressions we ran so far, is estimated for 2009. In 2009, the provisions of the new Forest Code had to be implemented to the full extent – therefore, it is reasonable to concentrate our investigation on this year. The previous period, as mentioned, was characterized by centralized forest governance and is less interesting for us. Our dependent variable is the regional area covered by reforestation activity (new forest plantations, etc.). As opposed to the baseline regression, we exclude three regions from the sample: the cities of Moscow and St. Petersburg (which have no forest area) and Tiumen (this region has a very complex forest governance system involving two of its autonomous regions, which makes the analysis and the correct interpretation of data problematic). In some of the specifications including additional variables we also run regressions excluding additional observations, if for the new control variables no data are available. Results are reported in Table 10.3 and are fully confirmed by semi-parametric analysis of Figure 10.2.

The baseline specification includes the following control variables. First, we control for the size of the area covered by forest (obviously, if it is

*Table 10.3* The impact of political regimes on reforestation activities, dependent variable: reforestation area, 2009, OLS

|  | *(1)* | *(2)* | *(3)* | *(4)* |
|---|---|---|---|---|
| Forest area | 0.532*** | 0.449*** | 0.551*** | 0.508*** |
|  | (0.130) | (0.121) | (0.127) | (0.126) |
| GDP per capita | −0.003 | −0.006 | 0.008 | −0.004 |
|  | (0.004) | (0.005) | (0.010) | (0.005) |
| Population | −470.356 | 402.127 | −445.208 | −1,218.74 |
|  | (537.981) | (580.549) | (653.344) | (769.880) |
| Democracy | 677.517*** | 400.336* | 640.518*** | 642.063*** |
|  | (208.608) | (212.002) | (204.185) | (204.138) |
| Coniferous forest |  | 21,331.540*** |  |  |
|  |  | (6,681.084) |  |  |
| Deciduous forest |  | 2,580.09 |  |  |
|  |  | (3,231.071) |  |  |
| Temperature |  |  | 478.995 |  |
|  |  |  | (711.173) |  |
| Rainfall |  |  | 211.533** |  |
|  |  |  | (100.904) |  |
| Transfers for forest restoration |  |  |  | 0.165** |
|  |  |  |  | (0.076) |
| Transfers for salaries |  |  |  | 0.061 |
|  |  |  |  | (0.066) |
| Constant | −13,736.877** | −14,375.238** | −39,024.275* | −13,877.834** |
|  | (5,475.941) | (6,302.128) | (21,160.763) | (5,459.184) |
| Observations | 76 | 76 | 76 | 75 |
| R-squared | 0.664 | 0.713 | 0.707 | 0.684 |

Note: see Table 4.1.

Source: Computed by authors using the data of Rosstat, Russian Census 2010, Russian Forest Agency and Moscow Carnegie Center.

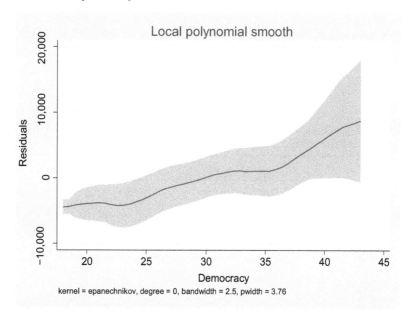

*Figure 10.2* Local polynomial smooth, effect of democracy on the unexplained variation in reforestation

Source: Computed by authors using the data of Rosstat, Russian Census 2010, Federal Forest Agency and Moscow Carnegie Center.

larger, reforestation activity should also be larger). Second, we control for the GDP per capita – economic development is likely to have implications for reforestation activity. Third, we control for the size of the population – this parameter increases forest disturbance by human activity and calls for greater reforestation effort. All three variables are for 2009. Fourth, we also include the key variable of interest – our democracy index (we use the value for the period from 2001–2010 since we are interested in long-term characteristics of the regional political systems). Further specifications add a number of control variables: (a) composition of the forests (share of deciduous and coniferous forests, which could determine the need for reforestation activity from the biological point of view); (b) average long-term July temperature and rainfall (to account for climate features, which again affect how much reforestation is needed); and (c) transfers paid by the federal government for forest activity of the regions (we include transfers paid for reforestation and for salaries of forest officials, which obviously affect the incentives these officials have to care for the forests).

Regardless of specification, we find the same outcome: democracy is increasing the reforestation activity in the region. Furthermore, as Table 10.4

Table 10.4 The impact of political regimes on reforestation activities conditional on bureaucratic agency, dependent variable: reforestation area, 2009, OLS

| | (1) | (2) | (3) | (4) | (5) | (6) |
|---|---|---|---|---|---|---|
| Forest area | 0.423*** | 1.139*** | 0.447*** | 0.731** | 1.591*** | 0.450*** |
| | (0.094) | (0.066) | (0.115) | (0.270) | (0.090) | (0.080) |
| GDP per capita | 0.003 | 0.012 | -0.001 | -0.018 | -0.024 | -0.001 |
| | (0.004) | (0.024) | (0.004) | (0.036) | (0.026) | (0.004) |
| Population | 5,544.56 | -536.472 | -779.146 | -901.468 | -236.057 | -249.465 |
| | (3,623.534) | (544.893) | (652.185) | (1,561.714) | (1,037.880) | (666.563) |
| Democracy | 520.809* | 229.552** | 795.111** | 453.782 | 267.284** | 794.999*** |
| | (295.177) | (104.722) | (300.587) | (319.408) | (125.262) | (277.493) |
| Constant | -13,322.54 | -5,253.203* | -16,354.710* | -5,492.30 | -2,480.50 | -18,277.761** |
| | (7,962.134) | (2,714.081) | (8,473.311) | (9,612.859) | (3,558.213) | (6,959.905) |
| Size of bureaucracy | Above median | Below median | | | | |
| Share of bureaucrats with short tenure | | | Above median | Below median | | |
| Share of bureaucrats with long tenure | | | | | Above median | Below median |
| Observations | 37 | 37 | 34 | 34 | 39 | 35 |
| R-squared | 0.55 | 0.37 | 0.547 | 0.531 | 0.427 | 0.638 |

Note: see Table 4.1.

Source: Computed by authors using the data of Rosstat, Russian Census 2010, Russian Forest Agency and Moscow Carnegie Center.

shows, in this case bureaucratic agency has no effect. Thus, the hypotheses suggesting a positive effect of democratization on replenishment of natural resources seem to be confirmed.

## 10.6 Summary

This chapter provided a substantially more favorable picture of the consequences of democratization in Russian regions. When we look at the public policies implemented by regions with different regimes in the resource sector, we establish that democracies are more likely to care for reproduction of natural resources and to use resources as a factor generating economic growth. The last finding (obtained from the analysis of the mineral resource sector) also differs substantially from what the previous literature has shown; we hypothesize that the reason for these differences is that our paper investigated an era of substantially more centralized Russian federalism. While in the past regional populism was the main problem, the period we investigated made excessive rent-seeking or compliance with formal requirements of the center the main problem – and sub-national democracy to some extent limited these negative effects.

### Notes

1 Legally, in Russia mineral resources belong to the state, which gives private companies the exploration rights. According to the federal constitution, mineral resources are the property of the federation, but in the 1990s, many regional constitutions disregarded it and declared resources regional property. If large companies (like Gazprom) dominate the regional economy, they typically have a de facto unlimited control over resources.
2 We do not include democracy squared in the set of covariates since otherwise the interpretation of the interaction term would be very difficult. We acknowledge this approach as a certain limitation of results reported in this chapter.

# 11 Religiosity as identity formation

The previous chapters of this book investigated how democratization in Russian regions affected economic growth, public policy, economic liberalization and subjective and objective well-being. In contrast, this chapter intends to capture more subtle effects of democratization – those that are associated with identity formation and self-perception through the choice of confession and the actual level of religiosity. Wide literature on democratization indicated the importance of self-identity, especially regionally concentrated, as the potential basis for collective action and as an important aspect of civil society. As Philippe Schmitter stated,

> The root hypothesis is that for an effective and enduring challenge to authoritarian rule to be mounted, and for political democracy to become and remain an alternative mode of political domination, a country must possess a civil society in which certain community and group identities exist independent of the state and in which certain types of self-constituted units are capable of acting autonomously in defense of their own interests and ideals.
>
> (Schmitter 1991, p. 6)

Therefore, the role of the growth of self-identification is endogenous to the regime transition. It is interpreted as both an important precondition for regime change and the consequence of democratization, as well as an already established aspect of consolidated democracy, as a final arrival point of transition. The identities are linked to regions, and the higher level of democracy is associated with increase in a higher level of regional self-identification. (The referendums on Scotland and Catalonia are probably some of the best recent examples of regional self-identification within the context of consolidated European democracies.) Self-identification is also important because it is linked to collective action: '. . . these identities and interests must not only be dispersed throughout the country, they must also be capable of being concentrated when the occasion demands, that is, they must be organized for coherent collective action' (Schmitter 1991, p. 6). However, while the cultural-political identities are both prerequisite and the outcome of democratization, it is still possible to distinguish various levels of their gradual development. *Religion* can be safely considered one of the contextual factors of transition due to its historical presence in Slavic lands dated to back to the 9th century and even earlier for Paganism. It provides a historical context, is reflected in culture and can be described as a very weak and passive form of self-identification. In contrast *religiosity* – actual and *conscious* choice of self-identification – is a strong and *active* form of identity that is formed after certain freedom was already given to the society; in other words, it is the outcome (*consequence*) of democratization. Religiosity is, therefore, a new phenomenon that came into play *after* the regime transition and presents useful tools to make such a differentiation between causes and outcome. The division between the two is, thus, crucial for the discussion of the causes and consequences of democratization.

The role of religion in post-Communist Europe posed a few puzzles to the academic discussion on the interaction between transition and the role of religion in society. While in consolidated Western democracies, religiosity has declined and society in this respect is passive, the post-Communist transition was associated with active recuperation of religious traditions and their regular practices. The religious resurrection and the growth of popular interest in religion paralleled by participation in religious rituals in post-Communist societies became the topic of academic discussions (see, for example, Need and Evans 2001). This has been interpreted as the reaction to almost a century of suppression of religion on the part of totalitarian regime (Need and Evans 2001).

This phenomenon is definitely not limited to or unique to Russia. A number of Central Eastern European post-Communist states experienced rapid growth of the importance of various religions and of active interest on the part of the population (mainly four played the most prominent role – Catholicism, Orthodoxy, Judaism and Islam). Recuperation of religion and growing religiosity became part of identity formation after the fall of Communism in 1989 (see, for example, Ochman 2013). It is important, however, that this phenomenon is not reduced to sheer religious self-identification (*religion* as such), but to active *participation* in religious rituals and institutions (that is, *religiosity*). Thus, the clear distinction between religion and religiosity is to be made.

Religiosity as a way of self-identity formation seemed to be geographically and chronologically heterogeneous. For example, the study by Need and Evans (2001) on the religiosity of Catholic and Orthodox post-Communist states in the 1990s demonstrated that Catholics were more active and regular practitioners than Orthodox. This could be explained by stating that the role of Communism in, for example, Russia had deeper roots and that more efforts were delegated at elimination of the religion, and it explains why this Orthodox country exhibited a lower level of religious activity. Thus the recuperation of the religion indeed had passed over the stage of the so-called 'spiritual vacuum' of the 1990s, where people actively joined various Eastern Asian sects (Obydenkova 2015). It took more time for post-Communist society to develop identification with historically present religions, such as Orthodox Christianity, Islam, Judaism, Paganism and to a lesser degree Buddhism.

For Russian sub-national regions, this aspect is equally important because most of the regional identities in Russia (with the exception of ethnic regions) were relatively weak by the end of the USSR due to the ideological homogenization and immigration policies carried out by the Soviet government to achieve the assimilation of ethnic groups. Even the territorial-administrative division into sub-national regions that had been established over the USSR and remained until now often went not along the ethnic groups living together but across their territories. The propaganda of atheism during the Soviet period and the elimination of different confessions (not only Christians, but also Islamic as well as various forms of Paganism especially common for the Siberian region) were also meant to contribute to the elimination of any cultural-religious identities to achieve homogenization of all people in one nation-state.

The theoretical framework of the influence of democratization on identity formation, or in this case rather recuperation of cultural-religious identities, received substantially less attention in the literature than other aspects of our investigation; therefore, in this case the theoretical underpinning of our research is much weaker. Still, there are a number of conjectures we could formulate and test. Most importantly, as argued earlier, we differentiate between religion and religiosity. This difference is crucial not only for this chapter but for the entire book. Religion is associated with the large historical presence of a certain confession within a specific geographic region.[1] Thus, religion may well be interpreted in this context as the passive presence of a powerful historical tradition, the presence of the cultural social capital. In contrast, religiosity implies active and regular participation in activities of churches or mosques or the like. The difference between religion and religiosity lays down an important ground for further discussion. Religiosity also reflects the freedom to practice religion; the possibility provided by the government to participate in related rituals; the sheer permission to establish a synagogue, a mosque, a church or another religious organization that provides people with the freedom of choice to participate there or not; and also the freedom to choose another religion and change the confession (a tendency very common for transitional societies that experienced the atheism propaganda of the previous totalitarian regime). The longer the totalitarian regime was in place, the more religious traditions were erased as a result of it. While the freedom to exercise religious beliefs and rituals and the choice of religion are taken for granted in consolidated democracies, it is a relatively new phenomenon for the post-Soviet Russia. Given the historical presence of five main confessions in pre-revolutionary Tsarist Russia that had been suppressed over the Soviet regime, the resurrection of the various religious traditions and their practice present an important outcome of the regime transition that took place since the later 1980s.

We look in particular at how democratization affected the development of *religiosity* in Russian regions. In the USSR, religion and church were under the strict control of the government; in the early 1990s, democratic Russia experienced a true revival of religious feelings. The new Constitution of the Russian Federation was adopted in 1993 and was followed by a number of laws. One of the most important laws defining the place of religion as an institution and legalizing religious pluralism was the law of 1997. The 1997 law has identified such religions as Islam, Judaism, Buddhism and Orthodox Christianity as especially significant throughout the history of Russia and prescribed that they should be respected as such. Other religious minorities are recognized by this law as 'ancient pagan cults' with some territorial-regional dimension compounded of Neopaganism and Tengrism.[2] A number of studies have demonstrated radical growth in believers and practitioners of various religions in Russia across different confessions. The First Religious Self-identification Survey was conducted in 2012 across 79 out of 83 regions and covered a total population of 143,200,000 (Arena Survey 2012). This chapter applies a number of indicators of religiosity at the sub-national level, extracted from very recent public opinion surveys.

## 11.1   Religiosity and democracy

The main departure point is that after the collapse of Communism, the wide population was left without any ideology or system of beliefs, without the very sense of life. The existentialism at this point became a crucial turning point in culture, linking past experience with newly arrived influences. The search for self-identification started even earlier in the 1980s, when the legitimacy of the Communist regime became questioned and then rejected. While this search for self-identity and the meaning of life and for new values of life started at the point of regime legitimacy crisis, the development of regime transition and the search for identities overlapping with religiosity presented some of the most interesting and unpredicted results across a few post-Communist states.

In terms of interconnection between democratization and religiosity, the relations are multi-directional. The arguments on this interconnection can be grouped in contradictory groups: first, along with the prior discussion, we assume that a higher level of democracy may be associated with higher religiosity (as part of the self-identity formation process); second, a higher level of democracy may lead to less religiosity (according to the secularization theory of modern democratic societies); and less democracy may be associated with more religiosity (as *modern* non-democratic regimes find religion a useful tool of manipulation).

As to the first group, the arguments on the end of Communism in 1989 and the rise of the religious confessions were discussed in the literature on post-Communist transitional societies (Need and Evans 2001; Ochman 2013). To sum up these arguments, first, the end of the anti-religious propaganda conducted by Communism may increase the interest for religion and the active participation in religious life. Second, the liberal democracy does respect the freedom of rights to various beliefs; therefore, more truly regional democratic government would let people exercise the right to religious beliefs that had been denied by the previous totalitarian regime. Third, after the end of the totalitarian regime and after the disappearance of the ideology, the society starts the process of self-identity formation or identity recuperation.[3] Religiosity becomes an important aspect of self-identity formation, even more crucial with the disappearance of official ideology.

On the other hand, some arguments may suggest quite the opposite link. The rises of democracy are associated with a higher level of education and then later with a more secular style of life (therefore, lower religiosity). Second, the democratic regime allows for the freedom of social gathering, common actions as part of the formation of active civil society (which might eliminate the need of the population to use religious life as part of 'getting together' social clubs – this phenomenon had been noticed in consolidated democracies).

Finally, if we consider the regional autocracies (the least level of democracy), then one might conjecture that regional governors try to cooperate with the dominant religion in the region (e.g., the Orthodox Church or Islam) to secure the sympathy of the population and also to be able to better control the population through cooperation with the religious institutions. This intention can be implemented through local and regional mass media, radio and television that are influential in general and even more in transitional societies. Thus, people might be simply manipulated to be drawn into religious life (as part of a co-existence strategy between political and spiritual leaders). Thus, three directions between the level of democracy and the level religiosity can be theoretically argued to exist.

The existing literature linking religion and democracy is rich, but it mostly looks either at variation across religious denominations (see chapter 4) or at the impact of the extent of religiosity on the likelihood of democratic consolidation (e.g. Canetti-Nisim 2004). This approach is applicable for countries where the position of religion in the society is well-established and much more robust than the political system: this is the standard case of informal institutions changing more slowly than formal rules, which has been systematically analyzed in the literature in various contexts (Williamson 2000; Roland 2004). The Russian case, however, is different: here religiosity is a very recent phenomenon which emerged as part of the transition process. Therefore, the opposite direction of causality is worth studying: political regimes could affect the extent of religious revival in individual regions. In order to understand this effect, another important observation should be made: in Russia religiosity often developed as part of the general ethnic or national self-identification. Public surveys frequently indicate that people identify themselves as orthodox not because of particular beliefs but because they interpret the orthodoxy as a necessary element of 'being Russian'; this is one of the main challenges for studying religiosity in Russia.

There are three possible mechanisms of this effect. The first mechanism is associated with *the use of religion by regional elites as a legitimization instrument.* Russia is, certainly, not a theocracy, where religion and state are closely linked to each other. However, there have been numerous attempts of regional governments to identify themselves as supporters of conservative values – which also included reference to religion. In the 2010s, there is some evidence that this form of conservatism is on the way to becoming the dominant ideology of Russia (although the outcome of this process remains to be seen, see e.g. Englstroem 2014). In the 2000s, the period we study, the Russian federal government did not explicitly appeal to any ideology, but some regional governments did. Reference to 'conservative' values is more attractive to authoritarian governments, since in the Russian context these values are understood and interpreted as contradicting 'Western' liberalism and democracy. Of course, not every attempt of regional governments to cultivate a particular ideology succeeded; the extent to which the regions managed to achieve this task remains to be seen. On the other hand, another direction of influence is possible: the regional governor might claim to be religious to be better accepted by the regional population, to gain their trust and support. Thus, if the population is already religious, it is beneficial for the governor to adjust to it and to create a better image.

The second mechanism, to some extent, contradicts the previous one. Religion can serve as a tool of spontaneous self-organization in authoritarian regions. It is easier for the regional governments to establish control over other types of social organizations and institutions than over religion. This can also explain why a governor might choose to picture himself as religious. It would help to establish better contact with local religious organization and, thus, to establish cross political-spiritual elite dialogue and consensus. As a result, people are more likely to find refuge in the religious life, especially if the regional authoritarian regime exhibits a high level of rent-seeking. Certainly, the values promoted by this 'religious self-organization' are not necessarily compatible with Western-style democracy. An excellent example is the Northern Caucasus. In this region authoritarian regimes emerged which were strongly backed by the federal government (as part of the 'pacification' strategy for the Northern Caucasus) and often tried to establish links to 'official' Islam in these regions. A response to the dominance of rent-seeking regimes was the spread of 'alternative' Islam, often much more radical than the 'official' one. Therefore caution is required in terms of normative interpretation of our conclusions: development of 'religious' self-organization does not necessarily promote civil society.

The third mechanism is associated with freedom of information in democratic regimes. In Russia, as mentioned, the positions of religions were not established ex ante, but rather emerged as an outcome of, among other things, the active proselytism of religious organizations. Some religions (like the dominant Orthodox Church), of course, had a major advantage in this respect. In autocracies, however, the activity of religious organizations (as of all other organizations) can be restricted by the regime, and, as a result, if this regime itself does not use conservative values as the foundation of its ideology, spread of religious practices and beliefs is more limited. While the previous two mechanisms suggested that the extent of religiosity should be stronger in non-democratic regions than in democratic ones, the last mechanism allows us to suggest the hypothesis that the extent of religiosity should be weaker. In what follows, we provide an empirical test of these hypotheses.

The scarce literature on the growth of religiosity as self-identification in post-Communist societies is also highly inclusive to the role played by some important intervening variables that are meant to have significant impact on religiosity – education and urbanism. Some studies demonstrate that religiosity as self-identification in post-Communist Poland is negatively influenced by education, thus confirming the secularization theory (modernization explanation of democracy) (see Need and Evans 2001). In contrast, other studies arrive at a different conclusion – that neither urbanism nor education had any influence at all on the level of religiosity in post-Communist societies (White et al. 2000 looked at Bulgaria, Slovakia, the Czech Republic and Ukraine). Including the education and urbanization of the population in the analysis of Russian regional society contributes further to these debates through providing very different findings.

## 11.2    Data: passive and active religiosity

Religiosity is one of the most challenging phenomenon to capture numerically and to measure. Religiosity is a constellation of many aspects, starting from intellectual acceptance of religion as an important part of life or history or culture, to recognition of traditional religious values, to the active stage of actual participation on a regular basis. In order to measure religiosity, we use the results of a large-scope survey covering almost all Russian regions, which was implemented by the FOM in 2013 (earlier data are, unfortunately, not available). The survey was based on representative samples within each region and several questions pertaining to religiosity. Conveniently, this dataset reflects different aspects of religiosity that can be subdivided into 'passive' and 'active'. The 'passive religiosity' includes such issues as opinion, perception, acceptance of religion as important, recognition of religious values, etc. In contrast, the so-called 'active religiosity' is the actual regular participation in religious rituals. This division is crucial for the analysis as it offers a much more nuanced approach to the phenomenon of religiosity through disentangling it into different aspects and allows considering this phenomenon in depth. Of all the questions raised by the survey, we have selected six to be used for our analysis as the most accurate ones.[4]

First, the subjects were asked whether they find religion 'important'. This question demonstrates the general attitude of the subjects regarding the role religion is supposed to play – without specifying any particular social or behavioral features derived from it. Second, the subjects were asked about whether they actually try to follow religious beliefs. In this case, the level of religiosity is higher – religion is not merely considered to matter, but the subjects at least attempt to follow its norms and rituals in their everyday life (although the question does not specify whether the subjects always succeed in their attempts to follow religious norms). Following religious requirements is possible, however, even if one does not consider religion as important and merely accepts its norms as part of one's cultural heritage. Third, the survey included a question on whether the subjects play an active role in the religious community they belong to. This is probably the strongest form of religiosity – in this case the subjects do not merely passively accept the norms of religion and try to implement it, but make religious activity a crucial part of their life. We have to note that at least in the Russian-Orthodox regions, religious communities were almost entirely destroyed during the Soviet era; therefore, actively participating in the life of a community is a conscious choice and not merely an attempt to follow standard practices.

Three further questions provide information on specific aspects of religiosity. First, the subjects were asked about the support of 'traditional values' (in particular, family). In this case religiosity is explicitly linked to conservatism, in line with the argument presented earlier. Second, the subjects were asked whether they treat other religions as sins. This is a question about religious tolerance. Tolerance as respect toward different faiths, religions and values is a crucial aspect of truly democratic society; thus, we include this variable as well.

The summary statistics suggest that there are substantial differences existing in Russia between these six aspects of religiosity. On average, 15% of Russians argue that religion is important for them; the lowest share (5%) is in Khabarovsk region in the Far East, and the highest (56%) in Dagestan, an Islamic region of the Northern Caucasus. Overall, 21% of Russians try to follow religious requirements – more than those who treat religion as important; the lowest indicator (4%) is in Chita (again, a Far East region) and the highest one (74%) in Northern Ossetia (an ethnic republic of the Northern Caucasus, which is, unlike all other ethnic republics of this part of Russia, traditionally an Orthodox-Christian region). Only 2% of Russians claim to actively participate in the life of religious communities, with the highest indicator being observed in Krasnodar (13%; Krasnodar is a region of Southern Russia with traditionally strong presence of the Cossacks). Less than 1% of Russians consider other religions as sins; somewhat surprisingly, the highest level of religious intolerance is in Buryatia, an ethnic Republic of Eastern Siberia and a traditionally Buddhist region. The results show that 20% of Russians treat traditional values as important; the lowest result is observed in Tyva (this ethnic republic is predominantly Buddhist as well) and the highest one in Northern Ossetia (42%).

While some indicators are positively and significantly correlated with each other, others are not. For instance, we observe significant and positive correlation between the share of those who try to follow religious requirements, on the one hand, and the shares of those who treat religion as important, who appreciate traditional values and who actively participate in the life of religious community, on the other. The share of those who appreciate traditional values is positively correlated with the share of those who treat other religions as sins. The share of those who consider religion as important, and the share of those who appreciate traditional values, are also positively correlated. The positive correlation across different aspects of religiosity implies that through disentangling religiosity, we investigate the same phenomenon from different angles.

Summing up, we need to carefully investigate each of the aspects of religiosity and cannot refrain ourselves to studying just one of them. This is what we attempt to do in the next section.

## 11.3   Empirical model and results

We run a series of regressions, where we use the indicators of religiosity presented earlier as dependent variables and the index of democracy as the key explanatory variable. We also add a number of further variables. First, we control for the level of education, which is typically expected to be negatively correlated with religiosity. Second, we control for the share of ethnic Russians – in ethnic regions religiosity frequently had deeper roots even during the Soviet era (and it is not coincidental that ethnic regions were regularly mentioned in our exposition of regions with very high levels of religiosity in the previous section). Third, we control for urbanization, which may serve as another indicator of modernization and typically implies weakening of religiosity and strengthening secularization. Fourth, we add the income per capita and the unemployment rate – the spread of religiosity could be connected to the hardships regional population experienced in the post-Soviet era. We use all regions for which data on religiosity is available: the FOM survey was not implemented in Chukotka and Ingushetia.

Table 11.1 reports the main findings of our estimations. We see that subnational democracy is not related to most aspects of religiosity: it suggests that the processes of formation of regional identities, at least associated with religious beliefs, were unrelated to the political development in the regions.

Table 11.1 The impact of democracy on religious attitudes of the regional population, full sample, OLS

| Dep. var. | Try to follow religious requirements | Importance of traditional values | Active participation in the life of the religious community | Importance of religion | Perception of other religions as sins |
|---|---|---|---|---|---|
| Income per capita | -0.003*** (0.001) | -0.001 (0.001) | 0.000 (0.000) | 0.000 (0.001) | 0.000 (0.000) |
| Unemployment | -0.743 (0.510) | 0.147 (0.382) | -0.194** (0.081) | 0.039 (0.493) | 0.062 (0.052) |
| Education | 96.350*** (32.952) | 68.160*** (19.989) | 1.088 (4.572) | 2.896 (18.077) | 2.363 (2.508) |
| Share of ethnic Russians | -14.665 (9.652) | -2.881 (5.000) | 1.384 (1.492) | -8.156 (5.897) | 1.033* (0.555) |
| Urbanization | -0.123 (0.146) | -0.044 (0.098) | -0.028 (0.044) | -0.078 (0.068) | -0.001 (0.012) |
| Democracy | -0.279 (0.242) | -0.079 (0.149) | -0.095*** (0.036) | -0.098 (0.139) | -0.011 (0.019) |
| Constant | 43.472*** (16.292) | 13.283 (9.356) | 7.399** (2.860) | 29.590*** (10.746) | -0.738 (1.286) |
| Observations | 77 | 77 | 77 | 77 | 77 |
| R-squared | 0.315 | 0.208 | 0.144 | 0.217 | 0.047 |

Note: see Table 4.1.

Source: Computed by authors using the data of Rosstat, Russian Census 2010, FOM and Moscow Carnegie Center.

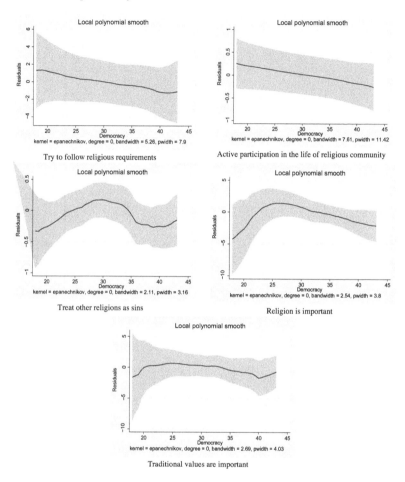

*Figure 11.1* Local polynomial smooth, effect of democracy on the unexplained variation in the indicators of religiosity

Source: Computed by authors using the data of Rosstat, Russian Census 2010, FOM and Moscow Carnegie Center.

If we use a semi-parametric approach (Figure 11.1), in some cases there appear to be stronger non-linear effects: for instance, share of those who treat other religions as sins is the highest in the 'intermediate' regimes, but, as mentioned, the overall level of religious intolerance is rather low, and therefore variation in this variable is less interesting. In the semi-parametric analysis, the weakest effect appears to be associated with the role of traditional values as a function of democracy – it means that the arguments linking the spread of religiosity to the attempts of the regional government to use it in connection with other 'conservative' values to legitimize a non-democratic system is not supported by our data.

There is, however, one variable for which we find a significant effect both in parametric and semi-parametric analysis: the share of those actively participating in the life of religious communities is negatively correlated with democratization. This is an unusual and worthwhile finding which seems to perfectly fit the argument of spontaneous self-organization and the role religion plays in this process in non-democracies. In democratic regions, where multiple opportunities of self-organization exist and civil society is strong, people are less inclined to invest their effort into religious life; in non-democratic regions, religious self-organization becomes the only opportunity they have for self-organization. We have to stress that the overall levels of active participation in religious life are very low, and therefore the extent to which religion can indeed offer an opportunity for self-organization should not be overestimated; but the finding is nevertheless intriguing and worth noticing.

Among the control variables, most are insignificant. An interesting and somewhat puzzling effect turns out to be associated with education: contrary to what we expected, education is positively and significantly correlated with some indicators of religiosity, in particularly the willingness to follow religious requirements. This is probably another indicator of the very specific path of development of religiosity in post-Soviet Russia: to some extent, its spread is driven by the interest of the educated group, trying to find new values and norms after the collapse of the USSR.

Our analysis thus far ignored the fact that Russian regions traditionally belong to different confessions. However, we need to account for it – it is possible that in regions where population belonged to particular confessions, the development of religiosity after the fall of Communism was different than in other regions or that Soviet rule was less successful in eradicating religious practices. Islamic regions are particularly interesting in this context because of the spread of radical Islamism Russia was exposed to during and after the Chechen wars (Wilhemsen 2005; Markedonov 2010), but also because of substantial evidence of stronger persistence of traditional institutions (Zelkina 1993). Therefore, we replicate our findings excluding all Islamic regions from the sample (see Table 11.2). The results are confirmed entirely.

Table 11.2 The impact of democracy on religious attitudes of the regional population, Islamic regions excluded, OLS

| Dep. var.: | Try to follow religious requirements | Importance of traditional values | Active participation in the life of the religious community | Importance of religion | Perception of other religions as sins |
|---|---|---|---|---|---|
| Income per capita | -0.003** | -0.001 | 0.000 | 0.000 | 0.000 |
| | (0.001) | (0.001) | (0.000) | (0.000) | (0.000) |
| Unemployment | -0.901 | -0.239 | -0.236*** | -0.208 | 0.055 |
| | (0.586) | (0.496) | (0.088) | (0.312) | (0.085) |
| Education | 95.313** | 45.257** | -0.858 | 10.318 | 2.335 |
| | (39.637) | (20.368) | (5.239) | (14.627) | (3.616) |
| Share of ethnic Russians | -8.997 | -4.757 | 1.420 | 0.337 | 0.934 |
| | (13.141) | (6.941) | (1.693) | (4.733) | (0.714) |
| Urbanization | -0.157 | 0.009 | -0.032 | -0.087 | -0.001 |
| | (0.151) | (0.112) | (0.047) | (0.056) | (0.013) |
| Democracy | -0.298 | -0.105 | -0.098** | -0.149 | -0.013 |
| | (0.255) | (0.161) | (0.038) | (0.094) | (0.021) |
| Constant | 43.121** | 19.682 | 8.353*** | 25.353*** | -0.43 |
| | (19.222) | (12.122) | (2.918) | (8.955) | (1.846) |
| Observations | 71 | 71 | 71 | 71 | 71 |
| R-squared | 0.269 | 0.122 | 0.147 | 0.144 | 0.033 |

Note: see Table 4.1.

Source: Computed by authors using the data of Rosstat, Russian Census 2010, FOM and Moscow Carnegie Center.

## 11.4 Bureaucratic agency

The last step of our analysis, as always, involves the discussion of bureaucratic agency. The approach we take in this case is exactly the same as in previous chapters, and we estimate the regressions using the share of those who actively participate in the religious life of their community as the dependent variable. Results reported in Table 11.3 suggest that there is no significant difference in the effects of democracy depending on the tenure

*Table 11.3* The impact of democracy on religious attitudes of the regional population conditional on bureaucratic agency, full sample, OLS, dependent variable: active participation in the life of the religious community

|  | *(1)* | *(2)* | *(3)* | *(4)* | *(5)* | *(6)* |
|---|---|---|---|---|---|---|
| Income per capita | 0.000 | 0.000 | 0.000 | 0.000 | 0.000 | 0.000 |
|  | (0.000) | (0.000) | (0.000) | (0.000) | (0.001) | (0.000) |
| Unemployment | −0.031 | −0.311** | −0.288** | −0.148 | −0.01 | −0.202* |
|  | (0.097) | (0.122) | (0.116) | (0.243) | (0.180) | (0.115) |
| Education | −0.036 | 0.053 | −0.13 | −0.021 | −0.061 | −0.033 |
|  | (0.038) | (0.083) | (0.111) | (0.047) | (0.069) | (0.048) |
| Share of ethnic Russians | 2.281 | 0.761 | 0.888 | 0.295 | 0.971 | 2.588 |
|  | (1.995) | (2.323) | (2.147) | (2.835) | (2.362) | (2.851) |
| Urbanization | 0.009 | −0.098 | −0.077 | −0.003 | 0.036 | −0.052 |
|  | (0.025) | (0.088) | (0.074) | (0.064) | (0.051) | (0.063) |
| Democracy | −0.097 | −0.075** | −0.058 | −0.115 | −0.152** | −0.102* |
|  | (0.070) | (0.035) | (0.042) | (0.069) | (0.065) | (0.059) |
| Constant | 4.309 | 10.825 | 15.012* | 8.516 | 5.491 | 9.532 |
|  | (2.773) | (6.526) | (7.982) | (5.999) | (4.802) | (5.821) |
| Size of bureaucracy | Above median | Below median |  |  |  |  |
| Share of bureaucrats with short tenure |  |  | Above median | Below median |  |  |
| Share of bureaucrats with long tenure |  |  |  |  | Above median | Below median |
| Observations | 38 | 38 | 36 | 34 | 39 | 37 |
| R-squared | 0.257 | 0.218 | 0.274 | 0.172 | 0.131 | 0.214 |

Note: see Table 4.1.

Source: Computed by authors using the data of Rosstat, Russian Census 2010, FOM and Moscow Carnegie Center.

of bureaucrats; we do find, however, a substantial difference depending on the size of bureaucracy. Religious self-organization as a response in regional non-democratic regimes seems to happen only in regions with relatively small bureaucracies.

The result seems to fit our main argument. Self-organization in non-democracy is feasible only if the extent of control of the regime over social activity is to some extent limited. Even the most authoritarian Russian regions are, of course, very far from exercising totalitarian control over the life of their inhabitants, but in some regions the government may be better able to undermine strong and independent religious communities than in others. This is what we find: if the region has stronger bureaucratic capacity (i.e., larger bureaucracy), the ability of religion to self-organization beyond the control of the state is limited. Only if the bureaucratic capacity is weak can the regional population use religious self-organization as the substitute for other forms of civil society (compare similar discussion about vodka market in chapter 9). Since, as mentioned, most non-democratic regions also have large bureaucracies and strong bureaucratic capacity (see chapter 4), the actual feasibility of religious self-organization in non-democratic regimes in Russian regions should not be over-estimated.

## 11.5  Summary

The aim of this chapter was to investigate the effects of sub-national political regimes on religiosity in Russian regions. We study religiosity as one of the aspects of identity formation. For most of the dimensions of religiosity, no significant effects of sub-national political regimes could have been established, as the first two tables demonstrated. However, there are a few highly important findings to be discussed.

The first finding is related to the most important aspect of religiosity – that is, active and regular participation in religious communities. The results demonstrated that across all regions and all confessions, the regional population is more active in participation in religious communities in non-democratic regions. This finding is also relevant for the regions with relatively weak bureaucratic capacity (when bureaucrats have shorter tenure and have less time to establish control over the society). The interpretation for this important discovery is in line with literature on active religiosity as a getaway for the population. That is, religious self-organization may serve as a way out from authoritarian control and as a substitute for other forms of civil society.

Furthermore, the standard control variables added more insights for literature on religiosity as self-identification and democratization. As the theoretical overview of the chapter demonstrated, the previous studies indicated two trends: either education negatively connected with religiosity or has no correlation at all. Our analysis demonstrated the existence of another possible direction – education can actually increase significantly the level of religiosity. This is complimentary to the previous studies, not contradictory. The previous studies analyzed the period of the 1990s, when the situation was critically different and the relationship between religiosity, education and democratization was different. In contrast, our study focuses on the longer period and demonstrates a more established and consolidated trend analyzing religiosity in 2013 – that is, 25 years after the fall of Communism in 1989. Also, previous studies focused on both Catholic and Orthodox nation-states of Central Europe, while our analysis is on religious pluralism within a single state. More importantly, our discovery is in line with aforementioned literature that demonstrated that the relationship between democracy and religiosity in the post-Communist world was not the same as in the Western consolidated democracies. Thus, the chapter contributed further information and new findings to the nascent academic discussion on identity formation and religiosity as part of the outcomes of the regime transition in the post-Communist world. Regional identities are often considered as indispensable elements of civil society that are critical for the development of democracy. As Schmitter stated:

> . . . for political democracy to become and remain an alternative mode of political domination, a country must possess a civil society in which certain community and group identities exist independent of the state and in which certain types of self-constituted units are capable of acting autonomously in defense of their own interests and ideals.
>
> (Schmitter 1991, p. 6)

This brings us to another consequence of democratization – the formation of civil society and the importance of its regional dimension.

## Notes

1 Random opinion polls in, for example, southern Europe (Italy and Spain) would show that people without hesitation call themselves 'Catholics'. Being Catholic for them, however, does not imply going regularly to churches and practicing it on a daily or weekly basis. It often implies the celebration of Christmas, to a lesser degree Easter and major events in one's life (such as weddings, baptisms and funerals).
2 Neopaganism is related to pre-Christian Slav Paganism, while Tengrism is related to Turco-Mongol nations within Russia that have been present since the 13th-century Turco-Mongol invasion into Slav territories. The law was translated into English and cited in a number of sources. See, for example, Lewis (2011).

3 After seven decades of the Communism, we can tentatively argue that when it comes to post-Soviet Russia, the society most likely faces the need for identity formation. In contrast, in states with less experience of Communist (Eastern Central Europe and the Balkans), it is more likely to address from the perspective of identity recuperation.

4 We have eliminated others that are more related to superstitions and practicing magic (clearly not related to religiosity). We have also excluded the question on whether individuals 'want to have more faith' – it allows multiple interpretations and is difficult to analyze unambiguously. The questionnaire also contains a number of more specific questions regarding particular rituals (e.g., reading the Bible) – we have excluded them as well, since we expect them to be covered to a substantial extent by the questions we kept in our analysis.

# 12 Emergence of civil society
## Electoral behavior and social protests

This chapter has a double purpose. First, it focuses on the importance of sub-national democracy within a non-democratic nation-state. Does the sub-national democracy matter within an autocratic nation-state? If yes, how does it matter and how can it manifest itself? How can it influence the dominant regime at the national level? Does an eventually non-democratic and highly centralized state swallow nascent regional democracies? Or is it possible for regional democracy to produce spillover mechanism at the national level and contribute to the democratization of the nation-state as a whole? This chapter addresses these questions through the analysis of two forms of manifestation of sub-national democracies – electoral behavior and social protests – as both had exhibited specific territorial patterns across the regions.

Throughout the book we have tried to clearly emphasize an important feature of our investigation: sub-national political regimes are fundamentally different from the national ones, since they are always the product of the interplay with federal authorities. Indeed, for example, expectations regarding political stability, which determined our results concerning economic growth (see chapter 8), were driven precisely by this feature. In this case, however, one also has to look at the reverse link: how sub-national regimes influence the national political arena. In more decentralized federations the mechanism of this influence is straightforward: regional governments maintain representation at the federal level (both through lobby organizations and through seats in the upper chamber of the federal parliament) and affect federal decisions. In Russia one could observe this mechanism in the 1990s: in the early 1990s, ethnic republics were a major player in the conflict between the president and the parliament (Sheinis 2005); in the late 1990s, regional governors played an important role in all coalitions competing for Yeltsin's succession (Lussier 2002). However, if we look at the 2000s, we see less evidence of the direct influence of regional politics on federal politics given the strong recentralization pressure by Putin. Does it mean, however, that sub-national regime variation became irrelevant for federal political decisions?

Second, this chapter also addresses one of the important consequences of democratization – the emergence of civil society. In this chapter, we focus on two pronounced aspects of civil society – their active participation in political life and people's attempt to influence politics, their understanding of the importance of political events. To address these issues, we analyze the outcomes of federal elections and social protests across the sub-national regions. Elections and protests are the most obvious tools of action of civic society and the sheer signs of its existence. That does not imply that protests or specific voting behavior are initially successful as it might take time for the impact of civil society to become obvious. However, what is critically important is that both participation in elections and protests are the signs of a newly emerged civil society that was practically absent during Communism and did not automatically come to life after the fall of the totalitarian regime. The 70 years of totalitarianism did erase the tradition of civil society (moreover, it is even questionable if civil society actually existed in Tsarist Russia). If the regional population votes against the party in power and if the social protest takes place as a reaction to electoral falsification, regardless of their efficiency, these are the important aspects of the emergence of civil society as a consequence of the democratization period.

While addressing these issues, we face a certain empirical challenge. As mentioned in chapter 3, the Carnegie index for democracy we use provides a parameter measuring the freedom of elections, which also takes into account federal electoral campaigns. Thus, we may find a correlation between federal electoral outcome and the index by construction of the former. To deal with this problem, we use the electoral results of the first large election after the period for which the index was computed – the State Duma (lower chamber of the federal parliament) elections of 2011. These elections are also interesting as one of the turning points in the history of the Russian political system: the elections were followed by mass protests (especially in Moscow), with people challenging the electoral falsification and the authoritarian rule of Putin.

Both electoral protests and street mass protests were perceived as two aspects of the same phenomenon – the awakening of civil society. At that moment, these protests were often discussed as a 'window of opportunity' for democratizing Russia and even as the beginning of the color revolution in Russia (Wolchik 2012). The scholars anonymously agreed on the unexpected nature of these mass protests for both national government and international observers[1] as the 'number of participants far exceeded past opposition protests, bringing hundreds of thousands of Russians out into the street for the first time in several years' (Volkov 2012, p. 56). While previously there were some dispersed protests mainly involving some labor unions and environment-protections issues, they are incomparable with the protests from December 2011 to May 2012 in terms of magnitude and importance (Volkov 2012, p. 55). While the later wave of these protests in 2012 took place mainly in capitals, this chapter raises the question regarding the protests of December 2011 that spread all over Russia: To what extent can these protests be considered the consequence of the post-Soviet transition period in Russia? What role did the sub-national level of democracy play in this event, if any at all? The chapter starts the analysis with regional behavior in federal elections and then proceeds with post-electoral protests in the regions.

## 12.1  Regional logic of federal elections

The electoral system for the State Duma changed several times during the post-Communist history of Russia. In 2011, the State Duma was elected based on a proportional system. At that time, Russia used extremely restrictive regulation for political parties, which resulted in a very short list of contestants for 450 mandates in the Duma. Seven parties participated in the elections: the pro-Kremlin United Russia, which unambiguously supported Vladimir Putin (Reuter and Remington 2009); the Just Russia, a political structure established, according to the existing evidence, with substantial support of the presidential administration, but taking a somewhat more critical left-wing stance toward Putin's politics and including a number of opposition activists (March 2009); the Communist Party of the Russian Federation, which was the main opposition force in the second half of the 1990s and was still considered opposition to the Putin government in 2011 but at the same time was loyal to the existing regime in numerous instances; the Liberal-Democratic Party of Russia (LDPR), which took a populist nationalist stance, but supported Putin in almost all key decisions (Clark 1995); two liberal opposition parties (Yabloko, which traditionally received larger support among the Russian *intelligentsiya*, see White 2006, and the Right Cause); and a rather unknown Patriots of Russia party (on the Russian party system see Gel'man 2008). Of these seven parties, Patriots of Russia and Right Cause are less interesting for our analysis and received negligible support of the voters; we will, therefore, focus on the five other parties. Of these parties, one (United Russia) was clearly pro-Putin; one (Just Russia) had mixed attitudes toward Putin; two (Communist and LDPR) formally opposed Putin, but were known to de facto support him in many cases; and Yabloko could be treated as a clear opposition party, but appealing only to a small social group.

The main logic of the 2011 elections campaign became the contradiction between the 'pro-Putin' majority and the 'anti-Putin' opposition, which, however, had no clear representation among contestant parties (open opposition was not admitted to elections). Furthermore, elections were expected to be associated with massive manipulations and falsifications; this is, in fact, what has happened, as the available empirical evidence shows (Enikolopov et al. 2013). In this case, those opposing Putin had only a handful of choices: they could decide not to participate in elections (in Russia participation is not mandatory) or otherwise make their vote invalid (for example, by damaging the ballots), or they could vote for one of the opposition parties, even knowing that their criticism toward Putin did not manifest in real political action and being only partly supportive of these parties' programs.[2] The last alternative was favored by one of the opposition leaders, Aleksey Naval'nyi, who coined the slogan 'Vote for everybody except United Russia!' This behavior could be interpreted from two perspectives. On the one hand, it could be seen as an example of expressive voting – showing the Kremlin its disappointment, but at the same time knowing that the elected Duma has no impact on political decisions and thus the actual party programs do not really matter (Hillman 2010). On the other hand, this type of voting behavior could serve as an instrument of coining a new opposition alliance based on 'negative consensus' (rejection of Putin's regime) rather than on a positive one (support of a particular program) (Gel'man 2012). These attempts to unify opposition continued after elections (the so-called 'Coordination Council of Opposition' of 2012), although without any success.

Therefore, in our analysis we will look at the share of votes obtained by the key political parties in each of the Russian regions. Elections of 2011 were not free or fair, and therefore, while explaining the electoral outcomes, we have to include in our analysis two possible dimensions: the actual voting behavior and the extent to which the elections could have been falsified. The existence of a more democratic political regime in a region could have affected both dimensions. On the one hand, democratic regime should have made falsifications more difficult. Since these falsifications were almost always done in favor of the ruling party, it is reasonable to assume that in democratic regions the share of the votes for United Russia should be lower. On the other hand, democratic regime could be associated with differences in the structure of political preferences and of political knowledge. People living in democratic regions could be more dissatisfied with the developing authoritarian rule in Russia at the federal level and try to counteract it. They may also be better informed about the political landscape: in Russia voting for 'United Russia' often represented a 'default option' voters selected due to the lack of information. Thus, we hypothesize that the share of United Russia should be lower if the level of sub-national democracy is higher.

At the same time, we are less unambiguous about the increase of the share of other political parties. Communists, LDPR and to some extent Just Russia followed political programs clearly incompatible with democratic norms and values. It could have reduced the electoral support these parties received in democratic regions, even if their population followed the expressive voting logic (the discussion of whether it is acceptable to create alliances with the nationalists or with the Communist movements has been dividing Russian 'liberal' opposition during the entire period of its existence). However, if voters followed the Naval'nyi approach, the shares of all other parties except United Russia should also be higher in democratic regions.

## 12.2 Empirical model and results

We estimate a set of five regressions, using the share of votes individual parties obtained during the elections of 2011. The data on electoral outcomes are from the Russian official data of the Central Electoral Committee. We regress these variables on the level of sub-national democracy in the period from 2001–2010, as well as a set of control variables (all for 2010, i.e., a year preceding elections – most likely, this was the period when the expectations and assessments of the voters formed). We control for six variables. First, income per capita is used to account for the effect of economic wealth on voting patterns. In richer regions, the support of Putin could be lower if the demand for democracy at the federal level is stronger. Second, we control for the share of ethnic Russians – it could both influence the extent of nationalist feelings affecting voting and represent the political culture (see chapter 4). Third, we control for urbanization, which, again, is a proxy for self-organization of the society and demand for democracy (as in chapter 4). Fourth, we control for the TV coverage of the regional population – in Russia TV channels are under strict control of the federal government and are systematically used for political propaganda, which also happened during the 2011 elections. Fifth, we control for the infant mortality in the region as a proxy for social well-being. Sixth, we add a measure of education – again, as a proxy for demand for democratization and for political information.

The results of our empirical estimations are reported in Table 12.1. Figure 12.1 again used the semi-parametric approach resembling the analysis we applied in previous chapters. In any case, our findings are strongly consistent with the hypotheses we developed. The share of votes for United Russia is negatively and significantly correlated with the level of

*Table 12.1* The impact of democracy on electoral outcomes, 2011, OLS

| Dep. var.:<br>Share of. . . | United<br>Russia | Just Russia | LDPR | CPRF | Yabloko |
|---|---|---|---|---|---|
| Income per<br>capita | 0.106<br>(0.226) | −0.068<br>(0.131) | 0.146**<br>(0.071) | −0.214<br>(0.129) | −0.006<br>(0.029) |
| Share of ethnic<br>Russians | −34.794***<br>(6.894) | 6.947**<br>(2.999) | 11.427***<br>(2.062) | 13.028***<br>(2.912) | 1.903***<br>(0.561) |
| Education | 7.117<br>(25.498) | −13.725<br>(12.364) | −30.291***<br>(7.592) | 21.395<br>(17.106) | 15.859***<br>(4.921) |
| Urbanization | −0.066<br>(0.150) | 0.061<br>(0.054) | 0.038<br>(0.041) | −0.067<br>(0.072) | 0.030**<br>(0.013) |
| TV coverage | −0.095<br>(0.245) | −0.002<br>(0.195) | 0.114<br>(0.140) | −0.038<br>(0.145) | 0.02<br>(0.031) |
| Infant<br>mortality | 0.026<br>(0.486) | −0.165<br>(0.248) | 0.291<br>(0.175) | −0.223<br>(0.212) | 0.015<br>(0.048) |
| Democracy | −1.054***<br>(0.228) | 0.426***<br>(0.106) | 0.242***<br>(0.060) | 0.229*<br>(0.122) | 0.114***<br>(0.024) |
| Constant | 117.509***<br>(26.136) | −2.995<br>(20.863) | −14.688<br>(15.081) | 10.895<br>(16.381) | −10.094**<br>(3.859) |
| Observations | 79 | 79 | 79 | 79 | 79 |
| R-squared | 0.697 | 0.497 | 0.674 | 0.438 | 0.738 |

Note: see Table 4.1.

Source: Computed by authors using the data of Rosstat, Russian Census 2010, Central Electoral Committee of the Russian Federation and Moscow Carnegie Center.

sub-national democracy. The shares of votes for all other parties are positively and significantly correlated with the level of sub-national democracy. To reiterate, this result gives rise to two possible interpretations. On the one hand, the level of falsifications in favor of United Russia was lower in democratic regions. On the other hand, demand for democratization was stronger in democratic regions, and, as a result, their public was more likely to support the idea of the 'negative consensus' proposed by Naval'nyi. Figure 12.1 also suggests some non-linearity in the effects of democratization on the voting patterns for individual parties. Yabloko, for instance, enjoyed particularly high support in very democratic regions, but in regions with average and with low democracy levels the support of this party was roughly the same. It may indicate that Yabloko, as the only consistently democratic movement at the elections (in terms of both manifests and past track record), had sufficient appeal only to regions where the level of sub-national democracy was very high.

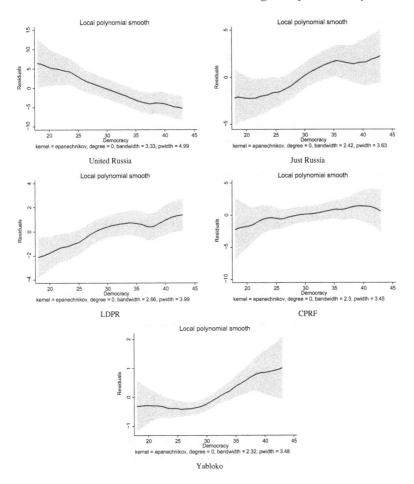

*Figure 12.1* Local polynomial smooth, effect of democracy on the unexplained variation in the electoral outcomes

Source: Computed by authors using the data of Rosstat, Russian Census 2010, Central Electoral Committee of Russia and Moscow Carnegie Center.

Table 12.2 reports how the effect on voting for United Russia changes depending on bureaucratic agency. Unlike previous results, however, we find that bureaucratic capacity and loyalty of the bureaucracy do not influence the fact that in more democratic regions the share of United Russia is also smaller. It could indicate that our results are to a greater extent driven by political preferences and not by the lack of falsifications, since the ability of the regime to falsify elections greatly depends on the bureaucratic capacity.

Table 12.2 The impact of democracy on the share of votes for United Russia, 2011, conditional on bureaucratic agency, OLS

| | (1) | (2) | (3) | (4) | (5) | (6) |
|---|---|---|---|---|---|---|
| Income per capita | 0.225 (0.360) | 0.55 (0.392) | -0.08 (0.277) | 0.758 (0.446) | 0.429 (0.518) | -0.036 (0.272) |
| Share of ethnic Russians | -44.242*** (11.643) | -27.449*** (8.867) | -44.041*** (10.453) | -32.907*** (7.320) | -32.780*** (9.643) | -35.163*** (12.238) |
| Education | -8.226 (47.275) | -48.219 (36.176) | 7.218 (31.292) | -65.316 (44.374) | -0.17 (49.041) | 8.501 (31.134) |
| Urbanization | -0.17 (0.207) | 0.116 (0.210) | 0.052 (0.172) | -0.309 (0.285) | -0.44 (0.292) | 0.021 (0.165) |
| TV coverage | -0.972** (0.450) | 0.189 (0.275) | 0.187 (0.249) | -0.211 (0.515) | -0.308 (0.270) | 0.055 (0.857) |
| Infant mortality | -0.692 (0.873) | 1.348 (0.950) | 0.022 (0.481) | -0.229 (0.927) | -0.418 (0.906) | 0.176 (0.518) |
| Urbanization | -1.113*** (0.397) | -1.415*** (0.270) | -0.804*** (0.265) | -1.101*** (0.339) | -0.999*** (0.342) | -0.962*** (0.334) |
| Democracy | 227.226*** (56.083) | 81.295*** (29.215) | 85.078*** (25.767) | 155.227** (57.542) | 160.433*** (33.772) | 95.73 (85.484) |
| Constant | 0.225 (0.360) | 0.55 (0.392) | -0.08 (0.277) | 0.758 (0.446) | 0.429 (0.518) | -0.036 (0.272) |
| Size of bureaucracy | Above median | Below median | | | | |

| | | | Above median | Below median | Above median | Below median |
|---|---|---|---|---|---|---|
| Share of bureaucrats with short tenure | | | | | | |
| Share of bureaucrats with long tenure | | | | | | |
| Observations | 39 | 39 | 37 | 35 | 39 | 39 |
| R-squared | 0.73 | 0.753 | 0.747 | 0.762 | 0.682 | 0.738 |

Note: see Table 4.1.

Source: Computed by authors using the data of Rosstat, Russian Census 2010, Central Electoral Committee of the Russian Federation and Moscow Carnegie Center.

## 12.3   Social protests

The importance of the social protests of 2011 and 2012 is difficult to overestimate – they were recognized as one of the pivotal points in the development of post-Communist society in Russia. They were even expected to turn into a color revolution and were recognized to be 'the largest since the demise of the USSR' (Wolchik 2012, p. 63). Some studies investigated the reasons for these protests and challenged the assumption that electoral fraud was the main cause for mass protests (Shevtsova, 2012, p. 21): 'There have been falsified elections before in post-Soviet Russia [. . .] Yet none led to mass opposition'. This also cannot be explained by the world financial crisis of 2008. Let us recall that the post-Soviet population in Russia witnessed major financial crisis in 1998, when many regular people lost all their assets maintained in banks. This was followed by further economic hardships that never brought people to the street protesting to the extent it happened in 2011. Given the previous regular experience with electoral fraud and frequently less active reaction of the population on much more severe economic hardships of 1990s, the reaction of the society in 2011 and the huge mass protests present a puzzle. So what made the difference in 2011? Why only 20 years later after the collapse of the USSR did society finally react in terms of these enormous mass protests? This section addresses this puzzle. The hypothesis is that the sub-national regional democracy that had been developing for over 20 years since the beginning of the regime transition in 1991 finally produced some form of civil society that manifested itself through social protests. This can be described as an actual consequence of the transition period and the demonstration of the emergence of civil society.

The protests, however, were unequally spread across the territory of Russia. Thus, it is reasonable to check whether the protests were affected by the resilience of local political regimes as well (the argumentation here is very close to what we have presented earlier – both preferences of the people and possible persecution by the local police play a certain role). Measuring participation in mass protests in Russia is a difficult task, but we used the data published by the RIA Novosti in January 2012 and based on the manifestations on December 10, 2011, to calculate two indicators: the share of participants of manifestations in the population of the capital city of the region (according to the police reports, most likely under-estimating the protests' size) and the share of participants of groups preparing protests in the social networks Facebook and VKontakte (a popular Russian alternative) in the total population of the city (this variable probably over-estimates the size of protests). The correlations between these values and the democracy index are presented by Figure 12.2.

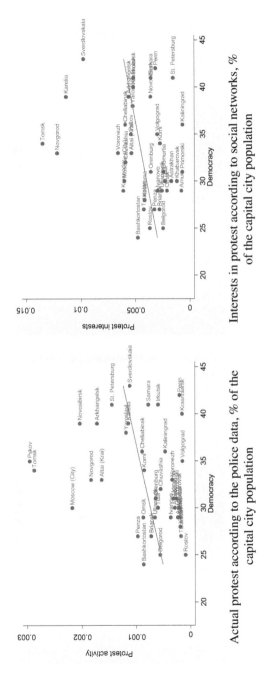

Actual protest according to the police data, % of the capital city population

Interests in protest according to social networks, % of the capital city population

*Figure 12.2* Mass protests after elections on December 10, 2011, and regional democracy of 2001–2010

Source: Computed by authors using the data of RIA Novosti and Moscow Carnegie Center.

We find that the regions with a higher level of democracy have rebelled stronger against the electoral falsification. Both graphs – on actual participation in the protest and on interest in protest – demonstrate a significant and positive correlation between the level of democracy and the participation in protests (the β coefficient in the regressions without control variables is significant at 5% level). Figure 12.2 presents two respective plots. The results are even more important because of limited information – RIA Novosti published the data only for 39 regional capitals with only most prominent protests. In a robustness check, we assumed that the participation in other regions was equal to zero and regressed this new variable on the democracy score. The significance of the β coefficient increased dramatically; if we use Tobit regressions (to accommodate for the fact that the data is censored at zero), the results are still highly significant.

This finding is in line with a number of other studies. Some scholars also stated that the electoral fraud was merely the catalyst, not the real cause. Among the actual causes of the social protest and first significant collective actions were distinguished two factors. First was described as a younger generation that 'was free of Soviet complexes, nostalgia, and fear', and the second was the rise of the Internet (Shevtsova 2012, p. 22). We argue that this younger generation was formed during a regime transition that was clearly very different from the Soviet regime and that this difference became crucial in the formation of civil society. Access to the Internet is associated with another related to democracy impact – traditionally described as 'freedom of mass media'. While the traditional mass media that still can be controlled by the central government cannot be described as independent, it was partially substituted by the independent electronic mass media and the variety of opinions and news coverage that can be found easily on the Internet. Thus, both causes are aspects of democracy and can be described as the consequences of the democratization that had led to the very nascent civil society in Russia 20 years later after the dissolution of the USSR. We argue that this consequence cannot be under-estimated. Within the context of consolidation of the non-democratic regime at the national level, the consequences of the sub-national democracies increase in terms of their importance.

## 12.4   Summary

This chapter analyzed the effect of sub-national democracy at the federal level in two different formats – participation in federal elections (as peaceful and legitimatized way of protest) and participation in actual social protest. We found that variation of democracy in Russian regions does indeed affect national politics by influencing the voting patterns of the Russian regional population. In spite of the centralization of Russian federalism under Putin, regional politics cannot be entirely neglected. While participation in elections is a well-established political tradition in modern Russia (that can be even traced back to the Communism), participation in social protests is a new phenomenon in the society. Mass media noticed that the whole period of regime transition in Russia, starting from the 1990s, was the first time when the society explicitly expressed its discontent as an organized collective action against consolidation of the regime and the dominance of United Russia.

## Notes

1 A few studies highlight this event as a 'surprise' and 'shock' for both national government and regime as well as for the international mass media (see for example Shevtsova 2012; Volkov 2012, Wolchik 2012; Krastev 2012).
2 In the past, there was also an option to vote 'against all candidates', but in 2011 it was already abolished.

# 13 Conclusion
## Integrative strategy of structure–agency approach

This book is the first attempt in the studies of democratization to integrate in a systematic way both structural and agency approach in the analysis of regime transition. Most importantly, so far the attempts to implement conceptual and empirical analysis of this integrative strategy were only addressed in the discussions of the causes of democratization. Our analysis took further steps and applied the integrative strategy also to explain the consequences of the regime transition. While the literature on the consequences of democratization is far less developed in political science than on the causes, the issue of the agency was not yet brought into discussion while analyzing the consequences of democratization in an empirical large-*n* study. The integrative strategy allowed arriving at the following theoretical and empirical conclusions regarding both causes and consequences of democratization.

## 13.1 Causes

The book has tested both classic and the most recent theories explaining the success or failure of democratization – modernization theory, path-dependency theory, the international dimension of democratization and the limiting factor. The first part of the book has attempted to take the 'integrative agenda' of structural and agency approaches further and to combine both in one coherent and systematic empirical analysis. The conclusions of this methodological and empirical experiment are the following.

In terms of traditional predictors for democracy, the results are not trivial. Only the part of the theory of modernization was confirmed. Out of four main explanatory variables, urbanization, income per capita, economic openness and education, only urbanization seems to be positively and significantly correlated with democracy. That can be explained partly in that democratization at the sub-national level is different from the national level due to the higher control variables. However, it is exactly one of the most important goals of this book – to demonstrate to what extent the theories of democratization can account for *sub-national* political development, and how much of sub-national regional processes can be explained by theories originated from cross-national studies. Yet another interesting conclusion is the confirmation that Russia was and remains largely a multi-ethnic state and that ethnicities indeed account for differences in success or failure of democratization. While there were a number of small-$n$ studies on different ethnic identities in Russia, this book is the first attempt to systematically control for the nexus of ethnicities-democracy as large-$n$ studies throughout the book. The analysis of the fourth chapter demonstrated the strongest significance of ethnicity (one of the proxies for political culture that we use in this book). Most importantly, the ethnic-related variable remains important throughout the book in confirmation of the theory on the importance of culture, society and political culture as part of the centuries' long historical heritage.

This historical-cultural heritage is critically different from historical legacy of Communism that was also investigated in the book. Communist legacies seem to have a significant negative impact on the level of democratization in the modern Russian regions. The discovery makes important implications for the literature on historical legacies and human capital and their role in establishment democratic regimes. The analysis indicates the impact of Communist era principles on the behavior of political elite and population in the 21st century. The findings of this chapter have important implications for another recent debate which was revived by the political events in Ukraine in 2014. After the collapse of the Soviet bloc, several former Communist countries introduced severe lustration laws, restricting the access of former party functionaries to power. Outside the post-Communist world, lustrations were used after the US invasion to Iraq. Generally, there are arguments both in favor of and against lustrations. On the one hand, lustration restricts access of former elite members to current politics, making democratic consolidation easier. On the other hand, lustration strengthens confrontation within the society, putting the civil peace at risk (as it, to some extent, happened in Iraq). Furthermore, lustration may create a shortage of human capital if the entire qualified bureaucratic personnel were to some extent connected to the former regime. Russia did not implement any restrictions on the former Communist elite members (it was hardly possible for a democratic government headed by a former first secretary of Sverdlovsk party organization). Our results show that the risks of not restricting access to the former adherents of the regime to the political scene after the transition starts are indeed non-negligible. It does not mean that a lustration is desirable – we do not investigate directly the human capital shortage effect and the impact on the civil peace – but our analysis at least provides some empirical evidence which could be used in the subsequent debate.

The analysis of the international dimension of democratization and the role of geography have been in the center of the scholars working on regime transition world-wide, but even more prominently it became the subject of analysis in the post-Communist world. Geography indeed proved to be an important channel for democracy-contagion that has spread across the borders and had distinguished regional patterns in cross-national analysis as well as in the regions of Russia. However, our analysis demonstrated that while geography does indeed play an important role of democratic diffusion, its significance can be found in the first years of the regime transition. If a state or a sub-national region experienced territorial centralization reform, the effect of geography becomes negligible. In terms of the general ability and willingness of external actors to influence regime transition in Russia, 2014 seems to mark an important milestone due to the Ukrainian crisis. Russia experienced a substantial decline in terms of its relations to the West at political, economic and social levels. Now political life is encapsulated from Western influences; also it is unlikely that sub-national regions will manage to maintain more intensive relations to the EU, even if they wanted to. There is evidence of sub-national administrations all over Russia going much further than even Putin's government in criticizing the West and restricting contacts with the European countries and the United States – at least at the rhetorical level.[1] In other cases, however, regions seem to be willing to maintain a more open system even within the boundaries imposed by Moscow. In addition, economic crisis in Russia and depreciation of the national currency, which are likely to result in a long-term economic stagnation, are also not conducive to developing linkages with foreign partners. While Russia claims to develop its ties to the Asian countries (especially China), it is doubtful that they will play any role at the sub-national level. Thus, the role of external factors for the regime transition in Russian regions is likely to decrease in the years to come.

Related to the international dimension of democratization is the theory of the limiting factor. While geography as a channel can become insignificant, the role and the importance of the limiting factor seem to become important not only in post-Communist regime transition but also beyond it as well. Moreover, the limiting factor mechanism works not only in cases when the external player is an autocratic state and geographically close located, but also in cases when the external actor is a democracy remote geographically.

The analysis of chapter 7 demonstrates that limiting factor may well affect regions located in the European part of Russia to develop the mechanism with Central Asian autocracies. Thus, the role of geography does not play any crucial role in the development of the limiting factor; neither does the nature of any external actor that might be involved.

The theory of limiting factor, while previously developed by us only within an article format, was taken a step further within this book project. Previously, while assessing the role of limiting factor, only structural factors had been considered. However, given the 'integrative strategy' of the book combining structural with agency approaches, the book discovers a further aspect of the limiting factor – the highly important role of the officials. As the analysis demonstrated, the limiting factor can be most efficient with a specific type of agency – when its size is relatively large and when the tenure of the officials is longer than average. That not only allows officials to work more efficiently for the executive, but also to get trained in blocking private entrepreneurs as 'intruders'. The later could have intervened into the business in order to diversify it. This would lead to the massive loss of monopolized control seized by the executive over this single economic source of development. Thus, retaining undivided control over the source does indeed require well-trained and long-tenured bureaucrats.

Producing and developing the dependence of the economic growth (limiting factor) of a state in question, any external player, be that democracy or autocracy, will limit the democratic development of that state. While the case of the regions of Russia that were analyzed in the book as an example are clearly related to external autocratic actors located in Central Asia, there can be different cases of limiting factor identified world-wide.

The modern post-Communist Eurasia also presents various forms of limiting factor beyond the case of the regions of Russia that had been analyzed in detail. One of the most prominent cases where the limiting factor can be well distinguished is Belarus. Belarus is located at the borders of the European Union and is marked by the well-developed geographic neighborhood, where the mechanisms of international diffusion of democratic norms, principles and values were expected to take place. Moreover, in the 1990s, Belarus, like many other post-Communist states, received generous funding from the European Union that was meant to help democratize the state and pass to market economy. The historical and cultural heritage of Belarus is also more favorable as compared to Russia or Moldova, for example. The historical presence of the protestant church, for example, was widely associated in the literature as the cultural environment highly favorable for flourishing democracy. In terms of size, which can also be associated with difficulties of democratization in post-Communism, Belarus is conveniently and relatively a small state. As for the natural resource curse perspective, Belarus has no natural resources at all – it lacks both oil and gas. Given its favorable for democratization geographic location, the generous aid of the EU, the size, the historical and cultural past and the absence of natural resources, Belarus was expected to be probably the best candidate out of all post-Soviet states for successful democratization. Thus, both the international dimension of democratization and the natural resource curse fail to explain the establishment and consolidation of autocracy in Belarus. So what went wrong in the case of this state and how can the theory of democratization be extended to account for it?

This is the case where the limiting factor theory is highly applicable. Three features of the limiting factor can be identified in the case of Belarus: (1) highly specific and localized source of economic development; (2) dependence of economic growth of a state on this source; (3) high costs of switching the source. First, Belarus is uncompetitive in the international market. Its food production and low-quality manufactured goods can be a trade source, let's say, within the EU's states. The only substantial source of economic development of Belarus is the cheap supply of Russian oil and gas and the special agreements on the transit of natural resources to the EU's states. This situation created total dependence of the whole economic development of Belarus on the transit agreements and supply agreements. The president of Belarus, Alexander Lukashenka, was actually elected and was an honest winner who defended his competitors in the democratic elections. However, once in power, Lukashenka seized total control over this single source of the revenue of the state, and the mechanism of limiting factor was in play, which eventually resulted in a strong and well-consolidated autocratic regime. Thus, the case of Belarus fits to the aspects of the limiting factor theory: (1) economic development is dependent on one single localized source; (2) it is concentrated in one single factor; (3) switching costs to another source or at least diversification are so high that they are practically impossible for a transitional state (with many economic problems and huge international debts and poor economic performance); (4) as a result, one single source is an easy prey for a leader in power; once seized, total control over economy is achieved and politics is manipulated. It might be tempting to consider the situation of Belarus as the result of the strong external autocratic player – Russia – that is responsible for the presence of the limiting factor and for autocracy. While the autocratic neighbor certainly is a contributing factor to the consolidation of autocracy, it remains only one of the explanations. Also the presence and economic support of one *autocratic* neighbor to the east of Belarus (Russia) could have been counter-balanced by the presence of strong *democratic* actor to the west of Belarus (the EU). Thus, the mere geographic proximity of certain economically strong neighbors cannot explain the eventual outcome of consolidation of autocracy.

Yet another example of internal limiting factor is shipping infrastructure, harbors and even migration. If the economy of the government is highly dependent on shipping, then simply by seizing total undivided control over the access to the harbors, the central government already can control the economic development and later the politics of a state. In some cases, this dependence is more complex: landlocked states frequently need the support of the foreign power to exercise their trade and other economic relations, and if this foreign power insists on dealing only with a particular political force or particular regime type, it substantially increases the chances for authoritarian consolidation. An interesting post-Soviet example is Tajikistan. This country's economic development in the last decade was entirely determined by the remittances of migrants, mostly working in Russia. Thus, a political regime of Tajikistan needs to keep friendly relations with Russia so that the Russian market would be open to its migrants. Thus, Tajikistan receives the financial ability to strengthen the power of the current regime. This is what happened to Emomali Rakhmon's presidency, which remained loyal to Russia in the political area and ultimately became a successful project of authoritarian consolidation.

However, the role of post-Soviet trade as a limiting factor could change in the years to come due to the overall political developments in Eurasia. On the one hand, in May 2014 Russia, Belarus and Kazakhstan have finally concluded the development of the Eurasian Economic Union (the first predecessor organization – the Customs Union – was set up in 2010); Armenia and Kyrgyzstan also plan to join the organization. The Eurasian Union aims to achieve an ambitious goal of wide-scope economic integration of its member countries and already managed to successfully abolish the customs borders between its members. The observed trade effects of the Eurasian Union have so far been small, yet it is reasonable to hypothesize that it could potentially encourage economic ties, particularly in the border regions. In this case, the dependence on post-Soviet trade could be preserved in the long run, which would potentially strengthen the limiting factor logic in the regions exposed to it.

Table 13.1 presents the empirical analysis across both causes and consequences of democratization and outlines the divide between the structural and agency approaches and their interrelated importance.

Table 13.1 Main results of the book

| Causes and consequences of democracy | Structural factors | Bureaucratic agency: size of bureaucracy | Bureaucratic agency: tenure of bureaucracy |
|---|---|---|---|
| **Causes** | | | |
| Modernization theory and cultural factors | – Urbanization has a positive effect<br>– Share of ethnic Russians has a positive effect<br>– Islamic legacy has a negative effect | Size of bureaucracy has a negative effect | Length of tenure of bureaucracy has a negative effect |
| Historical legacy of Communism | Share of CPSU members has a negative effect | Effect of CPSU legacy is driven by regions with small bureaucracy | Effect of CPSU legacy is driven by regions with bureaucracy with shorter tenure |
| Geography of external factors | Insignificant or not robust effect | | |
| Limiting factors | Trade with the FSU countries has a negative effect | Effect of the FSU trade is driven by regions with large bureaucracy | Effect of the FSU trade is driven by regions with bureaucracy with longer tenure |
| **Consequences** | | | |
| Economic growth | *U*-shaped effect: regions with high and with low levels of democracy have better growth performance than regions with intermediate regimes | *U*-shaped effect in regions with large bureaucracy; negative effect in regions with small bureaucracy | |
| Economic liberalization | *U*-shaped effect: regions with high and with low levels of democracy have higher investment risk than intermediate regions, but the result is not robust to outliers | | |

| | | | |
|---|---|---|---|
| Subjective well-being (happiness) | No effect | | |
| Objective well-being and health | Inverse *U*-shaped effect: alcohol consumption is lower in regions with high and with low levels of democracy than intermediate regions | Inverse *U*-shaped effect only in regions with small bureaucracy | |
| Public policy of mineral resources | Only democratic regions effectively use oil and gas to promote growth | The positive effect of democracy is present only in regions with large bureaucracy | The positive effect of democracy is present only in regions with short bureaucratic tenure |
| Public policy of environment | Democratic regions are more active in implementing reforestation activities | The effect is driven by the regions with small bureaucracy | |
| Identity formation | Democracy reduces the share of those who actively participate in the life of religious communities and has no effect on other aspects of religiosity | | |
| National politics and civil society | Democracy increases the vote shares for all parties except United Russia and decreases the vote share for United Russia | | |

Source: Compiled by authors.

## 13.2   Consequences

In the rich literature on the causes of democratization, the studies of structural and agency approaches have been used for the decades separately and in fewer cases together, combining large-$n$ studies for the former and small-$n$ studies for the latter. The book has been the first attempt to combine both in one single econometric analysis. In contrast to the literature on the cases, the studies on the consequences of democratization had *never* addressed the role of agency at all as a potential variable modifying the consequences. This book is the very first attempt to address the consequences of democratization through investigation into the impacts of democracy as dependent (and potentially modified) by the agency. The short-run consequences are less pronounced than the long-run, and they are far more difficult to capture at the sub-national level. This explains that for some cases, no interrelationship had been discovered. However, this is still important for further development of the theoretical literature on the consequences of democratization at the sub-national level.

When it comes to the economic consequences of democratization, the division between short-run and long-run results of political reforms is especially important. We admit that given the time frame of the book, we may only focus only on the short-run consequences. In the post-Communist world, the first decade(s) of the transition were marked by economic crisis and restructuring. Russia and its regions was not an exception to this rule. The financial crisis of 1998 was devastating for the population. The economic recovery came at a later stage, starting from the 2000s, and coincided with the presidency of Putin. This is the period we investigate in our study. The evidence is peculiar. The analysis demonstrated that the regions that are autocracies (with the minimum level of democracy) and the regions with the highest level of democracy perform economically much better than regions with an intermediate level of democracy. At the same time, if we look at economic reforms at the sub-national level, the situation is the opposite. We suggest that growth performance of democratic and autocratic regions is driven by expectations economic agents form regarding the stability of their economic policies and link it to the specifics of the design of Russian federalism.

We did not discover any interrelationship between the level of democracy in the region and subjective well-being (happiness). However, we also analyzed the impact of democratization on public health and looked at a crucial variable from this perspective – consumption of alcohol. It can be argued that health presents both objective and subjective well-being of the population. It is objective because it is an actual health issue and health-care system. It can also be considered as subjective because it is often explained as an expression of the dissatisfaction of life. The results are important for the context of the discussion: the most democratic regions and the most autocratic regions are associated with lower alcohol consumption than the regions with an intermediate level of democracy. Somewhat similarly, a high level of democracy is also associated with better public policy in terms of reforestation and forest management. It is somewhat peculiar that when it comes to the economic and well-being consequences of the regime transition, the pattern of the inverse *U*-curve seems to be the same: the most democratic and the most autocratic regions perform much better than the regions with average democracy. Introduction of the role of agency helps to clarify the mystery. It is suggested that the effect might be driven not only by the regime per se but also by the state capacity. The investigation into the nexus of democracy and state capacity should, thus, remain on the agenda for further studies.

The analysis also presented some important finding in regard of religiosity as one of the aspects of identity formation in post-Communist society. The regional population seems to be more active in participation in religious communities in non-democratic regions. This discovery is valid for both Muslim and, even more important, for non-Muslim regions. This can be found only in the regions with small agency. Participation in religious communities seems to be an actual substitute for other forms of civil society. Russia is not an exception in this respect among other post-Soviet countries, and their experience also calls for caution in interpreting our results: religious self-organization can be based on values very different from those needed to establish a successful democracy (in Central Asia similar logic of governmental control resulted in the predominance of Islamism as a form of informal self-organization; in Russia, however, we find our result to be also driven by multi-religious regions). While most of the regions are Orthodox-Christian and Islamic, there is also significant growth of regions with dominance of Paganism and Buddhism. However, another set of studies suggested that *active* religiosity may actually provide for the solid ground for the formation and consolidation of democratic tendencies in societies by forming the experience of collective gatherings and collective action. This argument became central for the studies of the transition of Central European societies. The analysis presented in the book is in line with literature stating that the relationship between democracy and religiosity in the post-Communist world are not the same as in the Western consolidated democracies. Thus, the book contributes new findings to the discussion on identity formation and religiosity as part of the outcomes of the regime transition in the post-Communist world.

Finally, the last chapter of the book directly addressed one of the most important motivations of the whole analysis: why sub-national political regimes matter at all within the context of non-democratic nation-states.

While it is clear that democracy is important, it is often taken for granted that democratization starts and gets consolidated at the national level first and then initiates the democratization of the regions often through decentralization reforms. However, recent work on sub-national regimes within democracies and autocracies demonstrated that this is not necessarily always the case. Democratization may start at the sub-national level and then proceed to the national level, as a spillover. Chapter 12 places this issue in the very center of the discussion: Do sub-national political regimes matter for the direction of national politics? Can they present an impediment for consolidation of autocracy? Through the analysis of the impact of sub-national electoral outcomes in federal elections, we can provide a positive answer to the aforementioned questions. Indeed, the analysis presented in chapter 12 demonstrated that sub-national variation of democracy had influenced national politics through specific voting patterns. This finding is even more impressive given the high level of territorial centralization reform conducted since the early 2000s and a consolidated centralized system that had been well established at the moment of the elections in 2011.

## 13.3    The role of agency

Our study of agency concentrated on the role sub-national bureaucracy plays in regime transition and in the way consequences of democratization are shaped. Bureaucracy, although generally recognized as an important element of regime transition (together with the elites and the population), rarely received sufficient attention in the scholarly literature. For the Russian case, the evidence is even more limited. Our findings suggest, however, that the characteristics of the bureaucratic machine are important in understanding the determinants and consequences of democratization. In particular, two features stand out as particularly important: the bureaucratic capacity (which we proxied by the size of bureaucracy) and the loyalty of bureaucracy to the incumbent (which, as we argued, should be higher for bureaucracies with on average longer tenure). One of the key conclusions of our book is that bureaucracy indeed matters. First, we find that bureaucratic capacity and loyalty are significantly increasing the chances of autocratic consolidation in the regions. This argument reveals a particular mechanism which explains the authoritarian outcomes of regime transition. Second, we show that for many other variables explaining the level of democratization, the effect is driven by the specific features of the regional bureaucracy. On the contrary, many causes of democratization also differ for regimes with large and with small bureaucracies.

Summing up, the book aspires to provide a number of useful theoretical and empirical findings for scholars working on democratization, post-Communism, Russia and its regions. The theoretical implications and combined research strategy, however, could appeal to a broader audience interested in theory of democracy and regime transition world-wide as well as those working on sub-national regimes. In this case, three contributions of the book should be highlighted. First, the causes and the consequences of democratization at the sub-national level should be analyzed only taking specific center-periphery relations in a particular country into account. Since the organization of these relations differs greatly in various countries, where sub-national regimes were observed – from Mexico, Argentina and Brazil to India, Indonesia and Nigeria – sub-national democratization could produce different outcomes. Second, sub-national democratization, just like national, is not isolated from external influences, even in relatively centralized countries, although these influences may take a specific form (e.g., a limiting factor). Third, agency matters – and, in particular, it is insufficient to look at high-level politicians; street-level bureaucrats are also of crucial importance. We see our investigation of Russia merely as a first step, which could be complemented by similar analyses of both national and sub-national regimes in other countries around the world.

## Note

1  To provide a few examples: in April 2014, Northern Ossetia opened a 'Museum of Atrocities by the US and NATO' (www.rg.ru/2014/04/20/reg-skfo/konflikt.html); in Evreyskaya Autonomous Oblast numerous local politicians protested against a discussion between the students of the local university and the US consul, which should have been devoted to the issues of intercultural communication and did not touch upon any political topics (http://news.mail.ru/inregions/fareast/79/society/17755747/). There are numerous similar cases reported from different parts of Russia.

# References

Acemoglu, D., and J. Robinson (2006a): Economic Backwardness in Political Perspective. *American Political Science Review* 100: 115–131.

Acemoglu, D., and J. Robinson (2006b): *Economic Origin of Dictatorship and Democracy*. Cambridge: Cambridge University Press.

Acemoglu, D., and J. Robinson (2012): *Why Nations Fail*. New York: Crown Business.

Acemoglu, D., Garcia-Jimeno, C., and J. A. Robinson (2014): State Capacity and Economic Development: A Network Approach. NBER Working Paper No. 19813.

Acemoglu, D., Naidu, S., Restrepo, P., and J. A. Robinson (2014): Democracy Does Cause Growth. NBER Working Paper No. 20004.

Adsera, A., Boix, C., and M. Payne (2003): Are You Being Served? Political Accountability and Governmental Performance. *Journal of Law, Economics and Organization* 19: 445–490.

Ahrend, R. (2012): Understanding Russian Regions' Economic Performance during Periods of Decline and Growth – An Extreme Bounds Analysis Approach. *Economic Systems* 36: 426–443.

Aixala, J., and G. Fabro (2009): Economic Freedom, Civil Liberties, Political Rights and Growth: A Causality Analysis. *Spanish Economic Review* 11:165–178.

Akhmetov, A., and E. Zhuravskaya (2004): Opportunistic Political Cycles: Test in a Young Democracy Setting. *Quarterly Journal of Economics* 119: 1301–1338.

Alampiev, P. M. (1963): *Ekonomicheskoe Rayonirovanie SSSR*. Moscow, USSR: Izdatel'stvo Ekonomicheskoi Literatury.

Albalate, D., Bel, G., and F. Elias (2012): Institutional Determinants of Military Spending. *Journal of Comparative Economics* 40:279–290.

Alexander, J., and J. Gravningholt (2002): Evaluating Democratic Progress inside Russia: The Komi Republic and the Republic of Bashkortostan. *Democratization* 9:77–105.

Alexeev, M. (2000): Russia's Periphery in the Global Arena: Do Regions Matter in the Kremlin's Foreign Policy? PONARS Policy Memo 158.

Alexeev, M., and A. Chernyavskiy (2014): The Effect of Oil on Regional Growth in Russia and the United States: A Comparative Analysis. *Comparative Economic Studies* 56: 517–535.

Alexeev, M., and A. Chernyavskiy (2015): Natural Resources and Economic Growth in Russia's Regions. *Economic Systems*, forthcoming.

Allina-Pisano, J. (2010): Social Contracts and Authoritarian Projects in Post-Soviet Space: The Use of Administrative Resource. *Communist and Post-Communist Studies* 43:373–382.

Allison, R. (2008): Virtual Regionalism, Regional Structures and Regional Security in Central Asia. *Central Asia Survey* 27: 185–202.

Almond, G. A., and S. Verba (1963): *The Civic Culture: Political Attitude and Democracy*. Newbury Park, CA: Sage.

Almond, G. A., and S. Verba (1980): *The Civic Culture Revisited*. Boston, MA: Little Brown.

Ambrosio, T. (2009): *Authoritarian Backlash: Russian Resistance to Democratization in the Former Soviet Union*. Farnham, UK: Ashgate.

Andersson, K. P., and E. Ostrom (2007): An Analytical Agenda for the Study of Decentralized Resource Regimes. Working Paper, Sustainable Agriculture and Natural Resource Management Collaborative Research Support Program, Virginia Tech.

Arena Survey (2012): Atlas Religii I natcionalnostei Rossii / Arena: The Atlas of Religions and Nationalities of Russia. Available at http://sreda.org/arena. Accessed 14 October 2013.

Babayan, N. and T. Risse (Eds., 2015): Democracy Promotion and the Challenges of Illiberal Regional Powers. *Democratization*, special issue, forthcoming.

Backhaus, J. (2008): Gibt es Coase Theorem auch in den Neuen Laendern? Discourses in Social Market Economy no. 4.

Bader, J. (2015): China, Autocratic Patron? An Empirical Investigation of China as a Factor in Autocratic Survival. *International Studies Quarterly*, forthcoming.

Bader, J., Graevingholt, J., and A. Kästner (2010): Would Autocracies Promote Autocracy? A Political Economy Perspective on Regime-Type Export in Regional Neighborhoods. *Contemporary Politics* 16: 81–100.

Bader, M., and C. van Ham (2014): What Explains Regional Variation in Electoral Fraud? Evidence from Russia: A Research Note. *Post-Soviet Affairs*, forthcoming.

Bahry, D. (2005): The New Federalism and the Paradoxes of Regional Sovereignty in Russia. *Comparative Politics* 37:127–146.

Bahry, D., and B. D. Silver (1990): Soviet Citizen Participation on the Eve of Democratization. *American Political Science Review* 84:821–847.

Bahry, D., Boaz, C., and S. B. Gordon (1997): Tolerance, Transition, and Support for Civil Liberties in Russia. *Comparative Political Studies* 30:484–510.

Balmaceda, M. M. (2008): *Energy Dependency, Politics and Corruption in the Former Soviet Union: Russia's Power, Oligarchs' Profits and Ukraine's Missing Energy Policy, 1995–2006*. New York: Routledge.

Baracani, E., and Di Quirico, R. (Eds., 2013): *Alternatives to Democracy: Non-Democratic Regimes and the Limits to Democracy Diffusion in Eurasia.* Florence, Italy: European Press Academic Publishing.

Barbalich, K. (2009): Sugar and Democracy in Fiji: The Material Foundations of Post-Colonial Authoritarianism 1970–2005. Unpublished manuscript, Victoria University of Wellington.

Barro R. J. (1996): Democracy and Growth. *Journal of Economic Growth* 1: 1–27.

Baum, M. A., and D. A. Lake (2003): The Political Economy of Growth: Democracy and Human Capital. *American Journal of Political Science* 47: 333–347.

Beazer, Q. H. (2011): Risk in the Regions: Bureaucratic Discretion, Regulatory Uncertainty, and Private Investment in the Russian Federation. PhD Thesis, Ohio State University.

Becker, S. O., Boeckh, K., Hainz, C., and L. Woessmann (2015): The Empire Is Dead, Long Live the Empire! Long-Run Persistence of Trust and Corruption in the Bureaucracy. *Economic Journal*, forthcoming.

Berkowitz, D., and K. Clay (2005): American Civil Law Origins: Implications for State Constitutions. *American Law and Economics Review*, 7:62–84.

Besley, T., and M. Kudamatsu (2008): Making Autocracy Work. In: E. Helpman (Ed.): *Institutions and Economic Performance.* Cambridge, MA: Harvard University Press.

Besley, T., and R. Burgess (2002): The Political Economy of Government Responsiveness: Theory and Evidence from India. *Quarterly Journal of Economics* 117: 1415–1451.

Biryukova, L., and A. Novikova (2009): Bashkirskaya i Federal'naya Demokratiya Dvizhutsya s Raznymi Skorostyami. *Gazeta*, June 22.

Bisin, A., and T. Verdier (2010): The Economics of Cultural Transmission and Socialization. NBER Working Paper No. 16512.

Blanchard, O., and M. Kremer (1997): Disorganization. *Quarterly Journal of Economics* 112: 1091–1126.

Blanco, L., and R. Grier (2009): Long Live Democracy: The Determinants of Political Instability in Latin America. *Journal of Development Studies* 45: 76–95.

Boix, C. (2003): *Democracy and Redistribution.* Cambridge, UK: Cambridge University Press.

Boix, C., and S. C. Stokes (2003): Endogenous Democratization. *World Politics* 55:517–549.

Bollen, K. A. (1993): Liberal Democracy: Validity and Method Factors in Cross-National Measures. *American Journal of Political Science* 37: 1207–1230.

Borge, L.-E., Parmer, P., and R. Torvik (2013): Local Natural Resource Curse? CAMP Working Paper No. 5/2013.

Brader, T., and J. A. Tucker (2008): Pathways to Partisanship: Evidence from Russia. *Post-Soviet Affairs* 24: 263–300.

Brambor, T., Clark, W. R., and M. Golder (2006): Understanding Interaction Models: Improving Empirical Analysis. *Political Analysis* 14: 63–82.

Brewer, M. B. (1999): The Psychology of Prejudice: Ingroup Love and Outgroup Hate? *Journal of Social Issues* 55: 429–444.

Brown, J. D., Earle, J. S., and S. Gehlbach (2009): Helping Hand or Grabbing Hand? State Bureaucracy and Privatization Effectiveness. *American Political Science Review* 103: 264–283.

Brueckner, M. (2010): Natural Resource Dependence, Non-Tradables, and Economic Growth. *Journal of Comparative Economics* 38: 461–471.

Bruno, R. L., Bytchkova, M., and S. Estrin (2013): Institutional Determinants of New Firm Entry in Russia: A Cross-Regional Analysis. *Review of Economics and Statistics* 95: 1740–1749.

Buckley, N., Frye, T., Garifullina, G., and O. J. Reuter (2014): The Political Economy of Russian Gubernatorial Election and Appointment. *Europe-Asia Studies* 66: 1213–1233.

Buckley, N., Garifullina, G., Reuter, O. J., and A. Shubenkova (2014): Elections, Appointments, and Human Capital: The Case of Russian Mayors. *Demokratizatsiya* 22: 87–116.

Bulte, E., and R. Damania (2008): Resources for Sale: Corruption, Democracy and the Natural Resource Curse. *B. E. Journal of Economic Analysis and Policy* 8(1).

Bunce, V. (2003): Rethinking Recent Democratization: Lessons from the Postcommunist Experience. *World Politics* 55: 167–192.

Bunce, V. (2005): The National Idea: Imperial Legacies and Post-Communist Pathways in Eastern Europe. *East European Politics and Societies* 19: 406–442.

Cabrales, A., and E. Hauk (2011): The Quality of Political Institutions and the Curse of Natural Resources. *Economic Journal* 121: 58–88.

Cai, H., and D. Treisman (2004): State Corroding Federalism. *Journal of Public Economics* 88: 819–843.

Cameron, D. R., and M. A. Orenstein (2012): Post-Soviet Authoritarianism: The Influence of Russia in Its Near Abroad. *Post-Soviet Affairs* 28: 1–44.

Canetti-Nisim, D. (2004): The Effect of Religiosity on Endorsement of Democratic Values: The Mediating Influence of Authoritarianism. *Political Behavior* 26: 377–398.

Carbone, G. (2009): Consequences of Democratization. *Journal of Democracy* 20: 123–137.

Carothers, T. (1999): *Aiding Democracy Abroad: The Learning Curve.* Washington, DC: Carnegie Endowment for International Peace.

Carothers, T. (2004): *Critical Mission: Essays on Democracy Promotion.* Washington, DC: Carnegie Endowment for International Peace.

Caselli, F., and G. Michaels (2009): Do Oil Windfalls Improve Living Standards? Evidence from Brazil. NBER Working Paper No. 15550.

Cincotta, R. P. (2008): How Democracies Grow Up. *Foreign Policy.* Available at www.foreignpolicy.com/articles/2008/02/19/how_democracies_grow_up. Accessed 31 May 2014.

Clark, T. D. (1995): The Zhirinovsky Electoral Victory: Antecedence and Aftermath. *Nationalist Papers* 23: 767–778.

CNSI (2005): *Neformal'naya Ekonomika Lesopol'zovaniya v Irkutskoy Oblasti: Sotsiologicheskiy Rakurs.* St. Petersburg, Irkutsk, Russia: CNSI.

Collier, P., and A. Hoeffler (2009): Testing the Neocon Agenda: Democracy in Resource-Rich Societies. *European Economic Review* 53: 293–308.

Colton, T. J. (2000): *Transitional Citizens: Voters and What Influences Them in the New Russia*. Cambridge, MA: Harvard University Press.

Coppedge, M., Gerring, J., Altman, D., Bernhard, M., Fish, S., Hicken, A., Kroenig, M., Lindberg, S. I., McMann, K., Paxton, P., Semetko, H. A., Skaaning, S.-E., Staton, J., and J. Teorell (2011): Conceptualizing and Measuring Democracy: A New Approach. *Perspectives on Politics* 9: 247–267.

Coppieters, B. (Ed., 1996): *Contested Borders in the Caucasus*. Brussels, Belgium: VUB Press.

Corden, W. M., and J. P. Neary (1982): Booming Sector and De-industrialization in a Small Open Economy. *Economic Journal* 92: 825–848.

Corey, J. (2009): Development in US States, Economic Freedom and the 'Resource Curse'. Fraser Institute Study in Mining Policy.

Corrales, J. (2009): Changes in Regime Type and Venezuela's New Foreign Policy. Unpublished manuscript, Florida International University.

Darden, K. (2001): Blackmail as a Tool of State Domination: Ukraine under Kuchma. *East European Constitutional Review* 10: 67–71.

Darden, K. (2008): The Integrity of Corrupt States: Graft as an Informal Political Institution. *Politics and Society* 36: 35–59.

de Figueiredo, R., and Z. Elkins (2003): Are Patriots Bigots? An Inquiry into the Vices of In-Group Pride. *American Journal of Political Science* 47: 171–188.

de Haan, J., Lundstroem, S., and J.-E. Sturm (2006): Market-Oriented Institutions and Policies and Economic Growth: A Critical Survey. *Journal of Economic Surveys* 20: 157–191.

De Silva, M. O., Kurlyandskaya, G. Andreeva, E., and N. Golovanova (2009): *Intergovernmental Reforms in the Russian Federation: One Step Forward, Two Steps Back?* Washington, DC: World Bank.

Deacon R. (2009): Public Good Provision under Dictatorship and Democracy. *Public Choice* 139: 241–262.

Denisova, I. (2010): Adult Mortality in Russia. *Economics of Transition* 18: 333–363.

Diaz-Cayeros, A., Magaloni, B., and B. R. Weingast (2003): Tragic Brilliance: Equilibrium Hegemony and Democratization in Mexico. Unpublished manuscript, Stanford University.

Dimitrov, M. K. (2009): Popular Autocrats. *Journal of Democracy* 20: 78–21.

Dininio, P., and R. Orttung (2005): Explaining Patterns of Corruption in the Russian Regions. *World Politics* 57: 500–529.

Dorn, D., Fischer, J. A. V., Kirchgaessner, G., and A. Sousa-Poza (2007): Is It Culture or Democracy? The Impact of Democracy and Culture on Happiness. *Social Indicators Research* 82: 505–526.

Dorn, D., Fischer, J. A. V., Kirchgaessner, G., and A. Sousa-Poza (2008): Direct Democracy and Life Satisfaction Revisited: New Evidence for Switzerland. *Journal of Happiness Studies* 9: 227–255.

Doucouliagos, C., and M. Ulubasoglu (2008): Democracy and Economic Growth: A Meta-Analysis. *American Journal of Political Science* 52: 61–83.

Druckman, D. (1994): Nationalism, Patriotism and Group Loyalty: A Social Psychological Perspective. *Mershon International Studies Review* 38: 43–68.

Dunning, T. (2005): Resource Dependence, Economic Performance and Political Stability. *Journal of Conflict Resolution* 49: 451–482.

Durlauf, S. N., Johnson, P. A., and J.R.W. Temple (2005): Growth Econometrics. In: P. Aghion and S. N. Durlauf (Eds.): *Handbook of Economic Growth. Volume 2*. Amsterdam, Netherlands: Elsevier.

Easterlin, R. (1974): Does Economic Growth Improve the Human Lot? Some Empirical Evidence. In: R. David and R. Reder (Eds.): *Nations and Households in Economic Growth: Essays in Honor of Moses Abramovitz*. New York: Academic Press.

Easterlin, R. (1995): Will Raising the Incomes of All Increase the Happiness of All? *Journal of Economic Behavior and Organization* 27: 35–47.

Easterlin, R., Angelescu McVey, L., Switek, M., Sawangfa, O., and J. Smith Zweig (2010): The Happiness-Income Paradox Revisited. *Proceedings of the National Academy of Sciences* 107: 22463–22468.

EDB (2013): *Prigranichnoe Sotrudnichestvo Regionov Rossii, Belarusi i Ukrainy*. St. Petersburg, Russia: EDB Center for Integration Studies.

Egorov, G., and K. Sonin (2011): Dictators and their Viziers: Endogenizing the Loyalty-Competence Trade-Off. *Journal of the European Economic Association* 9: 903–930.

Eickert, G. (2003): Patterns of Post-Communist Transformation. In: G. Eickert and S. Hanson (Eds.): *Capitalism and Democracy in Central and Eastern Europe*. Cambridge, UK: Cambridge University Press

Eifert, B., Gelb, A., and N. B. Tallroth (2002): The Political Economy of Fiscal Policy and Economic Management in Resource-Rich Countries. World Bank Policy Research Working Paper No. 2899.

Eifert, B., Gelb, A., and N. B. Tallroth (2003): Managing Oil Wealth. *Finance and Development* 40(1).

Englstroem, M. (2014): Contemporary Russian Messianism and New Russian Foreign Policy. *Contemporary Security Policy* 35: 356–379.

Enikolopov, R., Korovkin, V., Petrova, M., Sonin, K., and A. Zakharov (2013): Field Experiment Estimate of Electoral Fraud in Russian Parliamentary Elections. *Proceedings of the National Academy of Sciences* 110: 448–452.

Epstein, D. L., Bates, R., Goldstone, J., Kirstensen, I., and S. O'Halloran (2006): Democratic Transitions. *American Journal of Political Science* 50: 551–569.

Etkind, Alexander (2011): *Internal Colonization: Russia's Imperial Experience*. Cambridge, UK: Polity Press.

Evans, A. D. (2014): Local Democracy in a Hybrid State: Pluralism and Protest in Volzhskiy, Russia. *Post-Soviet Affairs* 30: 298–323.

Feng, Y. (1997): Democracy, Political Stability and Economic Growth. *British Journal of Political Science* 27: 391–418.

Fidrmuc, J. (2003): Economic Reform, Democracy and Growth during Post-Communist Transition. *European Journal of Political Economy* 19: 583–604.

Fish, M. S. (2001): The Inner Asian Anomaly: Mongolian Democratization in Comparative Perspective. *Communist and Post-Communist Studies* 34: 323–338.

Fish, M. S. (2002): Islam and Authoritarianism. *World Politics* 55: 4–73.

Freinkman, L., and A. Plekhanov (2009): Fiscal Decentralization in Rentier Regions: Evidence from Russia. *World Development* 37: 503–512.

Frey, B. S., and A. Stutzer (2000a): Happiness, Economy and Institutions. *Economic Journal* 110: 918–938.

Frey, B. S., and A. Stutzer (2000b): Happiness Prospers in Democracy. *Journal of Happiness Studies* 1: 79–102.

Frey, B. S., and A. Stutzer (2002): What Can Economists Learn from Happiness Research? Journal of Economic Literature 40: 402–435.

Frey, B. S., Benz, M., and A. Stutzer (2004): Introducing Procedural Utility: Not Only What, But Also How Matters. *Journal of Institutional and Theoretical Economics* 160: 377–401.

Frye, T. J. (2010): *Building States and Markets After Communism: The Perils of Polarized Democracy*. Cambridge, UK: Cambridge University Press.

Frye, T. J. (2012): In From the Cold: Institutions and Causal Inference in Postcommunist Studies. *Annual Review of Political Science* 15: 245–263.

Furman, D. (2010): *Dvizhenie po Spirali: Politicheskaya Sistema Rossii v Riadu Drughikh Sistem*. Moscow, Russia: Ves Mir.

Gaddy, C. G., and B. W. Ickes (2002): *Russia's Virtual Economy*. Washington, DC: Brookings Institute Press.

Gaman-Golutvina, O. (2008): Changes in Elite Patterns. *Europe-Asia Studies* 60: 1033–1050.

Garcelon, M. (1997): The Estate of Change: The Specialist Rebellion and the Democratic Movement in Moscow, 1989–1991. *Theory and Society* 26: 39–85.

Garcia-Guadilla M. P., and C. Perez (2002): Democracy, Decentralization, and Clientalism: New Relationship and Old Practices. *Latin American Perspectives* 29: 90–109.

Gates, S., Hegre, H., Jones, M. P., and H. Strand (2006): Institutional Inconsistency and Political Instability: Polity Duration, 1800–2000. *American Political Science Review* 50: 893–908.

Geishecker, I., and J. P. Haisken-DeNew (2004): Landing on All Fours? Communist Elites in Post-Soviet Russia. *Journal of Comparative Economics* 32: 700–719.

Gel'man, V. (1999): Regime Transition, Uncertainty, and Prospects for Democratization: The Politics of Russia's Regions in a Comparative Perspective. *Europe-Asia Studies* 51: 939–956.

Gel'man, V. (2008): Party Politics in Russia: From Competition to Hierarchy. *Europe-Asia Studies* 60: 913–930.

Gel'man, V. (2010a): The Dynamics of Sub-National Authoritarianism: Russia in Comparative Perspective. In: V. Gel'man and C. Ross (Eds): *The Politics of Subnational Authoritarianism in Russia*. Farnham, UK: Ashgate.

Gel'man, V. (2010b): Subversive Institutions and Informal Governance in Contemporary Russia. In: T. Christiansen and C. Neuhold (Eds.): *International Handbook of Informal Governance*. Cheltenham, UK: Edward Elgar.

Gel'man, V. (2012): The Regime, the Opposition and Challenges to Electoral Authoritarianism in Russia. Russian Analytical Digest No. 118.

Gel'man, V. (2013): Cracks in the Walls: Challenges to Electoral Authoritarianism in Russia. *Problems of Post-Communism* 60: 3–10.

Gel'man, V., Ryzhenkov, S., and M. Brie (2004): *Making and Breaking Democratic Transitions: The Comparative Politics of Russia's Regions.* Lanham, MD: Rowman & Littlefield.

Gennaioli, N., and I. Rainer (2007): The Modern Impact of Precolonial Centralization in Africa. *Journal of Economic Growth* 12: 185–234.

Gerber, T. P. (2000): Membership Benefits or Selection Effects? Why Former Communist Party Members Do Better in Post-Soviet Russia. *Social Science Research* 29: 25–50.

Gervasoni, C. (2010): A Rentier Theory of Subnational Regimes: Fiscal Decentralization, Democracy, and Authoritarianism in the Argentine Provinces. *World Politics* 62: 302–340.

Gevorkyan, N., Timakova, N., and A. Kolesnikov (2000): *Ot Pervogo Litsa: Razgovory s Vladimirom Putinym.* Moscow, Russia: Vagrius.

Giavazzi, F., and G. Tabellini (2005): Economic and Political Liberalization. *Journal of Monetary Economics* 52: 1297–1330.

Gibson, E. L. (2005): Boundary Control: Subnational Authoritarianism in Democratic Countries. *World Politics* 58: 101–132.

Gibson, J. L., Duch, R. M., and K. L. Tedin (1992): Democratic Values and the Transformation of the Soviet Union. *Journal of Politics* 54: 329–371.

Gill, B., and Y. Huang (2006): Sources and Limits of Chinese 'Soft Power'. *Survival: Global Politics and Strategy* 48: 17–36.

Gilson, R. J., and C. J. Milhaupt (2011): Economically Benevolent Dictators: Lessons for Developing Countries. *American Journal of Comparative Law* 59: 227–288.

Gimpelson, V., Kapelyushnikov, R., and A. Lukianova (2010): Employment Protection Legislation in Russia: Regional Enforcement and Labor Market Outcomes. *Comparative Economic Studies* 52: 611–636.

Giraudy, A. (2013): Varieties of Subnational Undemocratic Regimes: Evidence from Argentina and Mexico. *Studies in Comparative International Development* 48: 51–80.

Giuliano, E. (2006): Secessionism from the Bottom Up: Democratization, Nationalism, and Local Accountability in the Russian Transition. *World Politics* 58: 276–310.

Glazov, Y. (1988): *To Be or Not to Be in the Party: Communist Party Membership in the USSR.* Dordrecht, Netherlands: Kluwer.

Goldberg, E., Wibbels, E., and E. Mvukiyehe (2008): Lessons from Strange Cases: Democracy, Development and the Resource Curse in the U.S. States. *Comparative Political Studies* 41: 477–514.

Golosov, G. (2014): The Territorial Genealogies of Russia's Political Parties and the Transferability of Political Machines. *Post-Soviet Affairs* 30: 464–480.

Granville, B. (2010): Do Informal Institutions Matter for Technological Change in Russia? The Impact of Communist Norms and Conventions, 1998–2004. *World Development* 38: 155–169.

Guiliano, P., Mishra, P., and A. Spilimbergo (2013): Democracy and Reforms: Evidence from a New Dataset. *American Economic Journal: Macroeconomics* 5: 179–204.

Guriev, S., and E. Zhuravskaya (2009): (Un)happiness in Transition. *Journal of Economic Perspectives* 23: 143–168.

Hale, H. E. (2003): Explaining Machine Politics in Russia's Regions: Economy, Ethnicity and Legacy. *Post-Soviet Affairs* 19: 228–263.

Hanson, S. E. (1995): The Leninist Legacy and Institutional Change. *Comparative Political Studies* 28: 306–314.

Hardin, G. L. (2009): Environmental Determinism: Broken Paradigm or Viable Perspective? PhD Thesis, East Tennessee State University.

Harris, D. A. (1986): Reasons for CPSU Membership: Insights from Interviews with Emigrants. *Soviet Jewish Affairs* 16: 21–33.

Havrylyshin, O. (2007): Fifteen Years of Transformation in the Post-Communist World: Rapid Reformers Outperformed Gradualists. CATO Institute Development Policy Analysis No. 4.

Hayo, B. (2007): Happiness in Transition: An Empirical Study of Eastern Europe. *Economic Systems* 31: 204–221.

Hayo, B., and W. Seifert (2003): Subjective Economic Well-Being in Eastern Europe. *Journal of Economic Psychology* 24: 329–348.

Helliwell, J. F. (1994): Empirical Linkages between Democracy and Economic Growth. *British Journal of Political Science* 24: 225–248.

Hellman, J. S. (1998): Winner Takes All: The Politics of Partial Reform in Postcommunist Transitions. *World Politics* 50: 203–234.

Herrera, Y. M. (2005): *Imagined Economies: The Sources of Russian Regionalism.* Cambridge, UK: Cambridge University Press.

Hill, R. J. (1991): The CPSU: From Monolith to Pluralist. *Soviet Studies* 43: 217–235.

Hillman, A. L. (2010): Expressive Behavior in Economics and Politics. *European Journal of Political Economy* 26: 403–418.

Hiskey, J. T. (2005): The Political Economy of Subnational Economic Recovery in Mexico. *Latin American Research Review* 40: 30–55.

Hough, J. F. (1976a): Party 'Saturation' in the Soviet Union. In: P. Cocks, R. V. Daniels, and N. W. Heer (Eds.): *The Dynamics of Soviet Politics.* Cambridge, MA: Harvard University Press.

Hough, J. F. (1976b): Political Participation in the Soviet Union. *Soviet Studies* 28: 3–20.

Hughes, J. (1997): Sub-National Elites and Post-Communist Transformation in Russia. *Europe-Asia Studies* 49: 1017–1037.

Hutcheson, D. (2004): Protest and Disengagement in the Russian Federal Elections of 2003–2004. *Perspectives on European Politics and Society* 5: 305–330.

Inglehart, R., Klingemann, H.-D., and C. Welzel (2003): The Theory of Human Development: A Cross-Cultural Analysis. *European Journal of Political Research* 42: 341–380.

Inglehart, R., and C. Welzel (2005): *Modernization, Cultural Change, and Democracy. The Human Development Sequence.* Cambridge, UK: Cambridge University Press.

Inman, R. P., and D. L. Rubinfeld (2005): Federalism and the Democratic Transition: Lessons from South Africa. *American Economic Review* 95: 39–43.

ISANT (2003): *Samye Vliyatel'nye Lyudi Rossii 2003*. Moscow, Russia: ISANT.

Jacoby, W. (2006): Inspiration, Coalition, and Substitution. External Influences on Postcommunist Transformations. *World Politics* 58: 623–51.

James, A., and D. Aadland (2010): The Curse of Natural Resources: An Empirical Investigation of U.S. Counties. *Resource and Energy Economics* 33: 440–453.

James, A. G., and R. G. James (2011): Do Resource Dependent Regions Grow Slower than They Should? *Economics Letters* 111: 194–196.

Jennings, M. K., and R. G. Niemi (1968): The Transmission of Political Values from Parent to Child. *American Political Science Review* 62: 169–184.

Jennings, M. K., Stoker, L., and J. Bowler (2009): Politics across Generations: Family Transmission Reexamined. *Journal of Politics* 71: 782–799.

Johnson, R. N. (2006): Economic Growth and Natural Resources: Does the Curse of Natural Resources Extend to the 50 US States? In: R. Halvorsen and D. F. Layton (Eds.): *Explorations in Environmental and Natural Resource Economics*. Cheltenham, UK: Edward Elgar.

Kamrava, M. (2012): The Arab Spring and the Saudi-Led Counterrevolution. *Orbis* 56: 96–104.

Keating, M. (1988): *State and Regional Nationalism: Territorial Politics and the European State*. New York: Harvester Wheatsheaf.

Keating, M. (1995): Europeanism and Regionalism. In: B. Jones and M. Keating (Eds.): *The European Union and the Regions*. Oxford, UK: Clarendon Press.

Keating, M. (2002): Territorial Politics and the New Regionalism. In: P. Heywood, E. Jones, and M. Rhodes (Eds.): *Development in West European Politics*. Volume 2. London: Palgrave.

Keller, E. J. (1996): Structure, Agency, and Political Liberalization in Africa. *African Journal of Political Science* 1: 202–216.

Kenyon, T, and M. Naoi (2007): Policy Uncertainty in Hybrid Regimes: Evidence from Firm Level Surveys. *Comparative Political Studies* 43: 486–510.

Kopstein, J., and D. Reilly (2000): Geographic Diffusion and the Transformation of the Postcommunist World. *World Politics* 53: 1–37.

Kovzik, A., and M. Watts (2001): Reforming Undergraduate Instruction in Russia, Belarus and Ukraine. *Journal of Economic Education* 32: 78–92.

Krastev, I. (2012): An Autopsy of Managed Democracy. *Journal of Democracy* 23: 33–45.

Kryshtanovskaya, O., and S. White (1996): From Soviet Nomenklatura to Russian Elite. *Europe-Asia Studies* 48: 711–734.

Kryukov, V., Tokarev, A., and S. Yenikeyeff (2011): The Contest for Oil: Oil and Gas Management in Russia. In: P. Collier and A. Venables (Eds.): *Plundered Nations? Successes and Failures in Natural Resource Extraction*. Basingstoke, UK: Palgrave MacMillan.

Kubicek, P. (2009): The Commonwealth of Independent States: An Example of Failed Regionalism? *Review of International Studies* 35: 237–256.

Kusznir, J. (2008): *Der politische Einfluss von Wirtschaftseliten in russischen Regionen: Eine Analyse am Beispiel der Erdoel- und Erdgasindustrie 1992–2005*. Stuttgart, Germany: Ibidem-Verlag.

Kyland, F., and E. Prescott (1977): Rules Rather than Discretion: The Inconsistency of Optimal Plans. *Journal of Political Economy* 85: 137–160.

Lacina, B. (2009): The Problem of Political Stability in Northeast India: Local Ethnic Autocracy and the Rule of Law. *Asian Survey* 49: 998–1020.

Lada, A. (2013): Clash of Brothers in a Contagious World: Wars to Avoid Diffusion. Center for Economic and Regional Studies of the Hungarian Academy of Sciences Discussion Paper no. 2013/33

Lambert-Mogiliansky, A., Sonin, K., and E. Zhuravskaya (2007): Are Russian Commercial Courts Biased? Evidence from a Bankruptcy Law Transplant. *Journal of Comparative Economics* 35: 245–277.

Lankina, A., Libman, A., and A. Obydenkova (2015): Appropriation and Subversion: Pre-communist Literacy, Communist Party Saturation, and Post-Communist Democratic Outcomes. Unpublished manuscript, London School of Economics and Political Science and Universitat Pompeu Fabra.

Lankina, T. (2012): Unbroken Links? From Imperial Human Capital to Post-Communist Modernisation. *Europe-Asia Studies* 64: 623–643.

Lankina, T., and L. Getachew (2006): A Geographic Incremental Theory of Democratization: Territory, Aid, and Democracy in Postcommunist Regions. *World Politics* 58: 536–82.

Lankina, T., and L. Getachew (2012): Mission of Empire, Word or Sword? The Human Capital Legacy in Postcolonial Democratic Development. *American Journal of Political Science* 52:465–483.

LaPorte, J., and D. N. Lussier (2011): What Is the Leninist Legacy? *Slavic Review* 70: 637–654.

Leon, D. A., Saburova, L., Tomkins, S., Andreev, E., Kiryanov, N., McKee, M., and V. M. Shkolnikov (2007): Hazardous Alcohol Drinking and Premature Mortality in Russia: A Population-Based Case-Control Study. *Lancet* 369: 2001–2009.

Levitsky, S., and L. A. Way (2006): Linkage versus Leverage: Rethinking the International Dimension of Regime Change. *Comparative Politics* 38: 379–400.

Levitsky, S., and L. A. Way (2010): *Comparative Authoritarianism: Hybrid Regimes after the Cold War.* Cambridge, UK: Cambridge University Press.

Lewis, M. W. (2011): The Survival of Animism in Russia – and Its Destruction in the West. Geocurrents 2011. Available at http://geocurrents.info/cultural-geography/the-survival-of-animism-in-russia-and-its-destruction-in-the-west#ixzz2hhb6yV20. Accessed 14 October 2013.

Libman, A. (2010): Constitutions, Regulations, and Taxes: Contradictions of Different Aspects of Decentralization. *Journal of Comparative Economics* 38: 395–418.

Libman, A. (2011): Russian Federalism and Post-Soviet Integration: Divergence of Development Paths. *Europe-Asia Studies* 63: 1323–1355.

Libman, A. (2012): Democracy, Size of Bureaucracy, and Economic Growth: Evidence from Russian Regions. *Empirical Economics* 43: 1321–1352.

Libman, A. (2013a): Natural Resources and Sub-National Economic Performance: Does Sub-National Democracy Matter? *Energy Economics* 37: 82–99.

Libman, A. (2013b): Resource Curse, Institutions, and Non-Resource Sector. Unpublished manuscript, Frankfurt School of Finance & Management.

Libman, A., Kozlov, V., and A. Schultz (2012): Roving Bandits in Action: Outside Option and Governmental Predation in Autocracies. *Kyklos* 65: 526–562.

Libman, A., and A. Obydenkova (2013): Communism or Communists? Soviet Legacies and Corruption in Transition Economies. *Economics Letters* 119: 101–103.

Libman, A., and A. Obydenkova (2014a): Governance of Commons in a Large Nondemocratic Country: The Case of Forestry in the Russian Federation. *Publius: The Journal of Federalism* 44: 298–323.

Libman, A., and A. Obydenkova (2014b): International Trade as a Limiting Factor in Democratization: An Analysis of Subnational Regions in Post-Communist Russia. *Studies in Comparative International Development* 49: 168–196.

Libman, A., and A. Obydenkova (2015): CPSU Legacies and Regional Democracy in Contemporary Russia. *Political Studies*, forthcoming.

Libman, A., Schultz, A., and T. Graeber (2014): Tax Return as a Political Statement. Unpublished manuscript, Frankfurt School of Finance & Management.

Libman, A., and E. Vinokurov (2011): Is It Really Different? Patterns of Regionalization in Post-Soviet Central Asia. *Post-Communist Economies* 23: 469–492.

Lipset, S. M. (1959): Some Social Requisites of Democracy: Economic Development and Political Legitimacy. *American Political Science Review* 53: 69–105.

Lussier, D. M. (2002): The Role of Russia's Governors in the 1999–2000 Federal Elections. In: C. Ross (Ed.): *Regional Politics in Russia*. Manchester, UK: Manchester University Press.

Mahoney, J., and R. Snyder (1999): Rethinking Agency and Structure in the Study of Regime Change. *Studies in Comparative International Development* 34: 3–32.

Mainwaring, S., and A. Perez-Linan (2008): Regime Legacies and Democratization: Explaining Variance in the Level of Democracy in Latin America. Helen Kellogg Institute for International Studies Working Paper No. 354.

March, L. (2009): Managing Opposition in a Hybrid Regime: Just Russia and Parastatal Opposition. *Slavic Review* 68: 504–527.

Markedonov, S. (2006): Kavkaz v Poiskakh 'Svoei Zemli': Etnichnost' i Konflity v Regione. *Svobodnaya Mysl* 4: 70–76.

Markedonov, S. (2010): *Radical Islam in the North Caucasus. Evolving Threats, Challenges and Prospects*. Washington, DC: CSIS.

Marks, G. N. (2004): Communist Party Membership in Five Former Soviet Bloc Countries, 1945–1989. *Communist and Post-Communist Studies* 37: 241–263.

Matsuzato, K. (2004): Authoritarian Transformation in Mid-Volga National Republics: An Attempt at Macro-Regionology. *Journal of Communist Studies and Transition Politics* 20: 98–123.

McAllister, I., and S. White (1994): Political Participation in Postcommunist Russia. *Political Studies* 42: 539–615.

McMann, K. (2006): *Economic Autonomy and Democracy: Hybrid Regimes in Russia and Kyrgyzstan*. Cambridge, UK: Cambridge University Press.

Mehlum, H., Moene, K., and R. Torvik (2006): Institutions and the Resource Curse. *Economic Journal* 116:1–20.

Mendelski, M., and A. Libman (2014): Demand for Litigation in the Absence of Traditions of Rule of Law: An Example of Ottoman and Habsburg Legacies in Romania. *Constitutional Political Economy* 25: 177–206.

Michaels, G. (2011): The Long Term Consequences of Resource-Based Specialisation. *Economic Journal* 121: 31–57.

Mickiewicz, E. (1971): The Modernization of Party Propaganda in the USSR. *Slavic Review* 30: 257–276.

Mickiewicz, E. (2008): *Television, Power and the Public in Russia*. New York: Cambridge University Press.

Migue, J.-C., and G. Belanger (1974): Towards a General Theory of Managerial Discretion. *Public Choice* 17: 27–43.

Mikhailov, V. V. (2010): Authoritarian Regimes of Russia and Tatarstan: Coexistence and Subjection. *Journal of Communist Studies and Transition Politics* 26: 471–493.

Milner, H. V., and B. Mukherjee (2010): Democratization and Economic Globalization. *Annual Review of Political Science* 12: 163–81.

Mises, L. (1944): *Bureaucracy*. New Haven, CT: Yale University Press.

Mohtadi, H., and T. L. Roe (2003): Democracy, Rent Seeking, Public Spending and Growth. *Journal of Public Economics* 87: 445–466.

Morrison, K. M. (2012): What Can We Learn about the 'Resource Curse' from Foreign Aid? *World Bank Research Observer* 27: 52–73.

Moses, J. C. (2008): Who Has Led Russia? Russian Regional Political Elites, 1954–2006. *Europe-Asia Studies* 60: 1–24.

Moses, J. C. (2014): The Political Resurrection of Russian Governors. *Europe-Asia Studies* 66: 1395–1424.

Mousseau, M. (2000): Market Prosperity, Democratic Consolidation, and Democratic Peace. *Journal of Conflict Resolution* 44: 472–507.

Mueller, M. (2011): State Dirigisme in Megaprojects: Governing the 2014 Winter Olympics in Sochi. *Environment and Planning A* 43: 2091–2108.

Munck, G. L., and J. Verkuilen (2002): Conceptualizing and Measuring Democracy: Evaluating Alternative Indices. *Comparative Political Studies* 35:5–34.

Murphy, J. G., McDevitt-Murphy, M. E., and N. P. Barnett (2005): Drink and Be Merry? Gender, Life Satisfaction, and Alcohol Consumption Among College Students. *Psychology of Addictive Behaviors* 19: 184–191.

Myagkov, M., Ordeshook, P. C., and D. Shakin (2009): *The Forensics of Election Fraud: Russia and Ukraine*. Cambridge, UK: Cambridge University Press.

Need, A., and G. Evans G. (2001): Analysing Patterns of Religious Participation in Post-Communist Eastern Europe. *British Journal of Sociology* 52: 229–248.

Niskanen, W. A. (1973): *Bureaucracy: Servant or Master?* London: Institute of Economic Affairs.

Nureev, R. (Ed., 2010): *Ekonomicheskie Sub'ekty Postsovetskoi Rossii (Institucional'nyi Analiz): Desyat' Let Supstya*. Volume 3. Moscow, Russia: MONF.

O'Donnell, G. (1973): *Modernization and Bureaucratic Authoritarianism*. Berkeley: University of California Press.

Obinger, H. (2000): Politische Regime, politische Stabilitaet und Wirtschaftswachstum. *Swiss Political Science Review* 6: 1–26.

Obydenkova, A. (2006a): Democratization, Europeanization and Regionalization beyond the European Union: Search for Empirical Evidence. *European Integration Online Papers* 10: 1–39.

Obydenkova, A. (2006b): The EU-Russia Relationship: The Role of Transnational Regional Cooperation in Regime Transition in the Regions. Impact Beyond Members & Candidates. In: H. Koff (Ed.): *Deceiving (Dis)Appearances: Analyzing Current Development in Europe and North America's Border Regions.* Oxford, UK: Peter Lang.

Obydenkova, A. (2007): The International Dimension of Democratization: Test the Parsimonious Approach. *Cambridge Review of International Affairs* 20: 473–490.

Obydenkova, A. (2008): Regime Transition in the Regions of Russia: The Freedom of Mass Media: Transnational Impact on Sub-National Democratization? *European Journal of Political Research* 47: 221–246.

Obydenkova, A. (2010): Belarus as a Hybrid Regime. In: E. Baracani (Ed.): *Democratization and Hybrid Regimes: International Anchoring and Domestic Dynamics in European Post-Soviet States.* Florence, Italy: European Press Academic Publishing.

Obydenkova, A. (2011): A Triangle of Russian Federalism: Democratization, (De-) Centralization and Local Politics. *Publius: The Journal of Federalism* 41: 734–741.

Obydenkova, A. (2012): Democratization at the Grassroots: The European Union's External Impact. *Democratization* 19: 230–257.

Obydenkova, A. (2015): Religious Pluralism in Russia. In: F. Requejo and K.-J. Nagel (Eds.): *Politics of Religion and Nationalism: Federalism, Consociationalism and Secession.* Abingdon, UK: Routledge.

Obydenkova, A., and A. Libman (2012): The Impact of External Factors on Regime Transition: Lessons from the Russian Regions. *Post-Soviet Affairs* 28: 346–401.

Obydenkova, A., and A. Libman (2013): National Autocratization and the Survival of Sub-National Democracy: Evidence from Russia's Parliamentary Elections of 2011. *Acta Politica* 48: 459–489.

Obydenkova, A., and A. Libman (2014): Understanding the Foreign Policy of Autocratic Actors: Ideology or Pragmatism? Russia and the Tymoshenko Trial as a Case Study. *Contemporary Politics* 20: 347–364.

Obydenkova, A., and A. Libman (Eds., 2015a): *Autocratic and Democratic External Influences in Post-Soviet Eurasia.* Farnham, UK: Ashgate.

Obydenkova, A., and A. Libman (2015b): Understanding the Survival of Post-Communist Corruption in Contemporary Russia: The Influence of Historical Legacies. *Post-Soviet Affairs*, forthcoming.

Ochman, E. (2013): *Post-Communist Poland – Contested Pasts and Future Identities.* Abingdon, UK: Routledge.

O'Donnell, G.A. and P.C. Schmitter (1986): *Transitions from Authoritarian Rule – Tentative Conclusions about Uncertain Democracies.* Baltimore, MD: Johns Hopkins University Press.

Oleinik, A. (2005): A Distrustful Economy: An Inquiry into Foundations of the Russian Market. *Journal of Economic Issues* 39: 53–74.

Olters, J.-P. (2001): Modeling Politics with Economic Tools: A Critical Survey of the Literature. IMF Working Paper WP/01/10.

Ortmann, S., and J. Heathershaw (2012): Conspiracy Theories in the Post-Soviet Space. *Russian Review* 71: 551–564.

Ostrom, E. (1990): *Governing the Commons: The Evolution of Institutions for Collective Action*. Cambridge, UK: Cambridge University Press.

Ostrom, E. (1999): Coping with the Tragedy of Commons. *Annual Review of Political Science* 2: 493–535.

Ostrom, E. (2010): Beyond Markets and States: Polycentric Governance of Complex Economic Systems. *American Economic Review* 100: 641–672.

Ostrom, E. (2012): Why Do We Need to Protect Institutional Diversity? *European Political Science* 11: 128–147.

Oushakine, S. A. (2009): 'Stop the Invasion!': Money, Patriotism, and Conspiracy in Russia. *Social Research* 76: 71–116.

Owen, J. M. (2005): When Do Ideologies Produce Alliances? The Holy Roman Empire, 1517–1555. *International Studies Quarterly* 49: 73–99.

Owen, J. M. (2010): *The Clash of Ideas in World Politics: Transnational Networks, States, and Regime Change, 1510–2010*. Princeton, NJ: Princeton University Press.

Papaioannou, E., and G. Siourouins (2008): Democratization and Growth. *Economic Journal* 118: 1520–1551.

Papyrakis, E., and R. Gerlagh (2007): Resource-Abundance and Economic Growth in the United States. *European Economic Review* 51: 1011–1039.

Papyrakis, E., and O. Raveh (2014): An Empirical Analysis of a Regional Dutch Disease: The Case of Canada. *Environmental and Resource Economics* 58: 179–198.

Persson, T., Roland, G., and G. Tabellini (1997): Separation of Powers and Political Accountability. *Quarterly Journal of Economics* 112: 1163–1202.

Pertzik, V. A. (1984): Organisatsionno-Pravovye Problemy Territorial'no-Proizvodstvennykh Kompleksov. *Pravovedenie* 1: 65–75.

Petrov, N. (2005): Siloviki in Russian Regions: New Dogs, Old Tricks. *Journal of Power Institutions in Post-Socialist Societies* 2. Available at http://pipss.revues.org/331?for. Accessed 26 February 2015.

Petrov, N., and A. Titkov (2013): *Reiting Demokratichnosti Regionov Moskovskogo Tsentra Karnegi: 10 Let v Stroyu*. Moscow, Russia: Carnegie Endowment for International Peace.

Petrova, M., and R. H. Bates (2012): Evolution of Risk and Political Regimes. *Economics and Politics* 24: 200–225.

Plekhanov, A., and A. Isakova (2011): Region-Specific Constraints to Doing Business: Evidence from Russia. EBRD Working Paper No. 125.

Polishchuk, L. (2001): Legal Initiatives in Russian Regions: Determinants and Effects. In: P. Murrell (Ed.): *Assessing the Value of Law in Transition Economies*. Ann Arbor: University of Michigan Press.

Polishchuk, L., and A. Savvateev (2004): Spontaneous (Non)Emergence of Property Rights. *Economics of Transition* 12: 103–127.

Pop-Eleches, G. (2007): Historical Legacies and Post-Communist Regime Change. *Journal of Politics* 69: 908–926.

Pop-Eleches, G., and J. A. Tucker (2011): Communism's Shadow: Postcommunist Legacies, Values, and Behavior. *Comparative Politics* 43: 379–408.

Pop-Eleches, G., and J. A. Tucker (2014): Communist Socialization and Post-Communist Economic and Political Attitudes. *Electoral Studies* 33: 77–89.

Prendergast, C. (1993): A Theory of 'Yes Man'. *American Economic Review* 83: 757–770.

Pridham, G. (2000): Confining Conditions and Breaking with the Past: Historical Legacies and Political Learning in Transitions to Democracy. *Democratization* 7: 36–64.

Pridham, G. (2005): *Designing Democracy: EU Enlargement and Regime Change in Post-Communist Europe*. London: Palgrave.

Przeworski, A. Alvarez, M. E., Cheibub, J. A., and F. Limongi (2000): *Democracy and Development: Political Institutions and Well-Being in the World, 1950–1990*. Cambridge, UK: Cambridge University Press.

Przeworski, A. and F. Limongi (1993): Political Regimes and Economic Growth. *Journal of Economic Perspectives* 7: 51–69.

Rehm, J., and G. Gmel (2007): Alcohol Consumption and Public Health in Russia. *Lancet* 369: 1975–1976.

Reisinger, W. M., and B. J. Moraski (2012): Governance or Deference? A Survival Analysis of Russia's Governors under Presidential Control. In: W. Reisinger (Ed.): *Russia Beyond the Kremlin: Comparative Subnational Politics*. New York: Routledge.

Remington, T. F. (1988): *The Truth of Authority: Ideology and Communication in the Soviet Union*. Pittsburgh, PA: Pittsburgh University Press.

Remington, T. F. (2011): *The Politics of Inequality in Russia*. Cambridge, UK: Cambridge University Press.

Reuter, O. J., and N. Buckley (2014): Patrons, Clients and Technocrats: A Study of the Effects of Regime Type on Bureaucratic Appointment Strategies. Unpublished manuscript, University of Wisconsin – Milwaukee and Columbia University.

Reuter, O. J., and T. F. Remington (2009): Dominant Party Regimes and the Commitment Problem: The Case of United Russia. *Comparative Political Studies* 42: 501–526.

Reuter, O. J., and G. Robertson (2012): Sub-National Appointments in Authoritarian Regimes: Evidence from Russian Gubernatorial Appointments. *Journal of Politics* 74: 1023–1037.

Rigby, T. H. (1976): Soviet Communist Party Membership under Brezhnev. *Soviet Studies* 28: 317–337.

Rivera, S. W. (2000): Elites in Post-Communist Russia: A Changing of the Guard? *Europe-Asia Studies* 52: 413–432.

Robinson, J. A., Torivk, R., and T. Verdier (2006): Political Foundations of the Resource Curse. *Journal of Development Economics* 79: 447–468.

Rochlitz, M. (2013): Elections vs. Appointments: Comparing Incentive Pattern for Russian Governors under Putin. Unpublished manuscript, National Research University Higher School of Economics.

Rodrik, D. and R. Wacziarg (2005): Do Democratic Transitions Produce Bad Economic Outcomes? *American Economic Review* 95: 50–55.

Roland, G. (2004): Understanding Institutional Change: Fast-Moving and Slow-Moving Institutions. *Studies in Comparative International Development* 38:109–131.

Ross, C. (2009): *Local Politics and Democratization in Russia*. London: Routledge.

Ross, C., and A. Campbell (2009): *Federalism and Local Politics in Russia*. London: Routledge.

Ross, M. L. (2001): Does Oil Hinder Democracy? *World Politics* 53: 325–361.

Rowley, C. K., and N. Smith (2009): Islam's Democracy Paradox: Muslims Claim to Like Democracy, So Why Do They Have So Little? *Public Choice* 139: 273–299.

Ryavec, C. V. (2003): *Russian Bureaucracy: Power and Pathology*. Lanham, MD: Rowman and Littlefield.

Saez-Marti, M., and A. Sjogren (2008): Peers and Culture. *Scandinavian Journal of Economics* 110: 73–92.

Samuels, D., and F. L. Abruico (2000): Federalism and Democratic Transition: The 'New' Politics of the Governors in Brazil. *Publius: The Journal of Federalism* 30: 43–61.

Sandler, B. (1997): Do Border Economies Generate Comparative Advantages for Small- and Medium-Sized Enterprises? Evidence from the Maquiladora Industry. Kiel Working Paper No. 806.

Schmitter, P. C. (1991): An Introduction to Southern European Transitions from Authoritarian Rule: Italy, Greece, Portugal, Spain, and Turkey. In: G. O'Donnel, P. C. Schmitter, and L. Whitehead (Eds.): *Transitions from Authoritarian Rule. Southern Europe*. Baltimore, MD: Johns Hopkins University Press.

Schmitter, P. C. (1996): The Influence of the International Context upon the Choice of National Institutions and Policies in Neo-Democracies. In: L. Whitehead (Ed.): *International Dimension of Democratization: Europe and the Americas*. Oxford, UK: Oxford University Press.

Schultz, A., Kozlov, V., and A. Libman (2014): Judicial Alignment and Criminal Justice: Evidence from Russian Courts. *Post-Soviet Affairs* 30: 137–170.

Schultz, A., and A. Libman (2015): Is There a Local Knowledge Advantage in Federations? Evidence from a Natural Experiment. *Public Choice* 162: 25–42.

Sharafutdinova, G. (2006): When Do Elites Compete? The Determinants of Political Competition in Russian Regions. *Comparative Politics* 38: 273–293.

Sharafutdinova, G. (2013): Getting the 'Dough' and Saving the Machine: Lessons from Tatarstan. *Demokratizatsiya* 21: 507–529.

Sharafutdinova, G., and G. Kisunko (2014): Governors and Governing Institutions: A Comparative Study of State-Business Relations in Russia's Regions. World Bank Policy Research Paper No. 7038.

Sheinis, V. L. (2005): *Vzlet i Padenie Parlamenta: Perelomnye Gody v Rossiyskoy Politike*. Two Volumes. Moscow, Russia: Carnegie Center.

Shen, L. (2007): When Will a Dictator Be Good? *Economic Theory* 31: 343–366.

Shevtsova, L. (2012): Implosion, Atrophy, or Revolution? *Journal of Democracy* 23: 19–32.

Shlapentokh, V. (1989): *Public and Private Live of the Soviet People*. New York: Oxford University Press.

Shleifer, A., and R. W. Vishny (1993): Corruption. *Quarterly Journal of Economics* 108: 599–617.

Sidel, J. T. (2014): Economic Foundations of Subnational Authoritarianism: Insights and Evidence from Qualitative and Quantitative Research. *Democratization* 21: 161–184.

Simpser, A. (2013): *Why Governments and Parties Manipulate Elections: Theory, Practice, and Implications.* New York: Cambridge University Press.

Sirowy, L., and A. Inkeles (1990): The Effects of Democracy on Economic Growth and Inequality: A Review. *Studies in Comparative International Development* 25: 126–157.

Snyder, R. (2001): Scaling Down: The Subnational Comparative Method. *Studies in Comparative International Development* 36: 93–110.

Sonin, K. (2003): Why the Rich May Favor Poor Protection of Property Rights. *Journal of Comparative Economics* 31: 715–731.

Stoner-Weiss, K. (1997): *Local Heroes: The Political Economy of Russian Regional Governance.* Princeton, NJ: Princeton University Press.

Stoner-Weiss, K. (2000): Foreign Direct Investment and Democratic Development in the Russian Provinces: A Preliminary Analysis. *Policy Studies Journal* 28: 96–113.

Stoner-Weiss, K. (2006): *Resisting the State: Reform and Retrenchment in Post-Soviet Russia.* Cambridge, UK: Cambridge University Press.

Stutzer, A., and B. S. Frey (2006): Political Participation and Procedural Utility: An Empirical Study. *European Journal of Political Research* 45: 391–418.

Sullivan, J., and B. Renz (2010): Chinese Migration: Still the Major Focus of Russian Far East / Chinese North East Relations? *Pacific Review* 23: 261–285.

Tavares, J., and R. Wacziarg (2001): How Democracy Affects Growth. *European Economic Review* 45: 1341–1387.

Teorell, J. (2010): *Determinants of Democratization: Explaining Regime Change in the World, 1972–2006.* Cambridge, UK: Cambridge University Press.

Titma, M., Tooding, L. M., and N. B. Tuma (2004): Communist Party Membership: Incentives and Gains. *International Journal of Sociology* 34: 72–99.

Tolstrup, J. (2009): Studying a Negative External Actor: Russia's Management of Stability and Instability in the Near Abroad. *Democratization* 16: 922–44.

Tolstrup, J. (2015): Subnational Level: Russian Support for Secessionism and Pockets of Autocracy. In: A. Obydenkova and A. Libman (Eds.): *Autocratic and Democratic External Influences in Post-Soviet Eurasia.* Farnham, UK: Ashgate.

Tornell, A., and P. R. Lane (1999): The Voracity Effect. *American Economic Review* 89: 22–46.

Torniainen, T. J., Mashkina, O. V., Saastamoinen, O. J., and V. N. Petrov (2010): The New Forest Legislation in Russia: The Leaseholders' Attitudes. *Journal of Natural Resources Policy Research* 2: 171–186.

Torniainen, T. J., and O. J. Saastamoinen (2007): Formal and Informal Institutions and Their Hierarchy in the Regulation of the Forest Lease in Russia. *Forestry* 80: 489–501.

Torniainen, T. J., Saastamoinen, O. J., and A. Petrov (2006): Russian Forest Policy in the Turmoil of the Changing Balance of Power. *Forest Policy and Economics* 9: 403–416.

Trochev, A. (2004): Less Democracy, More Courts: A Puzzle of Judicial Review in Russia. *Law and Society Review* 38: 513–548

Ulybina, O. (2014): Russian Forests: The Path of Reforms. *Forest Policy and Economics* 38: 143–150.

Unger, A. L. (1981): Political Participation in the USSR: YCL and CPSU. *Soviet Studies* 33:107–124.

Usacheva, O. (2011): Ekologicheskiy Aktivizm v Postsovetskoi Rossii i Zapadnom Mire. *SOTSIS* 3: 23–31.

Vachudova, M. A. (2005): *Europe Undivided: Democracy, Leverage, and Integration after Communism.* New York: Oxford University Press.

van der Ploeg, F. (2011): Natural Resources: Curse or Blessing? *Journal of Economic Literature* 49: 366–420.

Vardomsky, L. (2009): *Rossiiskoe Porubezh'e v Usloviyakh Golbalizatsii.* Moscow, Russia: Librokom.

Varshney, A. (1998): Why Democracy Survives. *Journal of Democracy* 9: 36–50.

Vasilyeva, O., and J. Nye (2013). When Does Local Political Competition Lead to More Public Goods? Evidence from Russian Regions. EERC Working Paper No. 13/09 .

Veenhoven, R. (2003): Freedom and Happiness: A Comparative Study in Forty-Four Nations in the Early 1990s. In: E. Diener and E. M. Suh (Eds.): *Culture and Subjective Well-Being.* Cambridge, MA: MIT Press.

Volkov, D. (2012): The Protesters and the Public. *Journal of Democracy* 23: 55–62.

Voslenskiy, M. (1991): *Nomenklatura: Gospodstvuyushchiy Klass Sovetskogo Soyuza.* Moscow, Russia: Sovetskaya Rossiya.

Walberg, P., McKee, M., Shkolnikov, V., Chenet, L., and D. A. Leon (1998): Economic Change, Crime, and Mortality Crisis in Russia: Regional Analysis. *British Journal of Medicine* 317: 312–318.

Weede, E. (1996): Political Regime Type and Variation in Economic Growth Rates. *Constitutional Political Economy* 7: 167–176.

Welzel, C. (2006): Democratization as an Emancipative Process. *European Journal of Political Research* 45: 871–896.

Welzel, C. (2013): *Freedom Rising: Human Empowerment and the Quest for Emancipation.* New York: Cambridge University Press.

Welzel, C., and R. Inglehart (2008): The Role of Ordinary People in Democratization. *Journal of Democracy* 19: 126–140.

Wendland, K., Lewis, D. J., and J. Alex-Garcia (2014): The Effect of Decentralized Government on Timber Extraction in European Russia. *Environmental and Resource Economics* 57: 19–40.

Wendland, K. J., Lewis, D. J., Alix-Garcia, J., Ozdogan, M., Baumann, M., and V. C. Radeloff (2011): Regional- and District-Level Drivers of Timber Harvesting in European Russia after the Collapse of the Soviet Union. *Global Environmental Change* 21: 1290–1300.

White, D. (2006): *The Russian Democratic Party Yabloko: Opposition in a Managed Democracy.* Aldershot, UK: Ashgate.

White, S. (1994): Communists and Their Party in the Late Soviet Period. *Slavonic and East European Review* 72: 644–663.

## 208    References

White, S. (2010): Soviet Nostalgia and Russian Politics. *Journal of Eurasian Studies* 1: 1–9.

White, S., and I. McAllister (1996): The CPSU and Its Members: Between Communism and Postcommunism. *British Journal of Political Science* 26: 105–122.

White, S., and I. McAllister (2004): Dimensions of Disengagement in Postcommunist Russia. *Journal of Communist Studies and Transition Politics* 20: 81–97.

White, S., Miller, B., Grodeland, A., and S. Oates (2000): Religion and Political Action in Postcommunist Europe. *Political Studies* 48: 681–705

Whitehead, L. (Ed. 1996*): International Dimension of Democratisation: Europe and the Americas*. Oxford, UK: Oxford University Press.

Wilhelmsen, J. (2005): Between a Rock and a Hard Place: The Islamization of the Chechen Separatist Movement. *Europe-Asia Studies* 57: 35–59.

Williamson, O. (2000): The New Institutional Economics: Taking Stock, Looking Ahead. *Journal of Economic Literature* 38: 595–613.

Wirminghaus, N. (2012): Ephemeral Regionalism: The Proliferation of (Failed) Regional Integration Initiatives in Post-Soviet Eurasia. In: T. Börzel, L. Goltermann, M. Lohaus, and K. Striebinger (Eds.): *Roads to Regionalism: Genesis, Design and Effects of Regional Organizations*. Aldershot, UK: Ashgate.

Wittfogel, K.A. (1957): *Oriental Despotism – A Comparative Study of Total Power.* Yale, CT: Yale University Press.

Wolchik, S. (2012): Can There Be a Color Revolution? *Journal of Democracy* 23: 63–70.

Wu, C. (2004): Regime Type, Structural Factors, and Economic Performance. PhD Thesis, University of Michigan.

Yakovlev, A. (2011): State Business Relations in Russia in the 2000s: From the Capture Model to a Variety of Exchange Models? BOFIT Discussion Paper No. 10.

Yakovlev, E., and E. Zhuravskaya (2013): The Unequal Enforcement of Liberalization: Evidence from Russia's Reform of Business Regulation. *Journal of the European Economic Association* 11: 808–838.

Yenikeyeff, S. (2014): *The Battle for Russian Oil: Corporations, Regions, and the State*. Oxford, UK: Oxford University Press.

Zaprudski, S. (2007): In the Grip of Replacive Bilingualism: The Belarusian Language in Contact with Russian. *International Journal of the Sociology of Language* 183: 97–118.

Zelkina, A. (1993): Islam and Politics in the North Caucasus. *Religion, State and Society* 21: 115–124.

Zubarevich, N. (2011): Chetyre Rossii. *Vedomosti*, December 30.

Zuckerman, A. S. (Ed., 2005): *The Social Logic of Politics*. Philadelphia, PA: Temple University Press.

Zweynert, J. (2007): Conflict Patterns of Thought in the Russian Debate on Transition: 1992–2002. *Europe-Asia Studies* 59: 47–69.

# Appendix
## Selected characteristics of Russian regions

*Table A1* Demographic variables

| | Share of ethnic Russians | Share of population with a university degree, % | Share of young in the regional population, % | Share of elderly in the regional population,% | Population, thousands of people | Urbanization, % |
|---|---|---|---|---|---|---|
| Adygeia | 63.64 | 25.47 | 18.27 | 22.57 | 441.80 | 51.59 |
| Altai Krai | 93.93 | 20.87 | 16.74 | 20.96 | 2,505.20 | 53.96 |
| Altai Republic | 56.63 | 22.64 | 24.50 | 14.02 | 203.60 | 26.73 |
| Amur | 94.33 | 22.27 | 18.76 | 17.32 | 863.20 | 66.41 |
| Arkhangelsk | 95.58 | 20.90 | 17.09 | 19.62 | 1,281.10 | 74.80 |
| Astrakhan | 67.57 | 22.57 | 18.20 | 19.80 | 1,006.50 | 67.30 |
| Bashkortostan | 36.05 | 21.48 | 19.18 | 19.35 | 4,075.90 | 61.28 |
| Belgorod | 94.37 | 25.75 | 15.97 | 23.18 | 1,518.20 | 65.65 |
| Briansk | 96.70 | 21.64 | 16.30 | 23.52 | 1,327.00 | 68.67 |
| Buriatia | 66.05 | 26.59 | 21.32 | 15.46 | 971.80 | 57.62 |
| Cheliabinsk | 83.80 | 24.43 | 16.92 | 21.20 | 3,527.70 | 81.86 |
| Chita | 89.91 | 20.14 | 21.24 | 15.75 | 1,126.90 | 64.60 |
| Chukotka | 52.49 | 25.15 | 22.12 | 7.91 | 52.40 | 65.24 |
| Chuvashia | 26.86 | 23.82 | 17.83 | 20.04 | 1,280.10 | 59.76 |
| Dagestan | 3.60 | 24.36 | 28.79 | 10.60 | 2,721.40 | 43.90 |
| Evreyskaia | 92.74 | 18.79 | 19.14 | 17.13 | 182.90 | 67.34 |
| Ingushetia | 0.78 | 25.42 | 33.36 | 7.85 | 427.80 | 42.16 |
| Irkutsk | 91.41 | 25.00 | 19.50 | 17.84 | 2,498.40 | 79.38 |
| Ivanovo | 95.58 | 22.94 | 14.61 | 25.18 | 1,103.00 | 81.29 |
| Kabardino-Balkaria | 22.52 | 26.60 | 21.83 | 15.88 | 872.00 | 56.66 |
| Kaliningrad | 86.43 | 29.59 | 16.00 | 20.42 | 942.20 | 77.46 |

(*Continued*)

*Table A1* (Continued)

| | Share of ethnic Russians | Share of population with a university degree, % | Share of young in the regional population, % | Share of elderly in the regional population,% | Population, thousands of people | Urbanization, % |
|---|---|---|---|---|---|---|
| Kalmykia | 30.21 | 27.03 | 21.89 | 14.90 | 292.30 | 44.01 |
| Kaluga | 93.08 | 26.09 | 14.99 | 23.91 | 1,024.70 | 75.20 |
| Kamchatka | 85.92 | 29.18 | 17.61 | 14.38 | 338.00 | 79.28 |
| Karachaevo-Cherkessia | 31.63 | 30.63 | 21.07 | 17.71 | 457.70 | 44.00 |
| Karelia | 82.19 | 23.06 | 16.45 | 20.42 | 677.60 | 76.45 |
| Kemerovo | 93.70 | 22.32 | 17.21 | 20.21 | 2,818.80 | 85.67 |
| Khabarovsk | 91.81 | 29.44 | 16.64 | 18.32 | 1,382.70 | 81.28 |
| Khakassia | 81.66 | 21.79 | 19.02 | 17.93 | 536.60 | 70.15 |
| Kirov | 91.88 | 20.10 | 15.62 | 22.64 | 1,418.70 | 72.75 |
| Komi | 65.08 | 22.11 | 18.21 | 15.34 | 960.50 | 75.93 |
| Kostroma | 96.60 | 26.09 | 15.87 | 23.47 | 700.30 | 68.64 |
| Krasnodar | 88.25 | 24.98 | 17.04 | 22.85 | 5,156.50 | 53.02 |
| Krasnoiarsk | 91.32 | 25.04 | 17.93 | 18.00 | 2,882.50 | 75.88 |
| Kurgan | 92.47 | 18.23 | 17.16 | 22.60 | 962.10 | 58.37 |
| Kursk | 96.48 | 23.83 | 15.59 | 24.73 | 1,178.40 | 62.99 |
| Leningradskaia Oblast | 92.75 | 25.49 | 14.24 | 23.27 | 1,688.60 | 66.07 |
| Lipetsk | 96.26 | 24.06 | 15.58 | 23.93 | 1,193.80 | 63.75 |
| Magadan | 84.13 | 30.34 | 17.35 | 13.28 | 169.80 | 93.99 |
| Mariy El | 47.40 | 22.53 | 17.55 | 19.09 | 712.20 | 62.95 |
| Mordovia | 53.36 | 25.30 | 15.58 | 22.27 | 862.60 | 59.46 |
| Moscow City | 91.65 | 50.01 | 13.04 | 22.23 | 10,932.60 | 100.00 |
| Moscow Oblast | 92.92 | 36.29 | 14.38 | 23.34 | 6,824.80 | 79.91 |
| Murmansk | 88.97 | 26.66 | 16.59 | 15.67 | 840.40 | 92.44 |
| Nizhny Novgorod | 95.15 | 27.05 | 15.02 | 24.12 | 3,414.00 | 78.42 |
| Northern Ossetia | 20.82 | 33.41 | 20.36 | 20.13 | 709.70 | 64.48 |
| Novgorod | 95.06 | 22.30 | 15.30 | 24.79 | 664.30 | 70.59 |
| Novosibirsk | 93.10 | 29.13 | 15.92 | 20.99 | 2,665.30 | 75.99 |
| Omsk | 85.83 | 24.01 | 17.20 | 19.63 | 2,021.80 | 70.23 |
| Orel | 93.91 | 25.46 | 15.53 | 24.34 | 822.40 | 64.65 |
| Orenburg | 75.88 | 21.91 | 18.21 | 19.97 | 2,097.40 | 58.67 |
| Penza | 86.80 | 22.92 | 15.10 | 24.16 | 1,419.70 | 65.97 |

| | | | | | |
|---|---|---|---|---|---|
| Perm | 87.11 | 20.71 | 17.75 | 20.03 | 2,721.50 | 75.20 |
| Primorski Krai | 92.52 | 29.18 | 16.44 | 19.20 | 2,009.10 | 76.59 |
| Pskov | 95.01 | 21.45 | 14.86 | 25.36 | 718.10 | 68.27 |
| Riazan | 95.11 | 24.27 | 14.46 | 26.24 | 1,190.10 | 69.99 |
| Rostov | 90.34 | 26.50 | 15.89 | 23.02 | 4,333.90 | 67.12 |
| Sakha | 37.84 | 27.20 | 24.52 | 10.93 | 954.80 | 64.15 |
| Sakhalin | 86.46 | 23.38 | 17.15 | 16.64 | 521.10 | 81.32 |
| Samara | 85.55 | 29.15 | 15.45 | 22.10 | 3,227.20 | 80.29 |
| Saratov | 87.55 | 25.91 | 15.94 | 22.94 | 2,591.90 | 73.97 |
| Smolensk | 94.66 | 23.16 | 14.66 | 23.59 | 1,020.90 | 71.63 |
| St. Petersburg | 92.48 | 43.85 | 12.83 | 24.23 | 4,744.90 | 100.00 |
| Stavropol | 80.89 | 25.79 | 18.18 | 20.79 | 2,753.30 | 56.51 |
| Sverdlovskaia Oblast | 90.65 | 24.29 | 16.24 | 21.31 | 4,374.60 | 84.82 |
| Tambov | 96.99 | 21.61 | 15.01 | 25.53 | 1,136.00 | 57.95 |
| Tatarstan | 39.71 | 27.35 | 17.94 | 20.22 | 3,773.80 | 74.58 |
| Tiumen | 73.32 | 28.85 | 20.14 | 11.58 | 3,315.90 | 78.31 |
| Tomsk | 88.10 | 24.01 | 17.05 | 17.99 | 1,035.80 | 68.86 |
| Tula | 95.31 | 23.31 | 13.76 | 26.79 | 1,613.80 | 80.49 |
| Tver | 86.60 | 21.71 | 14.91 | 25.79 | 1,412.90 | 73.71 |
| Tyva | 16.27 | 19.02 | 30.31 | 9.33 | 304.90 | 52.04 |
| Udmurtia | 62.22 | 23.63 | 18.21 | 18.58 | 1,545.20 | 69.70 |
| Ulianovsk | 73.58 | 22.57 | 15.72 | 22.22 | 1,338.00 | 73.20 |
| Vladimir | 95.58 | 22.92 | 14.78 | 24.67 | 1,484.50 | 78.17 |
| Volgograd | 90.01 | 25.15 | 16.25 | 22.76 | 2,646.40 | 75.46 |
| Vologda | 97.27 | 21.82 | 16.60 | 21.44 | 1,235.20 | 69.31 |
| Voronezh | 95.50 | 26.00 | 14.71 | 25.51 | 2,357.30 | 62.26 |
| Yaroslavl | 95.97 | 25.36 | 14.68 | 24.88 | 1,316.20 | 81.56 |

Sources: Computed by authors based on Rosstat and Census 2010; all indicators are annual averages for the period from 2001–2010, except share of ethnic Russians and share of population with a university degree, which are for 2010. These two indicators have been recalculated for this table; in regressions we use the variables varying from 0 to 1.

Table A2 Historical legacies and ties to post-Soviet countries

| | Share of post-Soviet trade, 2001–2010, % | Share of CPSU members, 1976, % |
|---|---|---|
| Adygeia | 12.13 | |
| Altai Krai | 65.41 | 7.50 |
| Altai Republic | 5.42 | |
| Amur | 0.61 | 8.43 |
| Arkhangelsk | 4.78 | 7.96 |
| Astrakhan | 25.55 | 7.78 |
| Bashkortostan | 14.62 | 6.59 |
| Belgorod | 59.94 | 7.50 |
| Briansk | 56.35 | 7.49 |
| Buriatia | 9.90 | 7.24 |
| Cheliabinsk | 31.64 | 7.05 |
| Chita | 1.55 | 7.20 |
| Chukotka | 0.27 | |
| Chuvashia | 25.22 | 6.25 |
| Dagestan | 47.07 | 7.51 |
| Evreyskaia | 1.72 | |
| Ingushetia | 5.87 | 5.98 |
| Irkutsk | 7.10 | 6.29 |
| Ivanovo | 53.50 | 9.66 |
| Kabardino-Balkaria | 24.25 | 8.44 |
| Kaliningrad | 2.79 | 11.79 |
| Kalmykia | 22.34 | 6.40 |
| Kaluga | 22.47 | 10.05 |
| Kamchatka | 0.65 | 11.32 |
| Karachaevo-Cherkessia | 45.53 | |
| Karelia | 2.90 | 7.03 |
| Kemerovo | 15.22 | 7.84 |
| Khabarovsk | 0.57 | 8.89 |
| Khakassia | 20.52 | |
| Kirov | 12.89 | 7.16 |
| Komi | 14.15 | 7.31 |
| Kostroma | 19.85 | 10.39 |
| Krasnodar | 11.44 | 7.54 |
| Krasnoiarsk | 5.55 | 6.30 |
| Kurgan | 64.45 | 7.81 |
| Kursk | 48.55 | 8.50 |
| Leningradskaia Oblast | 2.54 | |
| Lipetsk | 9.34 | 7.33 |
| Magadan | 0.24 | 10.41 |

| | | |
|---|---|---|
| Mariy El | 12.96 | 6.88 |
| Mordovia | 33.12 | 7.81 |
| Moscow City | 6.54 | 15.43 |
| Moscow Oblast | 14.56 | 9.76 |
| Murmansk | 1.27 | 9.47 |
| Nizhny Novgorod | 27.59 | 7.95 |
| Northern Ossetia | 28.73 | 8.23 |
| Novgorod | 6.10 | 9.91 |
| Novosibirsk | 41.65 | 6.97 |
| Omsk | 31.40 | 7.80 |
| Orel | 27.28 | 9.04 |
| Orenburg | 33.81 | 8.21 |
| Penza | 33.06 | 8.53 |
| Perm | 13.05 | 6.24 |
| Primorski Krai | 0.22 | 9.36 |
| Pskov | 3.35 | 9.18 |
| Riazan | 16.84 | 8.89 |
| Rostov | 37.38 | 8.58 |
| Sakha | 1.10 | 7.04 |
| Sakhalin | 0.69 | 8.52 |
| Samara | 15.05 | 8.62 |
| Saratov | 19.94 | 9.61 |
| Smolensk | 11.12 | 9.06 |
| St. Petersburg | 6.08 | |
| Stavropol | 21.44 | 7.26 |
| Sverdlovskaia Oblast | 17.15 | 6.48 |
| Tambov | 29.18 | 8.76 |
| Tatarstan | 16.24 | 7.55 |
| Tiumen | 7.43 | 6.29 |
| Tomsk | 19.09 | 6.98 |
| Tula | 12.27 | 8.95 |
| Tver | 21.55 | 11.03 |
| Tyva | 4.75 | 7.60 |
| Udmurtia | 18.76 | 7.44 |
| Ulianovsk | 35.03 | 9.44 |
| Vladimir | 24.83 | 9.05 |
| Volgograd | 25.34 | 9.33 |
| Vologda | 7.40 | 9.01 |
| Voronezh | 35.41 | 9.12 |
| Yaroslavl | 24.12 | 9.07 |

Source: Computed by authors based on Rosstat, Soviet CPSU Congress records and Soviet statistics.

Table A3 Geographic characteristics

| | Distance to Minsk, km | Distance to Baku, km | Distance to Astana, km | Distance to Tashkent, km | Distance to Moscow, km | Distance to Brussels, km | Average January temperature, Celsius |
|---|---|---|---|---|---|---|---|
| Adygeia | 1,374.03 | 926.15 | 2,432.79 | 2,390.18 | 1,254.03 | 2,736.00 | 0 |
| Altai Krai | 3,611.81 | 2,913.8 | 871.49 | 1,730.17 | 2,935.78 | 5,142.00 | −18 |
| Altai Republic | 3,813.07 | 3,022.54 | 1,005.73 | 1,740.19 | 3,137.06 | 5,354.00 | −17.7 |
| Amur | 6,256.89 | 5,893.00 | 3,855.38 | 4,516.96 | 5,620.18 | 7,561.00 | −28.8 |
| Arkhangelsk | 1,389.37 | 2,749.53 | 2,318.75 | 3,169.95 | 991.88 | 2,580.00 | −11.9 |
| Astrakhan | 1,678.37 | 672.00 | 1,793.34 | 1,786.14 | 1,275.45 | 2,579.84 | −1.1 |
| Bashkortostan | 1,833.52 | 1,656.47 | 1,109.39 | 1,789.71 | 1,166.75 | 3,427.36 | −8.2 |
| Belgorod | 716.04 | 1,528.93 | 2,425.91 | 2,703.34 | 577.97 | 2,254.61 | −6.8 |
| Briansk | 457.99 | 1,842.07 | 2,508.35 | 2,909.5 | 346.01 | 2,056.31 | −7.1 |
| Buriatia | 5,088.59 | 4,502.26 | 2,479.22 | 3,120.91 | 4,424.84 | 6,527.65 | −27.1 |
| Cheliabinsk | 2,167.09 | 1,845.34 | 804.23 | 1,649.32 | 1,497.41 | 3,743.92 | −12.6 |
| Chita | 5,395.38 | 4,895.92 | 2,864.39 | 3,524.05 | 4,738.86 | 6,796.52 | −30.5 |
| Chukotka | 6,582.96 | 7,476.69 | 5,666.9 | 6,710.59 | 6,198.07 | 7,157.87 | −29.2 |
| Chuvashia | 1,275.93 | 1,755.38 | 1,678.82 | 2,290.55 | 601.54 | 2,853.26 | −7.9 |
| Dagestan | 1,898.66 | 343.7 | 2,021.14 | 1,798.14 | 1,590.18 | 3,342.74 | −1 |
| Evreyskaia | 6,639.87 | 6,313.34 | 4,275.25 | 4,930.87 | 6,010.65 | 7,914.41 | −22.6 |
| Ingushetia | 1,736.29 | 517.69 | 2,189.01 | 2,015.52 | 1,493.16 | 3,143.82 | −5 |
| Irkutsk | 4,872.72 | 4,272 | 2,247.09 | 2,905.75 | 4,207.72 | 6,326.51 | −28.5 |
| Ivanovo | 912.66 | 1,952.04 | 2,072.46 | 2,667.12 | 249.38 | 2,463.46 | −8.4 |

| Region | | | | | | | |
|---|---|---|---|---|---|---|---|
| Kabardino-Balkaria | 1,646.74 | 618.53 | 2,251.7 | 2,111.25 | 1,431.72 | 3,042.24 | −1.4 |
| Kaliningrad | 466.6 | 2,685.55 | 3,363.45 | 3,831.15 | 1,088.77 | 1,163.68 | −0.4 |
| Kalmykia | 1,455.07 | 795.83 | 2,055.06 | 2,072.51 | 1,147.98 | 2,944.69 | −2 |
| Kaluga | 571.61 | 1,867.19 | 2,367.83 | 2,829.63 | 158.56 | 2,171.15 | −7.6 |
| Kamchatka | 7,306.78 | 7,596.8 | 5,581.94 | 6,445.85 | 6,783.14 | 8,226.991 | −16.4 |
| Karachaevo-Cherkessia | 1,503.83 | 768.36 | 2,317.37 | 2,234.72 | 1,322.45 | 2,893.27 | −2.2 |
| Karelia | 963.62 | 2,597.1 | 2,521.86 | 3,253.25 | 863.81 | 2,186.27 | −12 |
| Kemerovo | 3,662.09 | 3,121.01 | 1,076.51 | 1,994.45 | 2,988.13 | 5,164.37 | −19.2 |
| Khabarovsk | 6,770.45 | 6472 | 4,432.39 | 5,093.73 | 6,144.08 | 8,021.57 | −22.6 |
| Khakassia | 4051 | 3,416.67 | 1,378.15 | 2,154.05 | 3,377.49 | 5,554.17 | −19.7 |
| Kirov | 1,455.35 | 2,022.57 | 1,610.83 | 2,365.76 | 791.69 | 2,976.07 | −10 |
| Komi | 1,614.89 | 2,364.38 | 1,711.93 | 2,584.08 | 1,004.34 | 3,034.74 | −17.1 |
| Kostroma | 937.78 | 2,032.16 | 2,084.79 | 2,711.96 | 301.67 | 2,463.59 | −9.1 |
| Krasnodar | 1,283.04 | 1,026.58 | 2,487.71 | 2,477.35 | 1,197.4 | 2,637.39 | 0 |
| Krasnoiarsk | 4,034.12 | 3,563.46 | 1,517.71 | 2,380.25 | 3,357.5 | 5,487.95 | −25.1 |
| Kurgan | 2,407.63 | 2,022.89 | 626.23 | 1,605.76 | 1,732.29 | 3,969.4 | −14.6 |
| Kursk | 626.87 | 1,636.55 | 2,426.2 | 2,756.9 | 460.6 | 2,200.26 | −6.9 |
| Leningradskaia Oblast | 692.32 | 2,557.15 | 2,713.43 | 3,365.83 | 633.73 | 1,997.29 | −5.5 |
| Lipetsk | 812.93 | 1,563.74 | 2,176.66 | 2,555.16 | 372.94 | 2,412.89 | −7.8 |
| Magadan | 6,432.58 | 6,781.05 | 4,794.53 | 5,717.43 | 5,910.1 | 7,379.21 | −29.4 |
| Mariy El | 1,317.7 | 1,809.02 | 1,651.8 | 2,296.44 | 641.64 | 2,892.22 | −8.4 |
| Mordovia | 1,148.98 | 1,569.89 | 1,641.9 | 2,284.02 | 513.85 | 2,750.5 | −8 |

*(Continued)*

Table A3 (Continued)

| | Distance to Minsk, km | Distance to Baku, km | Distance to Astana, km | Distance to Tashkent, km | Distance to Moscow, km | Distance to Brussels, km | Average January temperature, Celsius |
|---|---|---|---|---|---|---|---|
| Moscow City | 676.07 | 1,926.95 | 2,275.29 | 2,795.41 | 0.00 | 2,255.91 | −6.7 |
| Moscow Oblast | 676.07 | 1,926.95 | 2,275.29 | 2,795.41 | 0.00 | 2,255.91 | −6.7 |
| Murmansk | 1,701.08 | 3,328.22 | 2,823.71 | 3,733.64 | 1,487.28 | 2,528.11 | −9.6 |
| Nizhny Novgorod | 1,073.37 | 1,817.72 | 1,885.03 | 2,471.72 | 397.51 | 2,645.84 | −8.7 |
| Northern Ossetia | 1,740.28 | 519.95 | 2,209.52 | 2,029.82 | 1,505.03 | 3,142.74 | −1.2 |
| Novgorod | 563.55 | 2,403.68 | 2,656.14 | 3,262.29 | 491.43 | 1,914.06 | −5.9 |
| Novosibirsk | 3,490.58 | 2,918.49 | 875.95 | 1,830.94 | 2,815.71 | 5,009.88 | −19.1 |
| Omsk | 2,914 | 2,370.7 | 442.04 | 1,557.06 | 2,237.99 | 4,464.35 | −17.5 |
| Orel | 572.57 | 1,742.02 | 2,405.46 | 2,794.8 | 326.41 | 2,174.07 | −7.4 |
| Orenburg | 1,854.31 | 1,325.39 | 1,133.83 | 1,588.15 | 1,229.09 | 3,460.46 | −8.4 |
| Penza | 1,153.79 | 1,467.4 | 1,808.07 | 2,242.6 | 556.34 | 2,758.71 | −7.7 |
| Perm | 1,833.81 | 2,008.57 | 1,232.47 | 2,073.86 | 1,160.51 | 3,364.37 | −12 |
| Primorski Krai | 7,070.37 | 6,527.66 | 4,528.31 | 5,049.31 | 6,421.94 | 8,411.099 | −16.2 |
| Pskov | 438.63 | 2,468.43 | 2,831.04 | 3,404.29 | 610.13 | 1,727.32 | −4.5 |
| Riazan | 792.79 | 1,748.74 | 2,146.84 | 2,624.07 | 184.43 | 2,392.46 | −8.3 |
| Rostov | 1,131.65 | 1,111.56 | 2,332.26 | 2,429.24 | 959.52 | 2,369.26 | −3.7 |
| Sakha | 5,460.23 | 5,625.18 | 3,625.66 | 4,551.28 | 4,888.61 | 6,579.68 | −35.6 |
| Sakhalin | 7,256.86 | 7,055.09 | 5,011.62 | 5,690.96 | 6,648.92 | 8,045.8 | −10.5 |
| Samara | 1,488.63 | 1,421.46 | 1,466.59 | 1,949.39 | 856.94 | 3,095.39 | −7.7 |

| Saratov | 1,267.85 | 1,270.4 | 1,760.28 | 2,102.09 | 725.87 | 2,867.68 | −7.4 |
|---|---|---|---|---|---|---|---|
| Smolensk | 307.29 | 2,071.35 | 2,635.59 | 3,099.23 | 368.91 | 1,900.29 | −6.8 |
| St. Petersburg | 692.32 | 2,557.15 | 2,713.43 | 3,365.83 | 633.73 | 1,913.1 | −5.5 |
| Stavropol | 1,429.56 | 823.59 | 2,277 | 2,240.09 | 1,230.75 | 2,847.23 | −2.2 |
| Sverdlovskaia Oblast | 2,093.06 | 1,982.92 | 947.98 | 1,840.37 | 1,417.03 | 3,646.87 | −15.4 |
| Tambov | 930.15 | 1,509.44 | 2,052.35 | 2,441.8 | 419.5 | 2,530.35 | −7.9 |
| Tatarstan | 1,392.51 | 1,710.19 | 1,557.19 | 2,176.26 | 720.33 | 2,970.11 | −8.1 |
| Tiumen | 2,387.52 | 2,175.15 | 768 | 1,787.65 | 1,711.54 | 3,924.64 | −16.1 |
| Tomsk | 3,551 | 3,095.02 | 1,063.7 | 2,039.94 | 2,881.69 | 5,043.5 | −22.9 |
| Tula | 657.2 | 1,784.28 | 2,285.43 | 2,735.42 | 172.66 | 2,262.66 | −7.5 |
| Tver | 621.81 | 2,087.37 | 2,379.06 | 2,938.55 | 161.52 | 2,153.8 | −6.5 |
| Tyva | 4,337.34 | 3,598.98 | 1,589.39 | 2,239.69 | 3,662.47 | 5,848.16 | −30.1 |
| Udmurtia | 1,642.95 | 1,841.14 | 1,345.4 | 2,079.42 | 966.88 | 3,205.3 | −9.9 |
| Ulianovsk | 1,353.31 | 1,549.35 | 1,587.14 | 2,116.17 | 703.41 | 2,951.08 | −7.5 |
| Vladimir | 855.85 | 1,879.58 | 2,101.04 | 2,653.76 | 179.83 | 2,429.32 | −7.8 |
| Volgograd | 1,309.69 | 1,012.58 | 1,938.87 | 2,101.52 | 914.55 | 2,859.29 | −5.2 |
| Vologda | 958.09 | 2,204.48 | 2,169.3 | 2,846.64 | 408.8 | 2,415.08 | −9.9 |
| Voronezh | 820.87 | 1,494.49 | 2,220.94 | 2,551.18 | 466.13 | 2,405.66 | −6.9 |
| Yaroslavl | 874.11 | 2,042.67 | 2,144.96 | 2,758.62 | 250.08 | 2,399.25 | −8.1 |

Source: Computed by authors based on various Internet sources (distances) and Rosstat (temperature).

Table A4 Characteristics of regional bureaucracy

| | Size of bureaucracy, people | Age of bureaucrats < 30 years, % of total bureaucracy | Age of bureaucrats above 50 years, % of total bureaucracy | Tenure of bureaucrats below 1 year, % of total bureaucracy | Tenure of bureaucrats above 15 years, % of total bureaucracy | Share of bureaucrats with a university degree |
|---|---|---|---|---|---|---|
| Adygeia | 4,926.1 | 26.9 | 21.5 | 6.7 | 28.3 | 91.1 |
| Altai Krai | 30,091.2 | 26.7 | 21.9 | 6.9 | 29.6 | 85.9 |
| Altai Republic | 4,964 | 31 | 17 | 8.6 | 23.9 | 86.9 |
| Amur | 11,976.4 | 25.5 | 21.7 | 7.8 | 28.3 | 90.9 |
| Arkhangelsk | 15,398.4 | 25.5 | 20.6 | 7 | 28.9 | 83.4 |
| Astrakhan | 11,996.5 | 30.5 | 20.1 | 8.2 | 26.2 | 86.4 |
| Bashkortostan | 32,208.1 | 31.6 | 16.7 | 9.9 | 23.7 | 82.4 |
| Belgorod | 17,173.1 | 29.5 | 20.1 | 6.4 | 32.3 | 90.7 |
| Briansk | 15,577.6 | 23 | 21.9 | 5.3 | 35.5 | 87.2 |
| Buriatia | 12,798.3 | 28.9 | 18.5 | 6.7 | 23.4 | 93.4 |
| Cheliabinsk | 30,198.3 | 29.6 | 19.5 | 8.4 | 24.3 | 85.1 |
| Chita | 16,270.5 | 29.3 | 20.3 | 7.5 | 21.9 | 87.2 |
| Chukotka | 2,490 | 27 | 21.1 | 8 | 20.3 | 73.8 |
| Chuvashia | 11,134.4 | 30.1 | 15.2 | 7.5 | 24.7 | 90.6 |
| Dagestan | 20,112 | 18.8 | 22 | 5.2 | 30.9 | 90.9 |
| Evreyskaia | 3,570.9 | 26.7 | 21.6 | 6.6 | 28.3 | 87.1 |
| Ingushetia | 3,856.6 | 26.2 | 19.2 | 5.2 | 22.9 | 90.4 |
| Irkutsk | 28,108 | 28.5 | 19.6 | 9.4 | 22.5 | 87.4 |
| Ivanovo | 11,484.4 | 22.5 | 25.3 | 6.4 | 32.6 | 85 |
| Kabardino-Balkaria | 7,526.1 | 27.9 | 18 | 7.7 | 23.6 | 94.5 |
| Kaliningrad | 12,437.1 | 24.8 | 24.7 | 7.2 | 31.4 | 83 |
| Kalmykia | 5,758.3 | 27.4 | 18.3 | 8.6 | 26.4 | 93.2 |
| Kaluga | 12,302.8 | 26.2 | 23.2 | 7.4 | 30.9 | 83.6 |
| Kamchatka | 7,118.3 | 27.1 | 18.5 | 6.9 | 24.3 | 86.6 |
| Karachaevo-Cherkessia | 5,907.6 | 29.3 | 20.1 | 8.9 | 20.3 | 92.2 |
| Karelia | 8,785.7 | 23.4 | 20.4 | 5.9 | 31.5 | 85.1 |
| Kemerovo | 24,052.7 | 27.1 | 20.9 | 6.6 | 27.4 | 85.2 |
| Khabarovsk | 18,814 | 25.5 | 24.3 | 7.3 | 29.2 | 88.4 |
| Khakassia | 7,492 | 23.9 | 21.8 | 5.9 | 27.8 | 89.1 |
| Kirov | 16,242.8 | 26.4 | 21.9 | 6.4 | 34.3 | 85 |

| | | | | | |
|---|---|---|---|---|---|
| Komi | 12,759.2 | 23.9 | 19.3 | 7.4 | 24.1 | 85.5 |
| Kostroma | 11,032 | 25.7 | 24 | 8.4 | 33.4 | 81.7 |
| Krasnodar | 41,793 | 33.2 | 17.5 | 9.9 | 23.7 | 88.8 |
| Krasnoiarsk | 35,724.8 | 29.3 | 18.8 | 7 | 24.9 | 85.8 |
| Kurgan | 12,906.9 | 26.9 | 18.9 | 8.1 | 28.4 | 80.6 |
| Kursk | 15,151.4 | 26 | 21.9 | 5.4 | 30.8 | 88.5 |
| Leningradskaia Oblast | 15,275.7 | 28.1 | 21.1 | 9.1 | 27.6 | 79.6 |
| Lipetsk | 12,282.2 | 29 | 21.4 | 8.5 | 30.2 | 88.4 |
| Magadan | 5,008.9 | 23.5 | 21.7 | 7.2 | 23.4 | 83.4 |
| Mariy El | 7,253 | 24.8 | 23.3 | 7 | 33.1 | 90.1 |
| Mordovia | 10,081.3 | 27.7 | 22.3 | 7.5 | 33.4 | 87.4 |
| Moscow City | 64,515.5 | 32.9 | 23.5 | 10.3 | 23.4 | 80 |
| Moscow Oblast | 50,744.9 | 30.5 | 22.8 | 10.5 | 23.4 | 82.2 |
| Murmansk | 10,495.7 | 24.9 | 20.7 | 6.1 | 28.2 | 86.1 |
| Nizhny Novgorod | 33,061.1 | 26.9 | 22.7 | 8.2 | 25.6 | 88.1 |
| Northern Ossetia | 7,827.6 | 21.6 | 23.7 | 6.4 | 29.1 | 93.9 |
| Novgorod | 9,237.5 | 26.7 | 23.2 | 6.3 | 35 | 81.4 |
| Novosibirsk | 26,790.9 | 28.4 | 24.3 | 8.7 | 28.8 | 86.9 |
| Omsk | 20,680.6 | 29.5 | 20.2 | 7.5 | 24.6 | 86 |
| Orel | 10,712.9 | 26 | 22.1 | 6 | 34.6 | 91.1 |
| Orenburg | 21,432.2 | 32.6 | 17.7 | 7.5 | 25.9 | 84.4 |
| Penza | 14,191.6 | 27.3 | 23 | 8.8 | 30.8 | 85.6 |
| Perm | 27,106.8 | 32.2 | 18.8 | 10.1 | 22.5 | 76.1 |
| Primorski Krai | 22,746.6 | 30.8 | 20.9 | 7.7 | 23.5 | 88.5 |
| Pskov | 11,159 | 22.4 | 23.1 | 7.3 | 36.3 | 81.2 |
| Riazan | 13,636.2 | 26.1 | 23.7 | 7.5 | 29 | 86.5 |
| Rostov | 39,557.7 | 31.3 | 19.3 | 8.6 | 25.2 | 87.4 |
| Sakha | 14,536.2 | 24.8 | 19.9 | 8.5 | 23.9 | 88 |
| Sakhalin | 9,728 | 26.3 | 24.6 | 8.8 | 22.7 | 82.9 |
| Samara | 29,081.7 | 30.4 | 18.7 | 8.5 | 22.5 | 86.3 |
| Saratov | 24,730.2 | 29.1 | 20.1 | 8.6 | 24.7 | 85.7 |
| Smolensk | 13,421.7 | 27.2 | 22.5 | 7.5 | 29.7 | 86.5 |
| St. Petersburg | 32,904.6 | 29.5 | 25 | 8.2 | 25.3 | 84.7 |
| Stavropol | 24,048.7 | 32.9 | 20 | 8.3 | 24.6 | 89.9 |
| Sverdlovskaia Oblast | 37,348.8 | 28.6 | 22.2 | 8.2 | 24 | 77.9 |
| Tambov | 13,672.9 | 25.7 | 24.2 | 5.2 | 35 | 86.4 |
| Tatarstan | 32,522.3 | 35.4 | 17.3 | 9.2 | 22.8 | 86.3 |

(*Continued*)

*Table A4* (Continued)

| | Size of bureaucracy, people | Age of bureaucrats < 30 years, % of total bureaucracy | Age of bureaucrats above 50 years, % of total bureaucracy | Tenure of bureaucrats below 1 year, % of total bureaucracy | Tenure of bureaucrats above 15 years, % of total bureaucracy | Share of bureaucrats with a university degree |
|---|---|---|---|---|---|---|
| Tiumen | 43,921.1 | 34.1 | 15.6 | 10.1 | 19.3 | 84.4 |
| Tomsk | 12,677.3 | 28 | 21.9 | 7.8 | 24.8 | 86.1 |
| Tula | 15,953.9 | 25 | 24.6 | 6.5 | 30 | 83.5 |
| Tver | 17,265.7 | 27.8 | 23.3 | 8.1 | 28.3 | 80.5 |
| Tyva | 5,550.6 | 23.8 | 13.8 | 6.2 | 24.3 | 83.5 |
| Udmurtia | 15,383.4 | 28 | 19.9 | 5.3 | 32.2 | 86.7 |
| Ulianovsk | 14,433 | 29.5 | 20.8 | 10.3 | 24.2 | 80.3 |
| Vladimir | 14,244.5 | 29.2 | 22.9 | 9.7 | 30.5 | 82.1 |
| Volgograd | 26,327.3 | 28 | 21.6 | 7.8 | 24.4 | 87.3 |
| Vologda | 15,529.7 | 31 | 18.1 | 6 | 30.5 | 82.7 |
| Voronezh | 20,508.4 | 23.8 | 24.9 | 6.3 | 32.9 | 90.3 |
| Yaroslavl | 14,042 | 29.8 | 21.4 | 6.8 | 30.2 | 85.1 |

Note: Computed by authors based on Rosstat. Size of bureaucracy is computed as the average number of values from 2001–2010; other indicators are for 2008.

*Table A5* Outcomes of elections 2011

| | Just Russia, % | LDPR, % | CPRF, % | Yabloko, % | United Russia, % |
|---|---|---|---|---|---|
| Adygeia | 8.46 | 7.75 | 18.23 | 1.77 | 61.00 |
| Altai Krai | 16.10 | 16.57 | 24.71 | 2.42 | 37.17 |
| Altai Republic | 10.32 | 10.65 | 21.55 | 1.54 | 53.33 |
| Amur | 10.28 | 20.97 | 19.18 | 1.88 | 43.54 |
| Arkhangelsk | 21.83 | 18.14 | 20.40 | 4.40 | 32.06 |
| Astrakhan | 14.56 | 8.33 | 13.26 | 1.01 | 60.17 |
| Bashkortostan | 5.45 | 5.20 | 15.65 | 1.25 | 70.50 |
| Belgorod | 11.58 | 9.65 | 22.42 | 2.08 | 51.16 |
| Briansk | 11.17 | 10.64 | 23.31 | 1.98 | 50.12 |
| Buriatia | 12.63 | 9.47 | 24.34 | 1.88 | 49.02 |
| Cheliabinsk | 16.63 | 11.77 | 14.63 | 3.46 | 50.28 |
| Chita | 14.10 | 19.18 | 18.64 | 1.70 | 43.28 |
| Chukotka | 5.40 | 11.24 | 6.70 | 1.71 | 70.32 |
| Chuvashia | 18.79 | 10.67 | 20.90 | 1.60 | 43.42 |
| Dagestan | 0.19 | 0.03 | 7.93 | 0.05 | 91.44 |
| Evreyskaia | 10.53 | 15.72 | 19.80 | 1.91 | 48.11 |
| Ingushetia | 2.32 | 0.41 | 2.94 | 0.77 | 90.96 |
| Irkutsk | 13.36 | 17.34 | 27.79 | 3.44 | 34.93 |
| Ivanovo | 15.60 | 14.78 | 22.52 | 3.48 | 40.12 |
| Kabardino-Balkaria | 0.20 | 0.08 | 17.63 | 0.07 | 81.91 |
| Kaliningrad | 13.26 | 14.10 | 25.54 | 5.50 | 37.07 |
| Kalmykia | 7.18 | 4.02 | 18.37 | 1.43 | 66.10 |
| Kaluga | 15.61 | 14.36 | 21.91 | 4.12 | 40.42 |
| Kamchatka | 10.06 | 18.61 | 17.08 | 4.11 | 45.25 |
| Karachaevo-Cherkessia | 0.47 | 0.28 | 8.82 | 0.13 | 89.84 |
| Karelia | 20.58 | 17.94 | 19.26 | 6.21 | 32.26 |
| Kemerovo | 7.96 | 12.34 | 10.51 | 2.18 | 64.24 |
| Khabarovsk | 14.09 | 19.82 | 20.49 | 3.65 | 38.14 |
| Khakassia | 13.67 | 16.01 | 23.63 | 2.67 | 40.13 |
| Kirov | 19.79 | 16.70 | 22.68 | 2.72 | 34.90 |
| Komi | 11.47 | 11.91 | 13.46 | 1.51 | 58.81 |
| Kostroma | 18.58 | 15.99 | 28.85 | 3.03 | 30.74 |
| Krasnodar | 10.81 | 10.45 | 17.56 | 2.02 | 56.15 |
| Krasnoiarsk | 15.86 | 16.99 | 23.60 | 3.23 | 36.70 |
| Kurgan | 14.47 | 16.88 | 19.63 | 1.99 | 44.41 |
| Kursk | 14.43 | 13.47 | 20.71 | 2.29 | 45.72 |
| Leningradskaia Oblast | 25.30 | 14.98 | 17.39 | 5.02 | 33.03 |
| Lipetsk | 16.73 | 14.40 | 22.89 | 2.50 | 40.09 |
| Magadan | 11.61 | 17.37 | 22.75 | 3.47 | 41.04 |
| Mariy El | 10.59 | 11.72 | 20.73 | 2.01 | 52.24 |
| Mordovia | 1.29 | 1.54 | 4.54 | 0.30 | 91.62 |

(*Continued*)

*Table A5* (Continued)

| | Just Russia, % | LDPR, % | CPRF, % | Yabloko, % | United Russia, % |
|---|---|---|---|---|---|
| Moscow City | 12.14 | 9.45 | 19.36 | 8.55 | 46.62 |
| Moscow Oblast | 15.87 | 14.34 | 25.54 | 6.10 | 32.83 |
| Murmansk | 19.67 | 18.11 | 21.76 | 4.77 | 32.02 |
| Nizhny Novgorod | 10.60 | 10.66 | 28.77 | 2.83 | 44.56 |
| Northern Ossetia | 6.03 | 2.23 | 21.72 | 0.25 | 67.90 |
| Novgorod | 28.05 | 11.48 | 19.51 | 3.12 | 34.58 |
| Novosibirsk | 12.69 | 15.70 | 30.25 | 4.31 | 33.84 |
| Omsk | 13.40 | 14.19 | 25.57 | 3.52 | 39.61 |
| Orel | 11.21 | 12.24 | 31.98 | 2.07 | 38.99 |
| Orenburg | 16.79 | 16.90 | 26.18 | 2.36 | 34.89 |
| Penza | 8.66 | 10.12 | 19.83 | 2.11 | 56.30 |
| Perm | 16.41 | 17.89 | 21.02 | 4.34 | 36.28 |
| Primorski Krai | 18.16 | 18.70 | 23.32 | 3.11 | 32.99 |
| Pskov | 16.41 | 13.93 | 25.13 | 5.10 | 36.65 |
| Riazan | 15.08 | 15.06 | 23.58 | 3.08 | 39.79 |
| Rostov | 13.26 | 10.16 | 20.85 | 2.86 | 50.22 |
| Sakha | 21.82 | 8.47 | 16.39 | 1.66 | 49.16 |
| Sakhalin | 11.77 | 15.98 | 23.43 | 3.42 | 41.91 |
| Samara | 14.19 | 15.72 | 23.13 | 3.96 | 39.37 |
| Saratov | 10.08 | 7.24 | 13.80 | 1.70 | 64.89 |
| Smolensk | 18.60 | 14.75 | 24.24 | 2.87 | 36.23 |
| St. Petersburg | 23.66 | 10.30 | 15.33 | 11.59 | 35.37 |
| Stavropol | 11.82 | 15.31 | 18.40 | 2.13 | 49.11 |
| Sverdlovskaia Oblast | 24.69 | 16.01 | 16.82 | 4.27 | 32.71 |
| Tambov | 6.02 | 7.09 | 16.46 | 1.43 | 66.66 |
| Tatarstan | 5.30 | 3.48 | 10.59 | 1.08 | 77.83 |
| Tiumen | 9.20 | 16.98 | 12.38 | 2.16 | 56.37 |
| Tomsk | 13.41 | 17.85 | 22.39 | 4.66 | 37.51 |
| Tula | 8.46 | 9.21 | 15.07 | 3.49 | 61.32 |
| Tver | 19.80 | 11.69 | 23.23 | 3.76 | 38.44 |
| Tyva | 6.71 | 2.08 | 3.93 | 0.52 | 85.29 |
| Udmurtia | 11.18 | 16.59 | 19.55 | 2.84 | 45.09 |
| Ulianovsk | 15.62 | 12.59 | 23.09 | 2.28 | 43.56 |
| Vladimir | 21.79 | 13.09 | 20.78 | 3.56 | 37.55 |
| Volgograd | 21.94 | 13.29 | 22.76 | 3.44 | 35.48 |
| Vologda | 27.15 | 15.43 | 16.78 | 3.46 | 33.40 |
| Voronezh | 14.47 | 8.88 | 21.85 | 2.20 | 50.05 |
| Yaroslavl | 22.63 | 15.48 | 23.99 | 4.79 | 29.04 |

Source: Computed by authors based on the Central Electoral Committee of Russia data.

Table A6 Economic characteristics

| | GDP, 2000 | GDP growth rate | Investment to GDP | Economic openness | Health system | Crime rate | Income per capita | Natural resources to GDP, 2005–2010 |
|---|---|---|---|---|---|---|---|---|
| Adygeia | 5,519.60 | 7.27 | 0.27 | 10.60 | 37.58 | 1,219.50 | 2,419.79 | 2.96 |
| Altai Krai | 46,736.80 | 4.83 | 0.16 | 17.44 | 46.30 | 2,470.90 | 2,681.55 | 0.97 |
| Altai Republic | 2,737.50 | 5.48 | 0.32 | 46.91 | 39.57 | 2,626.30 | 2,740.20 | 2.73 |
| Amur | 26,315.20 | 4.61 | 0.38 | 9.25 | 60.41 | 2,398.40 | 3,452.04 | 11.99 |
| Arkhangelsk | 61,806.90 | 6.84 | 0.32 | 29.46 | 53.68 | 2,246.00 | 4,469.14 | 33.02 |
| Astrakhan | 28,115.70 | 3.92 | 0.39 | 24.03 | 65.95 | 2,696.20 | 3,334.42 | 13.08 |
| Bashkortostan | 145,125.00 | 6.33 | 0.24 | 39.65 | 41.87 | 1,797.80 | 3,970.72 | 15.31 |
| Belgorod | 42,074.50 | 7.49 | 0.25 | 65.17 | 39.79 | 1,341.40 | 3,408.27 | 20.77 |
| Briansk | 24,650.50 | 4.78 | 0.17 | 33.22 | 36.72 | 1,968.00 | 2,873.91 | 0.16 |
| Buriatia | 21,574.50 | 4.30 | 0.18 | 15.06 | 39.32 | 3,042.30 | 3,363.25 | 8.07 |
| Cheliabinsk | 120,561.00 | 4.31 | 0.22 | 48.87 | 40.77 | 2,447.60 | 3,847.60 | 2.38 |
| Chita | 30,024.60 | 5.46 | 0.26 | 15.64 | 53.29 | 2,734.50 | 3,304.53 | 14.44 |
| Chukotka | 3,931.40 | 10.75 | 0.40 | 63.90 | 74.02 | 1,692.20 | 10,328.18 | 48.75 |
| Chuvashia | 22,995.10 | 3.97 | 0.26 | 10.18 | 47.21 | 1,910.20 | 2,460.93 | 0.22 |
| Dagestan | 20,921.10 | 12.61 | 0.31 | 7.50 | 37.77 | 498.40 | 2,749.87 | 1.54 |
| Evreyskaia | 3,784.00 | 8.05 | 0.31 | 5.40 | 36.18 | 3,000.40 | 3,477.13 | 1.26 |
| Ingushetia | 2,618.50 | 2.60 | 0.30 | 65.51 | 27.20 | 436.70 | 1,744.23 | 3.86 |
| Irkutsk | 103,013.80 | 5.54 | 0.19 | 51.11 | 48.40 | 3,156.10 | 3,898.21 | 8.24 |
| Ivanovo | 16,900.00 | 3.53 | 0.23 | 22.78 | 51.67 | 2,140.10 | 2,215.44 | 0.61 |
| Kabardino-Balkaria | 14,081.30 | 6.63 | 0.22 | 3.32 | 43.27 | 1,012.60 | 2,476.17 | 0.23 |

(Continued)

Table A6 (Continued)

| | GDP, 2000 | GDP growth rate | Investment to GDP | Economic openness | Health system | Crime rate | Income per capita | Natural resources to GDP, 2005–2010 |
|---|---|---|---|---|---|---|---|---|
| Kaliningrad | 23,290.30 | 7.72 | 0.30 | 150.90 | 35.64 | 2,280.00 | 3,728.45 | 10.04 |
| Kalmykia | 6,212.60 | -1.15 | 0.37 | 32.12 | 49.24 | 1,710.60 | 1,744.50 | 5.85 |
| Kaluga | 23,903.30 | 6.85 | 0.27 | 50.29 | 39.34 | 2,038.50 | 3,228.72 | 1.23 |
| Kamchatka | 18,140.70 | 1.76 | 0.20 | 16.29 | 51.99 | 2,355.50 | 6,314.14 | 5.83 |
| Karachaevo-Cherkessia | 5,461.50 | 6.50 | 0.27 | 6.30 | 33.50 | 1,191.90 | 2,352.30 | 3.27 |
| Karelia | 28,214.60 | 2.28 | 0.21 | 47.38 | 50.52 | 2,302.60 | 4,059.89 | 22.69 |
| Kemerovo | 88,728.10 | 3.86 | 0.23 | 53.67 | 47.17 | 2,027.50 | 4,222.42 | 52.31 |
| Khabarovsk | 64,794.80 | 4.53 | 0.27 | 45.06 | 59.55 | 3,512.50 | 5,335.96 | 7.70 |
| Khakassia | 17,418.10 | 2.17 | 0.20 | 84.58 | 38.02 | 2,846.50 | 3,107.69 | 16.62 |
| Kirov | 35,795.40 | 1.69 | 0.20 | 18.63 | 46.68 | 2,025.50 | 2,854.73 | 0.29 |
| Komi | 59,473.10 | 3.01 | 0.29 | 22.61 | 45.70 | 2,748.80 | 6,160.79 | 43.29 |
| Kostroma | 16,662.20 | 3.02 | 0.22 | 16.28 | 36.46 | 2,064.90 | 2,875.74 | 0.21 |
| Krasnodar | 137,125.30 | 5.82 | 0.37 | 24.93 | 42.56 | 1,338.00 | 3,439.25 | 2.00 |
| Krasnoiarsk | 214,662.70 | 4.49 | 0.19 | 44.67 | 50.36 | 2,644.40 | 4,651.13 | 9.41 |
| Kurgan | 18,705.20 | 3.78 | 0.20 | 16.44 | 28.32 | 3,158.70 | 3,004.96 | 1.00 |
| Kursk | 30,167.70 | 4.63 | 0.22 | 18.32 | 51.49 | 1,965.90 | 3,192.44 | 19.34 |
| Leningradskaia Oblast | 56,001.90 | 8.50 | 0.42 | 115.81 | 32.01 | 2,007.70 | 3,283.88 | 2.27 |
| Lipetsk | 48,067.70 | 4.69 | 0.26 | 65.53 | 40.62 | 1,462.60 | 3,457.83 | 1.27 |
| Magadan | 13,009.50 | 0.90 | 0.23 | 11.83 | 55.54 | 2,716.00 | 6,613.63 | 45.73 |

| | | | | | | | | |
|---|---|---|---|---|---|---|---|---|
| Mariy El | 11,207.60 | 5.32 | 0.23 | 11.92 | 34.54 | 2,538.80 | 2,184.18 | 0.28 |
| Mordovia | 17,553.40 | 6.08 | 0.32 | 8.89 | 51.03 | 1,478.40 | 2,401.69 | 0.18 |
| Moscow City | 1,159,034.00 | 5.68 | 0.11 | 83.91 | 74.10 | 1,834.70 | 12,409.54 | 4.45 |
| Moscow Oblast | 176,693.60 | 7.06 | 0.26 | 42.57 | 35.24 | 1,555.10 | 4,778.63 | 0.58 |
| Murmansk | 55,135.00 | 0.22 | 0.16 | 32.16 | 51.17 | 2,083.00 | 6,051.14 | 22.56 |
| Nizhny Novgorod | 105,055.90 | 4.50 | 0.24 | 28.72 | 45.61 | 2,440.00 | 3,694.44 | 0.14 |
| Northern Ossetia | 8,363.20 | 6.47 | 0.20 | 14.11 | 67.53 | 1,049.60 | 2,719.79 | 0.59 |
| Novgorod | 20,965.50 | 4.31 | 0.25 | 42.79 | 39.71 | 2,153.60 | 3,378.69 | 0.38 |
| Novosibirsk | 72,012.70 | 6.55 | 0.19 | 21.35 | 57.51 | 2,893.00 | 3,710.83 | 5.78 |
| Omsk | 46,028.40 | 7.52 | 0.18 | 42.35 | 55.77 | 2,240.80 | 3,890.36 | 1.24 |
| Orel | 22,160.80 | 3.17 | 0.20 | 31.08 | 38.86 | 2,038.20 | 2,874.62 | 0.12 |
| Orenburg | 76,343.30 | 5.45 | 0.20 | 45.75 | 50.42 | 2,046.80 | 2,975.94 | 45.69 |
| Penza | 25,218.70 | 4.74 | 0.25 | 7.81 | 38.23 | 1,521.20 | 2,740.59 | 0.88 |
| Perm | 124,142.20 | 3.52 | 0.22 | 31.76 | 54.63 | 3,598.00 | 4,797.54 | 17.08 |
| Primorski Krai | 62,088.50 | 5.59 | 0.21 | 50.13 | 53.19 | 2,925.00 | 3,928.06 | 2.69 |
| Pskov | 16,178.90 | 2.77 | 0.17 | 41.91 | 34.25 | 2,169.30 | 2,990.59 | 0.42 |
| Riazan | 27,956.50 | 3.79 | 0.24 | 25.44 | 54.40 | 1,120.10 | 2,981.11 | 0.75 |
| Rostov | 88,955.00 | 7.71 | 0.26 | 40.31 | 37.52 | 1,727.40 | 3,492.43 | 2.90 |
| Sakha | 81,960.40 | 3.40 | 0.34 | 36.21 | 51.50 | 1,914.30 | 6,222.54 | 49.95 |
| Sakhalin | 34,777.00 | 11.85 | 0.55 | 57.73 | 46.04 | 2,669.60 | 7,106.25 | 56.52 |
| Samara | 140,407.40 | 3.31 | 0.19 | 53.10 | 48.12 | 2,364.70 | 4,942.21 | 14.25 |
| Saratov | 63,068.20 | 5.44 | 0.20 | 26.90 | 51.36 | 1,723.40 | 2,839.69 | 4.82 |
| Smolensk | 28,140.60 | 4.50 | 0.25 | 36.38 | 59.77 | 2,301.90 | 3,260.91 | 0.86 |
| St. Petersburg | 188,243.00 | 7.65 | 0.24 | 74.29 | 79.54 | 1,734.90 | 5,846.21 | 0.11 |

*(Continued)*

Table A6 (Continued)

| | GDP, 2000 | GDP growth rate | Investment to GDP | Economic openness | Health system | Crime rate | Income per capita | Natural resources to GDP, 2005–2010 |
|---|---|---|---|---|---|---|---|---|
| Stavropol | 53,732.40 | 6.63 | 0.24 | 15.58 | 43.59 | 1,568.60 | 2,882.33 | 2.53 |
| Sverdlovskaia Oblast | 156,077.00 | 6.34 | 0.21 | 45.31 | 43.16 | 2,802.10 | 5,024.85 | 5.89 |
| Tambov | 23,387.30 | 5.03 | 0.25 | 7.65 | 34.30 | 1,585.60 | 3,117.10 | 0.08 |
| Tatarstan | 186,154.40 | 6.06 | 0.27 | 50.04 | 44.51 | 1,962.80 | 4,092.73 | 32.76 |
| Tiumen | 570,790.20 | 5.40 | 0.29 | 51.04 | 49.19 | 2,961.20 | 8,428.29 | 75.19 |
| Tomsk | 40,539.50 | 4.33 | 0.25 | 17.81 | 67.54 | 2,772.20 | 4,244.93 | 37.25 |
| Tula | 42,061.30 | 4.81 | 0.20 | 53.66 | 33.82 | 1,222.40 | 3,156.42 | 0.93 |
| Tver | 35,341.10 | 4.46 | 0.28 | 11.71 | 51.65 | 2,366.10 | 3,054.41 | 0.35 |
| Tyva | 3,594.10 | 4.27 | 0.14 | 3.39 | 42.81 | 2,711.00 | 2,430.76 | 8.40 |
| Udmurtia | 53,307.40 | 2.76 | 0.18 | 16.50 | 57.64 | 2,677.20 | 2,856.71 | 33.47 |
| Ulianovsk | 30,415.00 | 3.81 | 0.21 | 11.96 | 36.28 | 1,733.10 | 2,795.44 | 3.18 |
| Vladimir | 33,017.70 | 4.09 | 0.21 | 21.05 | 34.31 | 2,082.60 | 2,645.44 | 0.74 |
| Volgograd | 63,767.10 | 4.06 | 0.19 | 35.49 | 35.04 | 1,936.10 | 3,345.11 | 6.65 |
| Vologda | 69,195.50 | 2.25 | 0.25 | 48.82 | 48.88 | 2,528.70 | 3,686.80 | 0.11 |
| Voronezh | 49,523.90 | 4.63 | 0.25 | 18.54 | 52.05 | 1,565.70 | 3,094.17 | 0.89 |
| Yaroslavl | 41,756.20 | 4.48 | 0.24 | 20.44 | 58.72 | 2,498.30 | 3,674.38 | 0.26 |

Note: Computed by authors based on Rosstat data; all variable computed (if not indicated otherwise) as average for the period from 2001–2010. Indicators measured as follows: GDP 2000: millions of RUR; GDP growth: %; investment-to-GDP ratio: ratio of fixed capital investments (millions of RUR) to GDP (millions of RUR); economic openness: ratio of total foreign trade (millions of RUR) to GDP (millions of RUR); foreign trade is reported by Rosstat in millions of USD and was recomputed in RUR based on the average annual USD/RUR exchange rate set by the Russian Central Bank; health system: number of doctors per 10,000 people; crime rate: number of crimes recorded by the police per 100,000 people; income per capita: monthly income in RUR; natural resources to GDP: ratio of total output of mining industry (millions of RUR) to total GDP (millions of RUR), %.

*Table A7* Selected additional sources

| Dataset | Source |
|---|---|
| Carnegie index of democracy | Moscow Carnegie Center dataset, http://carnegieendowment.org/files/CP_Petrov_Rus_2013.pdf, accessed 3 December 2014 |
| Religiosity data | Atlas of Religions and Nationalities in Russia, http://sreda.org/arena, accessed 3 December 2014 |
| Happiness data | FOM public opinion surveys dataset, http://fom.ru/obshchestvo/10901, accessed 3 December 2014 Civil Society Development Foundation, http://civilfund.ru/mat/view/27, accessed 3 December 2014 |
| Investment risk data | RA Expert, http://www.raexpert.ru/ratings/regions/, accessed 3 December 2014 |

# Index